TECHNOLOGY MADE SIMPLE

AN IMPROVEMENT GUIDE
FOR SMALL AND MEDIUM LIBRARIES

KIMBERLY BOLAN AND ROBERT CULLIN

AMERICAN LIBRARY ASSOCIATION

CHICAGO   2007

Composition in Minion and Helvetica Condensed by ALA Editions using InDesign CS on a PC platform.

Printed on 50-pound white offset, a pH-neutral stock, and bound in 10-point coated cover stock by McNaughton & Gunn.

The paper used in this publication meets the minimum requirements of American National Standard for Information Sciences—Permanence of Paper for Printed Library Materials, ANSI Z39.48-1992. ⊗

Library of Congress Cataloging-in-Publication Data

Bolan, Kimberly.
    Technology made simple : an improvement guide for small and medium libraries / Kimberly Bolan and Robert Cullin.
        p. cm.
    Includes bibliographical references and index.
    ISBN 0-8389-0920-5
    1. Small libraries—Automation—Planning. 2. Small libraries—Information technology—Planning. 3. Libraries—Automation—Planning. 4. Libraries—Information technology—Planning. I. Cullin, Robert. II. Title.
    Z678.93.S6B65 2007
    025.00285—dc22   2006013191

ISBN-10: 0-8389-0920-5
ISBN-13: 978-0-8389-0920-1

Printed in the United States of America

11 10 09 08 07   5 4 3 2 1

CONTENTS

FIGURES

PREFACE

hile most librarians recognize the importance of information technology (IT), a large number continue to struggle with implementing and maintaining effective computer and technology-related services. How can librarians, who often perform multiple roles in the small and medium-sized library environment, navigate through this technology maze? To put it simply, How does one keep up? Many small and medium libraries are forced to make it up as they go along just to get by. Lack of sufficient knowledge, time, staff, or funding forces them to "wing it," which will ultimately prove detrimental to libraries and their patrons.

So the question is, How do small and medium libraries implement and maintain successful computer and technology-related services? Success is derived from these basic principles: assessment, planning, implementation, and continuous evaluation. Most important, it's about being practical, keeping it simple, and getting things done. *Technology Made Simple: An Improvement Guide for Small and Medium Libraries* will provide a no-nonsense, step-by-step handbook for the small or medium-sized library that will lead librarians to successful technology-related services; ones that will allow libraries to be ahead of the game instead of lagging behind or just getting by.

WHO NEEDS THIS BOOK?

This is a technology manual for the non- or semi-technical library worker. In particular, the text will deal with the complexities of developing, implementing, and maintaining computer services within the framework of a small to medium-sized public library. Thought has been given to flexibility and scale, with an understanding that every library is unique and faces individual challenges in addition to those common to libraries in general. This book is an appropriate resource for the library with no technology staff or one that is limited in size or knowledge. This book is also for the library professional who is ultimately responsible for oversight in this area and wants a firmer understanding of the topic so he or she can lead more effectively.

USING THE MATERIALS IN THIS BOOK SUCCESSFULLY

Technology Made Simple is intended to help librarians and their staff develop effective technology services that reflect individual library priorities, as well as supporting the development of the small and medium-sized library and its role within the community. In order to accomplish these goals, this book will focus on technology as it relates to:

- impact
- assessment
- learning
- planning
- staffing
- budgeting and purchasing
- implementation and marketing
- training
- policies
- evaluation

Establishing this kind of framework is essential in navigating through a technological world where everything is constantly changing. Once this approach is understood, it can be applied to any given project at any given time. *Technology Made Simple* is a practical guide that can be referenced at all stages of planning, development, implementation, and maintenance. Numerous tips, practical pointers, and best practices are offered, as are recommendations to various worksheets, resources, and model libraries. Bringing technology and customer service together (internally as well as externally) is emphasized throughout the text.

In order to make the ideas in this book more tangible, information from select public libraries across the United States is included in it. To further increase the usability and effectiveness of *Technology Made Simple*, a supplemental web page that includes ready-to-use worksheets and up-to-date information can be found at http://www.ala.org/editions/extras/Bolan09205/.

THE AUTHORS' VISION

Librarian-consultant Kimberly Bolan and technology vendor Robert Cullin have worked together for more than three years and feel their diverse backgrounds and working relationship will prove helpful and insightful to others. Over the past ten years, Kim has worked at both a hands-on and management level for network and computer services in small and medium-sized libraries. Most recently, she served as the assistant director in a medium-sized public library, and she currently works as an independent library consultant. Rob Cullin is the vice president and co-owner of e•vanced solutions, Inc., a software company that grew out of a cooperative LSTA grant and now focuses exclusively on developing productivity solutions for libraries. Rob's background is in software and hardware product development, and his passion is public libraries.

Their experiences working independently and together as a team have led them to write this book. They feel strongly that librarians need a how-to technology manual for vision, planning, and understanding, not a how-to manual for configuring a router and server. In writing *Technology Made Simple* they want to show readers that technology is an *essential* tool that will better define the importance of the public library within our communities. It is also their intention to make technology less overwhelming and confusing, so that it becomes a topic librarians are energized by, not threatened by. They are convinced that through successful planning and open-minded management, public libraries of all sizes can move strongly into the future, becoming places of greatness.

ACKNOWLEDGMENTS

This book was a partnership not only between the two of us, but also with many peers, friends, and family members. Our gratitude goes out to all those who contributed their time, talent, and energy to this project. Thanks to each and every one of you, as there would be no book without you.

To Renee Vaillancourt, Emily Moroni, Christine Schwab, and Jenni Fry for their support and patience with us through the long process.

To our research assistants Mel Campbell and Keri Thomas, who helped us compile and sort much of the information and resources in the book.

To Ava Ehde, Matt Gullet, Dan Nguyen, and Michael Stephens, who all contributed greatly to the book and brought additional perspective to the topics covered.

To e•vanced solutions, Inc., and particularly to Todd Cutler, who gave us patience and time to allow us to write the book.

To our parents and family, Linda and Jim Bolan, Dave and Jeanette Cullin, Ted, Nicky, Kelly, Chris, Grace, Elyse, and Kiernan, whose patience and love during the last couple of years has helped us survive, thrive, and complete this project.

Finally, a very special thanks to all the very talented librarians and library staff members who contributed information to this book. It would not be nearly as complete or as pertinent if it were not for their contributions, ideas, and leadership. It is clear that examples of great, forward-thinking libraries are out there in every state and country, and, many times, we need only to look next door for inspiration.

Why Do IT? 1

Technology always has and always will affect libraries. Making libraries vital and valuable to their communities is more and more dependent upon libraries being quality sources of technological access to users. As computers and information technology become increasingly prominent, libraries are looking at how new areas of technology-based service can be cultivated to make and keep libraries vital. These issues are crucial for libraries of all shapes and sizes. However, they can prove especially arduous for the small and midsized facility. Unfortunately, a library's desire to move forward is often hampered by limited resources, but frequently it is the library's *perception* of these "limitations" that becomes the limiter. The questions at hand are, How can small and medium libraries take a proactive and integrated approach to service and technology? How can they progress without anxiety and uncertainty?

THE ROLE OF LIBRARIES IN A TECHNOLOGICAL WORLD

In order to fully answer these questions and find a path to success, it is important to take a look at the role of *your* library in *your* community. For years, librarians have been discussing an integrated approach to books and technology, looking to merge the traditional and the new in a complementary way. In essence, it's about discovering how technology can provide new paths while also enhancing conventional approaches. How can your library secure its future within the community? It is not only about *what* to do, it is about *how* to do it.

What barriers prevent your library from moving forward? External obstacles may include lack of a political or community focus, funding deficiencies, and a shortage of technical resources. Internal hurdles usually involve lack of technological knowledge and skills, insufficient training, uncertainty about how to move forward, and an overall resistance to change. The traditional image of the library as a book storehouse can also be problematic. Is your library perceived as old-fashioned? Why? Is it a lack of technology, a lack of awareness within the community, or the combination of both? How do you change this perception? For the Whitman County (WA) Rural Library District, the impact of technology on the community's perception of the library has been huge. Technology has changed the type of staff the library hires and has attracted many new customers to the library. "Many in our community now see the library as very high-tech and they look to us for technology information," says Kristie Kirkpatrick, the library's director. By supporting the developing role of public libraries, identifying new services and strategies, and breaking down stereotypes, libraries can carve out a new place in today's society.

Where We Are

Public libraries exist to serve a wide range of users and needs. They continue to fulfill multiple roles covering the areas of information, lifelong learning, recreation and leisure, culture, and research. Over the past several decades, technology has trickled into libraries in various forms—card catalogs, microfiche, computers, electronic databases, the Internet, and multimedia collections, just to name a few. For some like the Euclid (OH) Public Library, technology services now dominate the reasons why patrons visit their library. Internet access, meeting room usage, and audiovisual materials are the top three reasons patrons cited for visiting that library. The fact that print materials did not make the top three reasons should not be seen as a negative. Even though patrons may come to the library for a technology reason, they may still leave with a book.

Though technology is a prominent aspect of library service, its role still seems to baffle funding sources, customers, and staff alike. Often technology is integrated in an unsystematic way, creating confusion and leaving patrons and staff wondering what it's all about. Lack of adequate awareness and understanding on the part of funding agencies, the public, and library staff have also created a shaky foundation for technology services, leading to disproportionate technology budgets, mismatched and discontinuous systems, insufficient technology planning, staff rejection of new technologies, and library technology being controlled by government agencies.

Implementing successful information technology practices in your library is a long-term project that takes years, not days or months. A step-by-step, open-minded, practical approach to planning encourages growth in staff knowledge and experience and allows time for all your stakeholders to adapt to technology, evolving needs, and a shifting terrain of resources. Many who grapple with these problems tend to gloss over the process or get too caught up in the details. Just remember that time, experimentation, and experience will lead the way. Also keep in mind that there isn't one cookie-cutter plan or process. Edward Elsner, director of the Delton District (MI) Library, says that his library's technology success has stemmed from focusing on using technology instead of letting technology use the library or determine how it provides services. Keep in mind that no plan or process is an island. Tweak and adapt your approach until you find the right balance.

Where We Are Going

Technology at the library means more than Internet access. Technology is vast and ever growing, and although the Internet plays a critical role, it is not the only component. Current research continues to reflect the importance of technology on all levels.

> As the 21st century begins, dozens of emerging technologies will challenge libraries on a more fundamental scale. These new technologies will challenge libraries to address

essential transformational issues including enhancing convenience and expediency, providing varying and overlapping information formats, extending operating hours and points-of-service, addressing permanency of materials, serving broader populations, and managing costs of services.[1]

When it comes to technology and its future, libraries of all sizes and budgets will take on a variety of pivotal roles, including those of a

center of information

technology literacy provider

access leveler (providing technology to all patrons regardless of age, race, socioeconomic status, disability, etc.)

hub for community information

Trying to recognize and enhance roles such as these is where libraries are at now. Many are moving in new directions, looking at how to successfully integrate tradition with technology. Others get stuck because of a lack of knowledge or resources, unwillingness to move forward, or fear of taking risks. Whether you need a little encouragement or a big push, the next several chapters are for you. The goal is to ease this transition, making technology enticing, practical, and straightforward. For many of you, this transition and new mind-set are about making things more manageable, lessening the intimidation factor, and getting a better handle on what's necessary to fully integrate technology into your library.

Keep in mind that technological innovations are there to support libraries, not replace them. Look for ways to *enhance* your services through technology, moving beyond the library's walls and working to serve your community in new ways. Look to technology in order to build community relationships, reach new users, and develop the role of your library as the neighborhood information hub. Think of yourself as an evangelist for technology. After all, you know information and how access to it can transform people, businesses, and communities. Position your library to be the place in your community most associated with information and technology. Showcase your library as a community and technology leader. Market your library as *the place*— the place where reluctant and confused customers are guided by dedicated, knowledgeable, and friendly staff who lead people through the mysteries of technology just as they have led people through the mystery of finding the right book.

Social Impact

Another important aspect of technology is equality of access. Libraries provide technology to patrons with a wide range of skills and knowledge levels. By providing strong customer service, a variety of programs, and an inviting overall environment (building, web page, etc.) where all groups can come to explore, libraries bridge the "digital divide." This divide comes in two varieties:

the gap between those with resources and those without—an economic gap

the gap between the tech-savvy and the tech-phobic—a knowledge gap

"Many small, rural libraries face additional challenges as they struggle to increase their capacity to provide access with limited resources, technical support, or community partnerships," says Mark Pumphrey, director of the Polk County (NC) Public Library. "We've connected our Polk County Library users to free public Internet access. We're helping to bridge the digital divide in our small county. We're affirming that the public library is the very best place to start on the path of discovery and learning."

PATRON AND STAFF NEEDS

Moving forward with technology in a systematic and productive manner means being aware of the technological needs of your end users—both *community* and *staff*. Rule number one is to know your customer. Successful technology implementations are the result of knowing the answers to the following questions:

> Who are your customers?
>
> What are their needs and wants?
>
> What will successfully aid them in accomplishing their tasks at hand?
>
> How do you bring knowledge about technology to them?

By and large, lack of funding is the most vocalized concern of libraries, yet equally worrisome and limiting is the public's inaccurate perception of public libraries and their vague place within our communities. Funding and public perception go hand in hand. In order to receive proper funding, your library must be valued. To be valued, it must offer services people love and can't live without. This involves fully understanding the people the library is serving and their actual (not perceived) needs. Once this occurs, successful technology-related services will not be far behind.

As varied as libraries are, so too are their customers. In order to figure out your customers' needs, look at where they fit in with respect to their technology know-how. Take a look at figure 1-1. Off the top of your head, what quadrant(s) do your library's patrons fall in? Do you find that they fall in one predominant category or in a variety of categories? In most communities, the majority will fall somewhere in the middle, with a little knowledge, some fear, and

FIGURE 1-1
Library Users' Technology Competence vs. Technology Resources Personally Available to Them

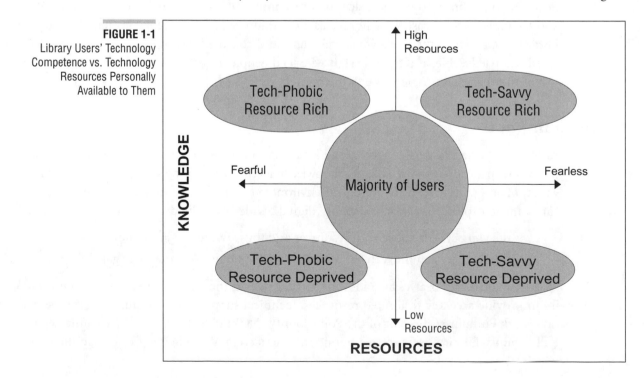

a few resources. The following sections of this chapter will provide you with a rudimentary breakdown of your customers, in general terms. See figure 1-2, which highlights the national averages for these categories of library patrons. This is a starting point for understanding the groups of users of your own library.

Adults

Typical library use by adults is either recreational, work related, or for personal education. Many adult users seek out the library for general computer use (e-mail, Internet, word processing), multimedia/audiovisual collections, in-depth research, or as a first step to connect with other organizations such as school libraries, special libraries, educational organizations, and businesses. Adult library users generally fall into one of three technology levels: novice, intermediate, and technically savvy. Novices need individual instruction, supporting resources, and group training options. Intermediate patrons are in transition, steadily developing skills and wanting to learn more. They need and crave instruction, desiring advanced levels and more specific topics. They also look for public access computers and, often, more sophisticated technologies.

Technically savvy patrons may occasionally find themselves in need of support or public access computers. They look for progressive technologies such as wireless support for their laptops. You may find it difficult to figure out what, if anything, your library can do for these technically savvy, resource-rich (TSRR) patrons. Appeal to their "techiness." Supply a variety of technology solutions, information, and outreach strategies, encouraging these customers to explore new as well as traditional elements of the library (the collection, library programs and services, etc.). Success with this group comes by providing fresh, convenient, progressive, and personalized services that appeal to their needs and technical expectations. These services can include online catalog access from home, online event calendars and program registration, online indexes of information (genealogy, local news, etc.), and wireless access, just to name a few. For example, look at TSRR parents who regularly bring their children to the library for story time. They might bring their laptops with them to do work, pay bills, and so on. Wireless Internet access allows them the freedom to wait for and watch over their children while working. They are using the library in a new way—on their own terms and with minimal impact on library resources. And as savvy as some of them are, most TSRR patrons can't keep up with the pace of change. They need a place to turn to for lifelong learning, a place where they can stay abreast of the latest and newest applications and technologies.

When it comes to the Internet alone, about 59 percent of American adults go online. According to a 2004 survey, 28 percent of American adults are "wireless ready" (i.e., they have used devices that allow them to connect to the Internet by wireless means).[3] So more than one-quarter of all adult Americans use wireless devices—either laptop computers with wireless modems or cell phones—that enable them to go online to surf the Web or check e-mail. In addition, about 41 percent of all Internet users have recently used a laptop that can connect wirelessly to the Internet or a cell phone that lets them send and receive e-mail. The obvious question is, What do these facts mean for libraries, and how can they help libraries define their users and those users' needs?

FAST FACTS
A "THIRD PLACE"

About 23 percent of adult American Internet users have gone online from a "third place," that is, a location other than home or work. Of that group of online Americans, 27 percent have used the Internet at school, 26 percent have used it at friends' or neighbors' homes, and 26 percent have used it at libraries.[2]

FIGURE 1-2
Demographics of Internet Users

Here is the percentage of each group who use the internet. As an example, 71% of adult women use the internet.

	USE THE INTERNET
Total Adults	73%
Women	71
Men	74
Age	
18–29	88%
30–49	84
50–64	71
65+	32
Race / ethnicity	
White, Non-Hispanic	73%
Black, Non-Hispanic	61
English-Speaking Hispanic	76
Community type	
Urban	75%
Suburban	75
Rural	63
Household income	
Less Than $30,000/year	53%
$30,000–$49,999	80
$50,000–$74,999	86
$75,000+	91
Educational attainment	
Less Than High School	40%
High School	64
Some College	84
College+	91

Here is the percentage of home internet users who have dial-up vs. high-speed connections at home. As an example, 34% of home internet users have dial-up connections.

	DIAL-UP	HIGH-SPEED
Home internet users	34%	62%

From http://www.pewinternet.org/trends/User_Demo_4.26.06.htm. Pew Internet and American Life Project, February 15–April 6, 2006 Tracking Survey. N = 4,001 adults 18 and older. Margin of error is ±2% for results based on the full sample and ±2% for results based on internet users. Please note that prior to the January 2005 survey, the question used to identify internet users read, "Do you ever go online to access the Internet or World Wide Web or to send and receive email?" The current two-part question wording reads, "Do you use the internet, at least occasionally?" and "Do you send or receive email, at least occasionally?" The Pew Internet and American Life Project bears no responsibility for the interpretations presented or conclusions reached based on analysis of the data.

Special Needs

Because they often have a higher level of technology anxiety than most, senior citizens are addressed here as a separate group even though they also fit into the adult classification. Due to their personal schedules and financial situations, many senior citizens regularly frequent their public libraries. A fact that surprises many is that an overwhelming majority of seniors have a strong desire to learn about technology and overcome their lack of knowledge and their fear. Many senior citizens want to use and understand technology and at least learn the basics. Consider your library's services such as computer classes and how-to programs that will appeal to them. Also, consider how you present and offer technology services. Special customer service training for staff about how to assist senior patrons with their technology use might be one possibility.

Just as it is important to analyze technology and the role it plays for patrons of all ages and socioeconomic levels, it is equally essential to address technology's role in the lives of users with special needs (i.e., learning and physical disabilities and restrictions). People with disabilities meet barriers of all types when it comes to computer use, including reading, writing, and searching the Internet. However, technology is helping to lower many of these hurdles. Hardware and software tools known as adaptive or assistive technologies have been developed to provide functional alternatives to standard operations. The questions to ask are, What patrons in your community are affected by disabilities, and how do libraries adapt and develop methods and strategies to serve patrons with these special needs?

Children

Children are the up-and-coming technology users. Computers and multimedia (movies, music, electronic games) are now an integral part of children's learning processes, and, unlike adults, they do not know life without these technologies. Research indicates that exposure to technology has significant educational value for children and is key to their development. Since children are the future of libraries, this is an indisputable reason for technological improvement and expansion. It can be difficult for adults to comprehend that many toddlers have already used a computer on a parent's lap or used a mouse by the age of 2. See figure 1-3 to find out how active children really are when it comes to computers. Surveys show that 31 percent of children between the ages of 0 and 3 have used a computer, 48 percent of children ages 0–6 have used one, and 70 percent of those in the 4–6 age range have used one. Even more mind blowing, more than two million American children between the ages of 6 and 17 have their own personal websites.[5]

FAST FACTS

KIDS AND TECHNOLOGY

In 2001, approximately 90 percent of Americans of ages 5–17 used computers, and 59 percent of them used the Internet. In both cases, these usage rates were higher than those for adults. Even kindergartners are becoming technologically savvy: one out of four 5-year-olds used the Internet in 2001.

A report based on 2002 data shows that 99 percent of public schools have Internet access, up from 35 percent eight years ago.[4]

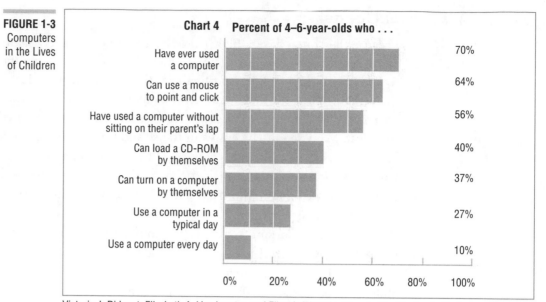

FIGURE 1-3
Computers in the Lives of Children

Victoria J. Rideout, Elizabeth A. Vandewater, and Ellen A. Wartella, "Zero to Six: Electronic Media in the Lives of Infants, Toddlers and Preschoolers," no. 3378 (Fall 2003): 5. The Henry J. Kaiser Family Foundation, http://www.kff.org. This information was reprinted with permission from the Henry J. Kaiser Family Foundation. The Kaiser Family Foundation, based in Menlo Park, California, is a nonprofit, independent national health care philanthropy and is not associated with Kaiser Permanente or Kaiser Industries.

Multimedia technology also heavily influences this age group. Over the past several years there has been an explosion in electronic media marketed directly at children ages 0–6. The most significant findings include

> Children 6 and under spend an average of two hours a day with screen media, mostly television and videos.

> A high proportion of very young children are using new digital media: 50 percent of those ages 4–6 have played video games, and 70 percent have used computers.

> Many parents see media as an important educational tool that is beneficial to their children's intellectual development.[6]

See figure 1-4 for additional information related to media use and young children.

Teens and Young Adults

Technology is *the thing* for teens and young adults. It is an integral part of their lives, and therefore it must play a large part in serving them at your library. In fact, you might hear teens say: "If it isn't online, it just doesn't matter." Whether in the form of computer hardware, software, audiovisual materials, or whatever comes along tomorrow, technology is where it's at for teenagers, both boys and girls alike. Studies show that children and teens are so computer-savvy and so comfortable with technology that they are leading the way, serving as technology pacesetters. Most teens have been online for quite some time now. They are

FIGURE 1-4
Media Use
by Children
Ages 0–6

In a typical day, the percentage of children who spend *more than an hour*:

ACTIVITY	AGE RANGE		
	0–6 YEARS	*0–3 YEARS*	*4–6 YEARS*
Watching TV	53	49	60
Listening to music	41	46	34
Watching videos/DVDs	34	33	35
Reading/being read to	30	30	31
Using a computer	7	3	11
Playing video games	4	1	7
Playing outside	72	68	78

Victoria J. Rideout, Elizabeth A. Vandewater, and Ellen A. Wartella, "Zero to Six: Electronic Media in the Lives of Infants, Toddlers and Preschoolers," no. 3378 (Fall 2003): 14. The Henry J. Kaiser Family Foundation, http://www.kff.org. This information was reprinted with permission from the Henry J. Kaiser Family Foundation. The Kaiser Family Foundation, based in Menlo Park, California, is a nonprofit, independent national health care philanthropy and is not associated with Kaiser Permanente or Kaiser Industries.

FAST FACTS

YOUTH AND THE PUBLIC LIBRARY

- 37.6 percent of youth often engage in school-related activities.

- 26.9 percent of youth often engage in recreation activities.

- 9 percent of youth often engage in personal information activities.

looking for a "connected" environment, and many are looking for access outside the home. (See figure 1-5 for a quick peek at the 18–24 crowd in comparison to other age groups who use the Internet away from home and work.) Whether surfing the Web, instant messaging (IM), podcasting, texting, e-mailing, blogging, or checking out the latest in DVDs, DVRs, and MP3s, technology is a magnet for this user group. This is the perfect opportunity to attract this critical user group to your library.

Traditionally speaking, most teens associate public libraries with recreational reading and homework-related activities. But many are gradually discovering that the library can also be a place where technology is freely and readily available in many forms, whether for word processing, e-mail, audiovisual resources, online gaming, or personal research. Understanding the need for efficient, up-to-date technology provided by knowledgeable staff is a necessity when it comes to serving this customer group. Unfortunately, providing technology and related services for teenagers and young adults can often be the most intimidating because they are the ones with the most tech know-how. Being caught in the middle between wanting to serve teens and not knowing exactly what to do and how to do it is a difficult situation. The important thing to realize is that you *can* do it with a little knowledge and persistence. Incorporating teen needs and wants into your library's technology planning is imperative for success today and tomorrow. After all, the teenagers of today are the taxpayers and voters of tomorrow.

Staff

Viewing and treating your staff as critical technological *customers* can provide extensive benefits to both your library and its patrons. Training staff at all levels and on a wide variety of technologies is vital. Equally critical is educating your employees about the importance of technology and how it fits into your library's mission. It is important that all your staff fully understand the magnitude of technology and its implications for customer service. Demonstrate how technology goes hand in hand with increasing efficiency and streamlining internal

FIGURE 1-5
Likelihood That
Americans Use
"Third Places"
to Access
the Internet

The percentage of American Internet users from each age group who go online from a "third place":

18–24	48
25–34	21
35–44	16
45–54	13
55–64	15
65+	10

Paul Harwood and Lee Rainie, "People Who Use the Internet Away from Home and Work," Pew Internet and American Life Project (March 2004): 6; http://www.pewinternet.org/pdfs/pip_other_places.pdf. The Pew Internet and American Life Project bears no responsibility for the interpretations presented or conclusions reached based on analysis of the data.

procedures and processes. Show your staff how technology can open up a multitude of options for increasing service to coworkers and patrons. When staff members are acknowledged as stakeholders, they gain a sense of accomplishment, see themselves as an important part of the team, grow less intimidated by technology, and ultimately become more dedicated to providing excellent service. They will become better equipped with the skills (technical as well as mental) that are necessary to provide enhanced service to the public, and they will work to strengthen the library's place within the community.

IMPACT OF TECHNOLOGY

What bearing does technology have on your library? Without a doubt, technology leads the way in

> increasing and improving services to patrons
>
> fulfilling the library's function as a local source of information for all types of patrons in all types of formats
>
> realizing the library's role as an equalizer for patrons (when services are free of charge)
>
> helping the library attract segments of the population that are often the hardest to attract—teens (ages 13–17), young adults (ages 18–24), TSRR adults
>
> increasing the library's efficiency by empowering staff, streamlining tasks, and ultimately saving time and money

In order to effectively use and ultimately lead with technology, you need to understand the role of the public library in the twenty-first century, be willing to move beyond tradition, and start to think outside the box. Recognize the relationship between your library and all your external and internal customers. How can technology function in their lives? "Probably the most cutting-edge thing we do [with technology] is not what we do, but how we think about it," says Danis Kreimeier, director of the Yorba Linda (CA) Public Library. "It's fully integrated into the way our library provides service. It is not additional, it's not only for 'grown-ups,' it's not scary, it's fun." No matter what its size, a library that is technologically progressive will be viewed as a critically important component of its community. This means more patrons, increased support, and additional funding. The goal is to add value to your library's resources and services while fostering a customer-centered approach.

DO YOU KNOW IT?

Libraries play a vital role. Your library can be the center of technology for the community, playing many roles but, most important, being a technology leader.

Know your patrons and staff. You have to know who you're serving before you can serve.

Technology will improve your library. Technology will enable your library to better serve its community.

NOTES

1. John Guscott, "These Emerging Technologies Will Change Public Libraries," *Library Futures Quarterly* (February 1, 2001; updated May 1, 2001), http://www.libraryfutures.com/freereports/technology.htm.

2. Pew Internet and American Life Project, "People Who Use the Internet Away from Home and Work" (March 2004), http://www.pewinternet.org.

3. Pew Internet and American Life Project, "28 Percent of American Adults Are Wireless Ready: A PIP Data Memo" (May 2004), http://www.pewinternet.org.

4. Ben Feller, "Youth Rides Technology Waves," *Capper's* 125, no. 25 (December 2003): 31; also available at http://www.infotrac.galegroup.com.

5. Victoria J. Rideout, Elizabeth A. Vandewater, and Ellen A. Wartella, "Zero to Six: Electronic Media in the Lives of Infants, Toddlers and Preschoolers," Henry J. Kaiser Family Foundation, Menlo Park, CA (Fall 2003), http://www.kff.org.

6. Ibid.

7. George D'Elia and June Abbas, "Impacts of Youth's Use of the Internet on Youth's Use of the Public Library," paper presented at the Annual Conference of the New York State Library Association, Rochester, NY, October 21, 2004.

Assess IT 2

The assessment phase is a critical part of the planning process, and although it may initially seem daunting and tedious (and may even seem a bit like overkill), have faith because it is well worth the effort. The goal of assessment is to get a sense of where your library and its overall vision stands in relationship to technology. Assessment is also the primary technique for finding gaps between where your organization is and where it wants to be. This chapter will show you how to assess technology on a variety of levels, from hardware and software to services and policies. It will present clear-cut, basic approaches for easily gathering information that will enable you to move your library in a direction that's relevant to the needs of your staff, your patrons, and your community.

WHAT IS ASSESSMENT?

The terms *assessment* and *evaluation* are often used interchangeably. For the purposes of this book, *assessment* refers to the measurement of a library's technology-related elements and services. For example, how many computers are installed in your library? How old are they? What software is running on them? How technically efficient are your staff? What technology-related policies are in place? *Assessment* also refers to gathering both formal and informal information from users. What do your "customers" (internal and external) want? How do they view and use technology in the library?

As used in this book, the term *evaluation* refers to the "feedback loop"—the study of the overall impact of technology on a library and its users. In other words, evaluation is *ongoing assessment*. Examples might include tracking the impact on public computer use after adding new hardware or software, or evaluating the skill level of your employees after holding a staff technology training session. And as with assessment, evaluation means gathering feedback from patrons and staff. Keep in mind that many of the ideas and tools presented in this chapter also apply to the discussion of evaluation in chapter 10.

A valuable assessment looks at things from both an internal perspective (data and opinions provided by the staff) and an external one (what those outside your organization perceive). In the end, the assessment will illustrate your technological progress. A good assessment will also guide you during the research, information gathering (see chapter 3), and planning (see chapter 4) stages with ease, giving you the informational tools to answer questions such as these:

Where are the gaps and overlaps in our library's service?

Are we actually doing what we think we're doing?

Where should the library focus its future efforts and resources?

How can we do what we're doing better?

An equally helpful, though often unrecognized, attribute of an assessment is the ability to use it to educate staff members about the place and importance of technology within the library. You'd be amazed at how much more valuable something becomes once it is documented on paper. The assessment allows technology personnel to see where things stand more clearly, which in turn enables them to more effectively share this information with others. This is a simple thing that can have a tremendous impact. Having a full knowledge and understanding of technology and its impact on your organization and community is a key to strengthening your library. In addition, being able to easily disseminate that information to others will give you greater credibility, lead to better decision-making, allow easier implementation, and help the library staff provide higher-quality customer service.

The key lesson to be learned here is that assessment should be a regular and essential part of your technology process. All too often, libraries skip the "inventory" phase due to lack of resources or enthusiasm, or they simply shrug it off as not being important. By establishing assessment practices and incorporating them into your daily activities, you will find that the rewards will far outlast your initial planning and implementation stages. Doing so will not only provide better day-to-day efficiency but will also bring long-term benefits. Being able to quickly and easily document your technology planning and the resulting accomplishments is always a plus at budget time or when looking to fund a new project.

TEAMWORK

Effective technology planning must be a collaborative process rather than simply the responsibility of an individual "techie," administrator, or consultant. Small and medium libraries often leave technology to one person's input, opinions, and decision-making, which is generally not the best way to proceed. Medium-sized facilities tend to leave technology solely in the hands of a technology "department," which is also not recommended. The best option is to create a diversified, well-rounded team. As a rule of thumb, teams perform better than individuals. They are able to

accomplish more than individuals (in a shorter period of time)

brainstorm ideas, options, and solutions

detect problems that might be missed by an individual or a single department

develop a strong, well-thought-out plan that incorporates input from a varied, well-represented group

assist in building a rapport among team members that will ultimately increase morale and produce high-quality results

Building a Team

Establishing a technology team does not have to be complicated or cumbersome. The first order of business is to define the common goal of the team (e.g., to find out how the library can better serve its customers with technology). Just by establishing a few simple guidelines, you can begin to form your team, making the best possible decisions about who to involve. The key ingredients for team building include

> keeping the group well rounded
>
> establishing a group that is the appropriate size for the library organization
>
> choosing the "right" facilitator

When building a team, include staff from more than one area or department, and possibly even a patron or two. Look for a balance of different personality types, strengths, and backgrounds, making sure the representatives are from all levels of the library. No matter what the team members' duties or status are in the organization, they should be knowledgeable about library operations, the general uses of technology, and how staff and patrons use the library and related technology. Don't overwhelm the group with "techie" members. Depending on the size of your facility, try to include only one or two people who are responsible for technology on a day-to-day basis.

In a very small rural library, a possible team might consist of a clerk who is responsible for technology, another clerk who specializes in something else, a supervisor, and even a patron. In a library where there are more staff, the team might include a circulation clerk, a reference librarian, a supervisor, a page/shelver, and one or more technology staff.

Don't get caught up in numbers. A team of three can be equally if not more effective than a team of six. Just because your library is small doesn't mean you can't utilize teams. In fact, if well chosen, small teams are generally more efficient and better at producing quick results and meeting tight deadlines. The important thing to remember is that your team's success is dependent on the skills and attitudes of its members.

Once the technology team has been formed, working by a few simple rules or guidelines will help ensure the team is a success. These team operating guidelines are as follows:

> Meetings will be held on an "as needed" basis.
>
> Goals and priorities will be established by the group with direction from library management.
>
> Everyone will keep an open mind, all opinions will be respected, and it's understood that it's okay to disagree.
>
> All team members will participate in discussion and assigned duties; no one dominates.
>
> The group will stay on task in regard to meetings and assigned duties.
>
> Team members will rotate as note taker (this person will take brief "minutes," preferably on a laptop, during meetings).
>
> Decisions will be made together as a group.

Linda Yoder, director of the Nappanee (IN) Public Library, emphasizes:

> Whenever possible and practical, try to involve the staff in the research and investigation of a new program, product, service. Asking input along the way helps reduce the "urge

to resist change" if staff are privy to the conversations. The opportunity for input builds accountability for helping to recognize potential pitfalls, so that if "hiccups" do occur there is more tolerance among staff since they were part of the process.

Choosing the "right" leader for the group is also critical to a team's success. In general, the role of a group leader or facilitator is to oversee the team, keeping everyone on task. As most of you know, this is not an easy or sought-after position. Running meetings, encouraging participation, providing motivation when needed, serving as a liaison between the team and decision-makers, and leading the group to reach its goals and objectives are what it's all about. Choose a team leader who best exhibits these leadership abilities. This person may very well be the one responsible for technology oversight and day-to-day operations, but be careful to keep an open mind because this might not be the case. Choose wisely because this step is key. If you are the person in charge of technology and the one putting the team together, be cautious about automatically assigning yourself as leader. Be honest about what strengths you can bring to the team; technology may be your strength, but serving as team leader might not be.

IDENTIFYING STAKEHOLDERS

The first task of a technology team must be to identify all the library's stakeholders: those people inside and outside the organization who have a vested interest in the library's technology. It is also wise to include staff members outside the technology team in the stakeholder analysis because they will provide a valuable outside perspective. Not only are employees stakeholders themselves, but their participation will assist in establishing their acceptance of the overall goal—technology planning and development.

The list of internal stakeholders might include staff, administrators, board members, volunteers, and Friends of the Library. These stakeholders are crucial when it comes to gathering information about the library and the community during the assessment phase. The team will want to collect ongoing feedback from these stakeholders and will share its planning ideas with them once the time comes.

Equally critical in this process is establishing the external stakeholders. To identify the members of this group, ask the following questions:

> Who in the community has a vested interest in technology in the library? In the library as a whole?
>
> Who can assist in making the library's technology plans and goals a reality?
>
> Who are the people that might be negative toward technology?
>
> Who are the most active or vocal members of the community? Of the library?
>
> Who is involved in other technology activities and organizations in the community?
>
> Who is missing? Who haven't you thought of?[1]

A sample list of external stakeholders might include patrons, existing and potential vendors and suppliers, politicians, business and technology leaders, competitors (bookstores, etc.), and educators. As with the internal stakeholders, the technology team may want to tap the external stakeholders for information during the assessment process, as well as keep them in the loop during the planning phase. (For additional information on stakeholders, gathering information from your community, and general planning for small and medium-sized libraries, visit the Northeast Kansas Library System and its New Pathways to Planning website, listed in appendix B.)

WHAT DOES THE LIBRARY HAVE?

Once all the key players (team members and stakeholders) have been identified, the next objective of the technology team is to find out what technology the library currently has. In other words, it's time to gather information. This part of the assessment provides the groundwork for future planning. The information gathered here is critical when attempting to see where a library has been, where it should be going, and how it will eventually get there. This is also an excellent learning opportunity for the team (and the rest of the library staff) as they help to identify both the quantity and quality of technology in the library, as well as engage stakeholders (staff, administrators, board, local government, the community) in the planning process. An assessment produced with the input and knowledge of multiple people (i.e., the technology team) will help a library to accomplish two very important technology goals: cross-training and shared knowledge. Small and medium libraries often make the mistake of putting just one person in charge of technology, from data collection to decision-making to troubleshooting. Getting started with team building and information sharing during these early stages will lead to a better understanding of organizational goals and objectives among your staff members and will broaden their perspectives and increase their flexibility, efficiency, and effectiveness. And because the information is collected by and shared with multiple staff members, the library will also reap the lasting benefits of improved support and troubleshooting.

It is important at this stage not to try to move too quickly or rush into the decision-making process. A library can only implement new technologies or services once the existing situation has been well documented and analyzed. Understanding the impact of new technologies upon your core technology infrastructure will ultimately produce a more solid, better-received product.

The information-gathering or "inventory" stage is generally where libraries of all sizes get sidetracked. There's certainly a lot to be documented, and this can quickly turn into an overwhelming task. Keep in mind that you don't have to be fanatical in order to produce a valuable assessment. Be organized, take it one step at a time, and record the basics. Use the worksheets in appendix A and refer to this book's web page at http://www.ala.org/editions/extras/Bolan09205/ for ways to quickly and easily capture the necessary information related to equipment and services. Putting extra effort into the assessment will pay off in the long run (i.e., in the planning, budgeting, and staffing phases). Having thorough, up-to-date information at your fingertips means being able to better illustrate the importance and need for technology. It also means easier planning and budgeting.

Hardware, Software, and Infrastructure

The primary tool in assessing your library's existing hardware, software, and network infrastructure is the inventory. Begin by creating comprehensive, itemized inventories of all key elements using a spreadsheet like Microsoft Excel or a database such as Microsoft Access. The key is to log the details electronically so the information can be quickly searched, sorted, and edited. Take into account that this information will be equally (or even more) valuable next

INVENTORIES

year and the year after that, so keep everything up-to-date by adding, deleting, and modifying your equipment and software lists on a regular basis. See appendix A for sample hard copies of the "Hardware Inventory Worksheet" (also to be used for network infrastructure) and the "Software Inventory Worksheet." Be sure to answer the specific questions pertaining to hardware and software. Refer to the "Hardware and Software Assessment/Analysis Worksheet" in appendix A for a sample list of questions. Please note that the questions to be answered on these worksheets are not simply questions on their own. Instead, look at them as guides that will ultimately lead to further questions and discussion during the analysis and planning phases. Always ask yourself, What can the library do with this number, this percentage, this piece of information?

When tackling an inventory, follow these basic tips to keep things simple, smooth, and successful:

Divide the responsibilities of the team.

Choose a software tool that enables you to easily and accurately gather and maintain inventory information from your desktops, servers, and laptops.

Establish a reasonable time frame for completion.

Skip over statistics that are too difficult to obtain. If you don't have the time or resources to devote to finding the answer, move on rather than bring the whole inventory process to a halt.

Move quickly and efficiently through the process. Don't prolong things.

Generalize statistics and counts when necessary. All of the information provided doesn't have to be exact. Remember, this is an internal assessment, not an official report to the state.

Look to surveys as outlined later in this chapter to help fill in the blanks and produce hard-to-find information.

It is especially important to keep staff informed and involved throughout the inventory process and from this point forward. Answer who, what, where, when, why, and how. This is the fastest way to gain their support. The following are questions frequently asked by staff about the inventory, along with some typical or appropriate answers.

Q: Why are we doing a technology inventory?

A: The library needs an accurate inventory of all hardware and software in order to implement a consistent replacement program and negotiate better pricing. More accurate information will also mean better support for both patrons and staff.

Q: What will be inventoried?

A: All technology-related items and information related to them, including computers, the software installed on them, and peripherals such as printers, scanners, network equipment, and telephone and fax devices. No personal files or information will be accessed in any way.

Q: When and where will the inventory be performed, and how long will it take?

A: The total inventory will occur between (date) and (date). Equipment will be inventoried at the location of the equipment on a specified date and time. Staff will be notified prior to the inspection. All passwords must be left with _____ _____ before the inventory. Each individual visit will require approximately (minutes/hours) to complete.

Q: Who will be performing the inventory?

A: _____ will be completing the work. _____ will serve as the contact person if you have questions.

Q: Will the inventory require installation of software on my computer?

A: Yes. A small program will be installed and left on the computer. This program will create a profile of the computer, which includes the hardware and network configuration and a list of installed software. This profile information, along with manually gathered information, will be stored in a centralized database.[2]

Another key element in the hardware and infrastructure assessment is the creation of a graphical depiction of the library, or a "technology floor plan." This will include the basic layout of technology in the library, including the locations and names of workstations, network points, electrical connections, and so on. This step can be as simple or as elaborate as needed for your organization. If you have a blueprint of your facility, consider using that as your foundation. If one is not available to you, see figure 2-1 for a simple alternative. Having an up-to-date visual of your technology layout is a helpful supplement to the inventory worksheets because it depicts the "geography" of the library, which will be critical during initial and ongoing planning as well as throughout the lifetime of maintenance and troubleshooting.

The Community

The next section of the assessment includes a discussion of your patrons. Begin by getting a general sense of who your users are. Basically, *who* is your library serving? What are the general demographics of your community? What are your current customers' use patterns? What are the technology literacy levels of users (and non-users)? What is the competency versus resource demographic? (Refer back to figure 1-1 in chapter 1.) Consult the "Patrons, Services, and Policy Assessment/Analysis Worksheet" in appendix A for a list of starter questions and discussion points that will help you determine who your current and potential technology users are. This information, when combined with the other elements of the assessment, will not only lead to a greater understanding of your library's customers but will also show the way to improved planning of service priorities, allocation of resources, education of stakeholders, and better-focused marketing efforts. (Later in this chapter, tips will be shared for determining the community's perception of technology in the library.)

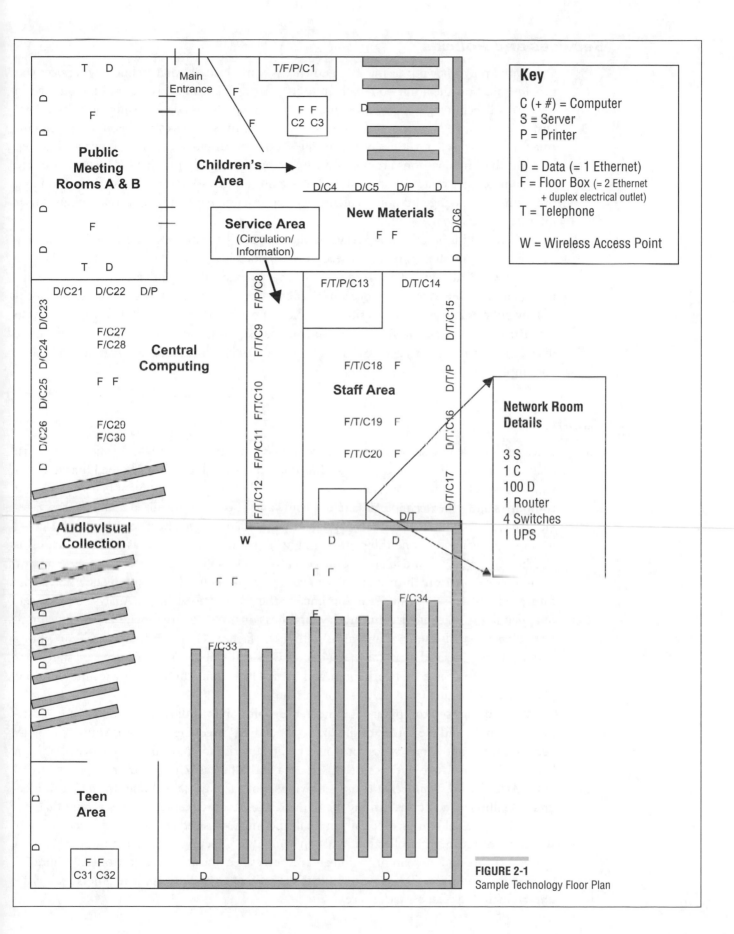

FIGURE 2-1
Sample Technology Floor Plan

Services and Policies

Once you know who your technology audience is, you must ask what technology services you provide and how the library offers them to its patrons. Basically, this piece of the puzzle is a review of all technology-related programs, services, and policies related to the library's external customers (i.e., your patrons). Refer again to the "Patrons, Services, and Policy Assessment/Analysis Worksheet" for a list of starter questions and discussion points. Once again, keep in mind that the questions are not all-inclusive but are merely provided as a starting point. For example, service items can include, but are not limited to, informal and formal training programs, circulating and noncirculating collections, and electronic tools that enhance user interactions, just to name a few.

When looking at technology-related policies at this stage in the game, begin by reviewing general policy questions; you don't need to get too detailed at this point. Basically, make sure you've covered all your policy bases. Look at what rules are already in place. Is everything up-to-date and useful? Where are revisions needed? Are new policies needed? Are existing technology policies and guidelines easily accessible or posted for patrons and staff? Again, refer to the "Patrons, Services, and Policy Assessment/Analysis Worksheet" in appendix A for sample questions to get you started. (See chapter 9 for additional information on creating, reviewing, and implementing policies.)

Facilities

Once you have a clear sense of what the library has in terms of services and policies, you must evaluate how it delivers these services. How does the technology "fit in" to the library? To get your answer, start with a space assessment. In a nutshell, a space assessment helps ensure that computers and other technologies are efficiently and effectively organized and that these "services" have been allocated sufficient space for your customers to effectively use them. Having technology available is one thing; arranging it in a way that is useful as well as practical is another. By reviewing and analyzing the general layout and location of technology resources, the library can increase the overall value of its assessment in terms of planning now and in the future. Follow the sample questions outlined in the "Facility Assessment/Analysis Worksheet" in appendix A. Take into account the layouts, locations, and square footage allotments for all technology-related resources and areas within the facility. Consider the general computing and technology-related areas for the public, as well as the library's training spaces, staff work and service areas, server/network room, and so on. Once again, this is where a technology floor plan is a valuable tool (see figure 2-1 for an example).

With advances in computer equipment, the evolution of audiovisual resources and multimedia formats, and the spread of digitization, defining "adequate space" for your technology becomes more and more critical. It would be no surprise to see technology space allocation become an area where libraries of all sizes make the biggest changes over the next several years. Already several universities are removing all of the physical volumes from their undergraduate libraries and transforming them into digital resource centers. Is this a trend that will soon affect public libraries, especially in small and medium-sized facilities that are continually stretched for room, with collections and departments competing against one another for shelf space? As more and more information and resources become available electronically, libraries of all shapes and sizes will need to reevaluate the ratio of technology space to other areas of the library, including that of stack space.

Speaking of the stacks, how much shelf space in your library is dedicated to books and magazines that deal with technology-related topics? Libraries often overlook this consideration during the assessment phase, yet it is important. Have you ever noticed how one of the largest sections in bookstores is always the computer and information technology section? In addition, pay close attention to the physical location of technology-related materials in your library. In particular, observe their proximity to service areas throughout the facility. Consider putting the technology books near heavily used computer areas so that users have a handy resource when they need help. This issue becomes more significant as libraries emphasize customer service and expand their repertoire of technologies. Close proximity and easy access for patrons to get to staff members (and vice versa) is imperative.

Staff

Staff are the key to effective technology assimilation and acceptance in any library, especially in a small to medium-sized organization where employees often take on a multitude of roles and duties. Analyzing how your library is "staffing" technology as well as measuring and evaluating your staff's technology skills and attitudes will aid in developing a stronger program that will meet the needs of the library and the community. In order to successfully assess technology competencies, staffing levels, and attitudes, you must first understand the basics. You can begin by answering the questions outlined in the "Staff Assessment/Analysis Worksheet" in appendix A. Start addressing general staff statistics such as the number of full-time and part-time employees, their involvement with technology, and projected staff growth. Next, tackle areas related to the technology proficiency of staff, their customer service skills related to technology, staff training opportunities, and equipment and software designated for the staff. (See chapter 5 for additional information on staffing.)

TRADITIONAL STATISTICS VS. STATISTICS FOR A NEW CENTURY

Libraries gather statistics on every aspect of their operations: door counts, circulation, reference transactions, acquisitions, technical services, program attendance, meeting room bookings, and so on. The question is, Has your library analyzed this information to see what it reveals about the use of technology in your library? In today's libraries it is critical to begin thinking out of the box in terms of statistics. You can begin by looking at traditional statistics in a new way to try to figure out how technology can help adapt and streamline processes, workflow, and customer service. For instance, has circulation leveled or dropped off but daily visitors keep increasing? Maybe this means the library is seeing more usage of computers. It is important not only to collect statistics but also to look at what the numbers are telling you. The message is sometimes hidden, but it can quickly be revealed if you open your mind and look at what is truly going on.

Libraries must also start collecting and analyzing data beyond that of traditional statistics. This may mean going beyond the figures gathered for your system and state reports. As the mission and purpose of public libraries change and grow, it becomes more and more important to find new ways of measuring service. For example, service is not always about circulation, although this is an important element; it's about "touches." In other words, how does the library reach out and "touch" its customers beyond checking out materials? A few examples of "new" types of information gathering include trying to answer the following questions:

How many Internet users does the library have daily? Monthly?

How many hits does the library's website get daily? Monthly? What pages are getting used the most?

How many patrons bring their own laptops into the library?

If the library is a wireless hotspot, how many wireless connections are made daily? Monthly?

What is the monthly circulation of audiovisual and technology-related collections?

What is the technology/computer training attendance for the public? (See figure 2-2 for sample computer training statistics.)

How many technology-related reference questions (i.e., bibliographic instruction as well as general assistance) do staff answer daily? Monthly? Annually? These questions can be tracked by a reference log.

Reference Log

A simple and often overlooked data collection tool is the detailed reference log. Of course, this tool is valuable not only for technology-related questions but for everything related to what's happening at the reference desk (specific materials people are asking for, services requested, etc.). Many libraries strip the reference statistics process down to tally sheets because they say they're too busy to collect anything beyond a hash mark. They claim they are saving time and money. The response to this thinking is, How can spending five to ten extra seconds to record information that leads to compelling documentation for services rendered—which in turn leads to increased support and funding—be a waste of time? Who's too busy for this?

A sample reference log is provided in figure 2-3. Use this as a guide in creating what works best for your facility. Modify it to work with your library's procedures and needs. General instructions for the completion of a reference log are as follows.

1. Provide a brief description of the question in the "Information Requested" box. Basically, follow the guidelines for your state outlining what is considered a reference question. For example, include electronic bibliographic instruction such as assistance searching the Internet, assistance finding technology-related materials such as computer instruction manuals, audiovisual/multimedia items, and so on.

2. Input how the question was handled in the "How Handled" box (i.e., how did you help the customer?). Hint: Develop a code system or list of abbreviations for staff, so there is consistency. That way, the information will be much clearer and easier to compile. Examples may include BI for bibliographic instruction, IS for in stock (i.e., the item requested was on the shelves), REF for referral to another library, H for placed a hold, and so on.

3. List non-reference questions too (even though you probably won't include them in reference counts for system or state reporting). They can be very telling. Simply check the "Non-Ref" box to indicate that it should not be counted in general reference statistics. Items such as technical assistance with public access computers (PACs), Internet, and databases are generally included here, for example, loading paper, rebooting computers, directional questions, and circulation inquiries. Assign a staff member the duty of creating a monthly compilation of relevant statistics.

FIGURE 2-2
Computer Training Statistics

MONTH	# OF OPAC CLASSES	ATTENDANCE OF OPAC CLASSES	# OF COMPUTERS FOR BEGINNERS CLASSES	ATTENDANCE OF COMPUTERS FOR BEGINNERS CLASSES	# OF BASIC INTERNET CLASSES	ATTENDANCE OF INTERNET CLASSES	# OF ADVANCED INTERNET CLASSES	ATTENDANCE OF ADVANCED INTERNET CLASSES	TOTAL # OF CLASSES	% INCREASE FROM PREVIOUS MONTH	TOTAL ATTENDANCE	% INCREASE FROM PREVIOUS MONTH
January	2	9	1	5	2	10	2	17	7		41	
February	4	23	2	10	2	11	3	18	11	57.1	62	51.2
March	3	16	2	8	4	20	2	9	11	0.0	53	-14.5
April	3	15	3	8	3	13	3	13	12	9.1	49	-7.5
May	2	15	2	10	4	31	2	11	10	-16.7	67	36.7
June	3	20	2	12	3	14	1	7	9	-10.0	53	-20.9
July	2	9	2	8	2	12	1	10	7	-22.2	39	-26.4
August	2	13	1	8	2	8	2	9	7	0.0	38	-2.6
September	2	11	1	6	2	14	1	7	6	-14.3	38	0.0
October	4	19	1	5	2	13	2	13	9	50.0	50	31.6
November	2	12	3	14	3	13	2	10	10	11.1	54	8.0
December	1	5	2	9	2	14	2	12	7	-30.0	40	-25.9
Total	30	167	22	103	31	178	23	136	106		584	

FIGURE 2-3
Reference
Questions
Log

INFORMATION REQUESTED	HOW HANDLED	NON-REF	INFORMATION REQUESTED	HOW HANDLED	NON-REF
1.			11.		
2.			12.		
3.			13.		
4.			14.		
5.			15.		
6.			16.		
7.			17.		
8.			18.		
9.			19.		
10.			20.		
COMMENTS/OBSERVATIONS:					

Adapted from the Webster (NY) Public Library's reference log.

4. Finally, at the bottom of the sheet, include general observations and comments related to patrons and their use of the library. This is a great way to gather qualitative information from staff.

Sampling Computer Usage

When gathering non-traditional statistics, you may need to be inventive. Remember that there are no magical formulas. Since many statistics are often virtually impossible to gather without spending an exorbitant amount of time and resources, sometimes it all boils down to being resourceful. You might want to use sampling methods. For example, when trying to analyze the number of public PCs needed in your library, you can perform a study of computer usage. Select three to five sample days and assign team members or staff to take timed samples (every half hour or hour) of how many computers are available or occupied at each sample point. Repeat the process as desired. The resulting information will allow you to assess capacity and how many or what percentage of the day computers are "booked."

Using your judgment and your own sampling will give you a much more accurate idea of your technology needs than "standard" formulas. What may be enough computers for Library A may not be enough for Library B, even though the two libraries may have similar population sizes, number of cardholders, and collections. Demographics vary widely, and, as a result, no two communities are alike.

When it comes to assessing the staff's computer needs, it can get a bit tricky. Consider this: a general rule of thumb is that full-time staff members with multiple job responsibilities receive their own computer. Part-time staff (twenty hours per week) with a variety of duties beyond circulation and reference share computers (one computer for every two part-time employees). In other words, this rule translates into one computer per full-time equivalent (FTE) for staff with numerous job responsibilities. This can be a general guideline for libraries trying to plan the number of computers per FTE, but again, this is not an exact science. It's all about using judgment. For instance, when it comes to a technical services or cataloging department, one computer per part-time employee might be necessary, depending on the workflow of the department, staff schedules, and so on. There are always questions and considerations that go beyond asking, How many FTEs does the library have? and these always end up determining what is best and appropriate for your library and its situation. This is what analysis is all about: figuring out how to translate raw data into answers about your library and its course for the future.

Other Methods

New software affords a simpler and more permanent path for non-traditional data collection. There are now a number of excellent software applications (both for-purchase and freeware) that will allow you to automatically capture valuable data such as computer usage, capacity loading, web statistics, wireless statistics, program statistics, meeting room use data, and so on. For example, when assessing the number of computer or Internet users, you can try any of the various PC reservation applications on the market. Most wireless solutions will also have some sort of log on counter for gathering data about the number of connections made. When dealing with web stats and counts, be wary of putting too much emphasis on statistics, because the underlying technology of the Internet makes this data entirely inaccurate and sometimes misleading. You should only use web statistics to garner a basic impression of your site's usage over time, the general popularity of pages, and so on, while remembering that even these assertions can be as inaccurate as the statistics themselves.

No matter what data are being collected, there is enough variety and growth in the software marketplace so that applications are available for libraries of all budgets and sizes. One last tip: always compare statistics from month to month and, ultimately, from year to year in order to see if there are increases, declines, recognizable patterns, and other trends.

GETTING INPUT

Equally critical during the assessment phase is getting input from as many stakeholders as possible. This is necessary in order to fully comprehend how technology in the library is viewed, understood, and acknowledged. Try approaches for obtaining input that will best suit your environment, and then gather the best data possible for your situation. You will notice that the techniques described in this section are neither complicated nor beyond a small or medium-sized library's scope. Again, it is all about being creative. Know up-front that one method of getting input will not be right for everyone. It doesn't take long to realize that your approach for internal customers (employees, volunteers) may be quite different from one for external customers.

So what are the benefits of going beyond inventories and assessment worksheets to gather input directly from stakeholders? Well, there are a number of them. Generally speaking, the greatest asset in any organization is its employees. Unfortunately, most libraries do not grasp the attitudes and perceptions of their staff, so by more actively involving them in the assessment phase (either directly or indirectly), libraries will begin to better understand the mindset of their employees. This step will also establish a positive rapport by demonstrating the library's willingness to listen and include staff in its planning. The technology team must be prepared to make a commitment to listen to the staff and follow up on what they have to say, thoroughly compile and analyze their responses, and openly share the results with decision-makers. These actions will lead to happier and more knowledgeable workers who can better serve themselves and the community. When collecting information from internal customers such as employees, three highly recommended approaches that will provide the most valuable feedback are technology evaluation surveys, internal focus groups, and personal observations from staff.

When it comes to external customers, this next level of assessment provides a library with a way to view the interests and needs of its community and then compare them to the goals, ideas, and capabilities of the library. There is no arguing that collecting information from the community can be time-consuming, but it is also essential in gathering valuable input and public support. It is also an excellent marketing tool and a perfect opportunity to draw administrators and other decision-makers into the planning process. There are numerous ways to gather data from your current and future patrons, from surveys to public meetings to focus groups. Again, choose the method that works best for your library, but remember that no matter what tools you decide to use, the most important step is to listen to what is being said. Both internal and external customers need to see the benefits of technology. By getting input, you will gather information as well as begin to build a technology relationship with users. With participation comes ownership and consensus, which ultimately lead to successful implementation.

Helpful Tools

When it comes to gathering information, there are a variety of simple tools that are both suitable and useful for the small and medium-sized library. The following are some key types, but they are by no means a complete list of options.

Surveys

The most common and generally the easiest of data collection methods is the survey, whether in paper or electronic format. Surveys provide an excellent way to validate or contradict what the technology team and library management thinks or believes. No matter what format you use, the survey should remain narrow, focusing on the topic at hand: technology. A good survey will gather basic data as well as reveal the participants' feelings, level of awareness, satisfaction, and other needs related to the topic. When it comes to surveying staff, keep their

TIPS FOR CREATING EFFECTIVE TECHNOLOGY SURVEYS

- Identify basic objectives for the survey before writing down a single question. Look at what has already been gathered in the inventory phase, find out where the holes are, where additional and supporting information is needed. One common mistake in surveys is asking too many questions that provide redundant or pointless data.

- Begin the survey with a brief overview of the objectives of the survey, and end the survey with a short explanation of how the information will be used.

- Keep questions simple and avoid wordiness and technical jargon. Be brief, direct, and clear.

- Keep the overall survey short and sweet. Include no more than fifteen to twenty questions if possible (definitely don't go beyond thirty).

- For quantitative questions use a scale such as frequency (Never, Rarely, Sometimes, Often, Almost Always), agree/disagree (Strongly Disagree, Disagree, Agree, Strongly Agree), or quality (Poor, Fair, Good, Excellent). No matter what you choose, be consistent.

- Consider incorporating at least one open-ended question for gathering input on suggestions for improvement, expectations, and opinions on specifics.

- Create questions that will not only bring forth data and open, honest responses but will also educate those taking the survey.

responses confidential and anonymous. Have one person on the team responsible for collecting and compiling the data. This might require a team member who is not on the staff. When it comes to conducting the survey, although staff will be required to complete any in-house surveys that come their way, you should also consider providing incentives to them in order to encourage positive attitudes and timely completion. Enticements for external customers may also be considered in order to maximize their participation and return rate. (See the sidebar "Tips for Creating Effective Technology Surveys" for more survey tips.)

Consider using online surveys to gather information from as many internal and external stakeholders as possible. Online surveys not only simplify the clerical work involved, but they typically are less expensive than paper forms and produce a higher response rate. There are numerous options for creating online surveys: from using a web editor, to freeware, to affordable subscription services. Consider options that allow you to not only generate surveys but also manage lists and notifications, track activity, and generate reports. (See the section on this chapter in appendix B for some vendors.) Many types will also allow you to print the surveys, which is a plus. This latter option might seem strange since this is a "technology" survey, but bear in mind that not everyone is online. Wouldn't it be a telling statistic in itself to analyze which types of stakeholders submit electronically versus on paper?

Focus Groups

Although it may seem tempting, it is important not to restrict your technology assessment to inventories and surveys. In order to produce a well balanced evaluation, you should supplement quantitative information with more qualitative findings that stem from meetings, observations, interviews, evaluations, and suggestions. Consider conducting focus groups first. These will provide a means of gathering in-depth information on opinions and attitudes.

They are also a good starting point because they are small in size and allow you to concentrate on getting the input of a specific group, such as teens, a neighborhood association, senior citizens, working moms, small business owners, and so on. Focus groups are generally small (between five to ten people) and informal, which also means they are less intimidating. They are also short term and allow you to zero in on a particular topic or topics. Keep the meetings relatively short, one or two hours in length; include both library and non-library users; and make arrangements for refreshments.

Assign a technology team member or two as moderators and ask a staff member from outside the technology team to serve as note taker for the meetings. Before holding any sessions, brainstorm topics for discussion and prepare an outline for the group. Use the "Technology Brainstorming Worksheet" in appendix A as a starting point. (Note: This worksheet is also a great reference tool when creating an assessment summary. It will also come in very handy when completing your needs analysis, as discussed in chapter 4.)

Presentations

A natural progression from focus groups is large group presentations and public meetings. Focus groups can provide an initial sounding board for the technology team, laying the groundwork for further discussion with the community at large. This is also an excellent opportunity to get top decision-makers actively involved in the assessment process. Have a member of the technology team partner with the library director or board member, and then approach local organizations such as the parent-teacher organization, Rotary Club, or home-school association and ask if you can attend one of their meetings as guest speakers. Also consider holding one or two open informational meetings at the library. No matter where and who you're addressing, always keep presentations brief, well organized, and to the point, remembering that the primary purpose is to hear what the community identifies as its important technology issues.

Suggestion Box

Suggestion boxes have been a permanent fixture in libraries for quite some time now. The key here is to look with a fresh eye on an "old" tool—from how the data are collected to how the tool is marketed. Instead of a box, why not place an easel pad or two near the computer and service areas asking library customers to write comments related to technology? When it comes to utilizing the traditional suggestion box, don't hide it; instead, give it a name like "Your Ideas" and, most of all, promote it! Make it stand out, let people know where it is, and train staff to encourage customers to submit information. Many staff fear "the box" because it is generally associated with negative patrons, complaints, and problems. Convince your staff to look at it as an assessment tool, not a means to disciplinary action. Additionally, take the suggestions seriously, follow through, and always respond to the "suggestee." Whether replying personally or in a section on the library's web page or bulletin board that addresses input, show you have paid attention. When customers see results from their ideas and suggestions, they will be more likely to lend you their time when it comes to giving feedback, and you have most likely created new library advocates as well.

Observations

Firsthand accounts and stories about user experiences with technology in the library are indispensable pieces of information for a technology assessment. Using the "Comments/

SURVEYS VS. FOCUS GROUPS

When compared to other data collection methods, surveys are generally the easiest type to implement. They also draw out more open and honest responses, which means that participants are more likely to express criticisms and concerns. One drawback to surveys is their lack of "interactivity." The feedback received in a survey is typically limited to the questions you ask, whereas a method such as a focus group provides an interactive forum that spurs a broader context of discussion. This often leads to a greater degree of feedback and assessment. The drawback to focus groups is the suppression of honest criticism (as generated with anonymous surveys) because many people are fearful of stating critical opinions in person. When all is said and done, no method is perfect. All have their pros and cons, so the lesson to be learned is to use an assortment of methods to get the best results.

Observations" section of the reference log, have the staff make notes about what they observe in regard to users and technology throughout the course of a day, week, or month. These notes may take the form of quick comments and remarks or more elaborate accounts and anecdotes. Staff should be encouraged to jot down their observations in an impartial, unbiased manner, whether positive or negative in nature, success stories or malfunctions and disappointments. Their remarks may range from how users are assisted and instructed on various technologies throughout the library to what the library "looks like" at different times of the day as far as activity levels go. One last tip: feel free to adapt the reference log for circulation staff so that all employees can participate. If necessary, replace the reference log method with something different; as long as it works for your library, that's all that matters.

Evaluations

Last but not least, don't forget about capturing input at the close of library programs via the evaluation process. What could be a better time for gathering information from a captive audience? Seize the moment! Hopefully you are already doing some type of evaluation for some or all of your library's programs, so this is not a new concept. Evaluations come in all shapes, but most commonly they are simple paper forms or quick exit interviews at the close of a library program. If neither of these collection methods works for you, consider trying something new such as the easel idea outlined in the "Suggestion Box" section of this chapter. Or even better, be original. When piggybacking on a program evaluation to capture other useful information for the library, don't limit yourself solely to technology-specific programs such as computer classes. Look to general programs that draw a variety of library users: story times, book discussion groups, travel logs, and so on.

   A written program evaluation should generally be short and sweet and primarily address the program at hand. If you decide to use the program evaluation as a dual-purpose assessment tool, add just *one* technology-related question at the end of the standard form that tackles what you want to know. Depending on your library and its needs, this question may be very focused and specific, such as, Would you like to see _____ at the library? It could also be a question such as, What technology would you like to see at the library? or What technologies do you use most frequently in the library? These would be followed by a list of options with check boxes. It might also be helpful to refer back to the sidebar "Tips for Creating Effective Technology Surveys" because many of the same rules apply for evaluations. The resulting information will also tie in nicely with your technology needs assessment, as discussed in chapter 4.

What Are Other Libraries Doing?

While library service has not traditionally been viewed as a competitive "business," you still should look at other public libraries in your state and from around the country to see how their technology and related services compare to yours. Gather both comparative library data (service population, library budget, technology budget, number of computers, etc.) and general technology-related information on services and practices. See how your library compares with others.

Where does your library succeed?

Where does it lag behind?

What information is useful for collecting in the planning stages?

What ideas are others implementing that might be beneficial to your library?

Some libraries exclusively compare themselves to neighboring libraries (within their own state) similar to their own size, but this can be very shortsighted. There's no doubt this information is useful and has its purpose, as it has been a standard part of needs assessments for years, but be careful how you analyze and use this data. See figure 2-4 for a sample library comparison and refer to appendix A for a copy of a "Library Comparison Worksheet." Also, be cautious when comparing your library to others based solely on one or two criteria (e.g., population, budget, staff size). Many libraries get caught up in numbers that are virtually meaningless unless one has the big picture. For example, Libraries X, Y, and Z might each have populations between 38,000 and 45,000 and budgets of $1 million. Libraries X and Y each only have 12–15 public PCs. On the other hand, Library Z, with the same population and budget, has 40 public PCs. Instead of accepting that your library (with a population of 41,000 and a $980,000 budget) should have no more than 15 public PCs (based on the majority response, of course), ask yourself, Why the difference between libraries? Think of how you can use this information. Investigate and find out the particulars. Don't just accept numbers at face value or go with the old saying that "the majority rules."

What is equally informative (and highly recommended), yet often disregarded, is to look at libraries outside your own library's immediate vicinity. You'd be amazed at what you will discover: other libraries can be great idea generators and confidence boosters. People tend to get caught up in how their particular region or state does things and to forget that there's a whole other library world out there. You might consider doing a simple comparison grid that includes your library and a handful of other similar facilities across the country. In addition, when gathering specific information about what other libraries are doing with technology equipment, services, and staffing, don't necessarily limit yourself to libraries similar to your own in size and budget. Look at smaller and larger facilities as well. Technological innovation and success are not limited by a library's size or budget. Just look at the model libraries listed in appendix C; these libraries are doing great things with technology. Search for libraries via the Web, magazine databases, and key resources such as WebJunction that specialize

FIGURE 2-4
Sample Library Comparison

LIBRARY	POPULATION	EXPENDITURES PER CAPITA	BOOKS PER CAPITA	LOANS PER CAPITA	REGISTERED BORROWERS AS % OF POPULATION	HOURS OPEN PER WEEK (unduplicated)	ATTENDANCE PER CAPITA (persons entering the library)	REFERENCE TRANSACTIONS PER CAPITA	STAFF PER 1,000 POPULATION	MICRO-COMPUTERS FOR PUBLIC USE
A	43,030	40.07	4.1	10.1	69.4	69.5	5.8	2.0	0.7	26
B	37,932	44.08	3.2	9.1	63.9	68	5.5	0.8	0.8	3
C	42,219	36.15	2.5	11.0	54.4	68	3.9	1.4	0.6	29
D	42,232	36.96	3.1	16.2	71.8	70	6.9	1.1	0.9	7
E	45,134	35.55	2.6	9.8	47.8	72	7.3	1.5	0.7	26
F	36,870	36.19	3.3	8.8	77.8	68	4.8	1.6	0.5	8

Adapted from Moline Public Library Needs Assessment, Moline, IL (November 2000).

in technology for smaller libraries.[3] On-site field trips are also highly recommended. Any evidence you can provide that demonstrates what other libraries are doing, and, in particular, how they're doing it successfully, will ultimately encourage support in your own library. Where there's a will there's a way, and remember, most ideas can be modified to meet your own library's needs and situation.

One word of caution: when comparing your library to others (no matter if they're local or out of state), don't base your future decisions (such as how many computers to add) exclusively on what other libraries your size have instituted. Keep in mind that these data reflect what others have done, not always what they *should have* done. And when looking at comparable libraries, don't stop at gathering comparative statistics. Find out exactly what these libraries are doing; visit their websites or contact them directly. Don't be afraid to ask about current plans, practices, and ideas.

SUMMARIZE YOUR FINDINGS

After the assessment team has gathered all the data, there will certainly be a massive amount of information to sort through. The key here is to begin organizing the data into a format that is manageable instead of overwhelming. The end result will be a technology assessment summary; this can take the form of a simple bulleted list or a more detailed report. (See the "Sample Technology Assessment Summary" in appendix A.)

No matter how your summary is presented, its content should be succinct and easy to understand because the summary will be one of the primary documents used during the remainder of the planning phase. In many instances, the summary is used as an introduction (or supplement) to the formal, written technology plan (see chapter 4). On the whole, a truly functional summary should do the following:

> Provide description, not opinion or argument.
>
> Be based on facts and focus on describing findings.
>
> Have an objective tone and avoid drawing conclusions or using statements such as "The library should be . . ." or "Knowing this, the library must . . ."
>
> Be clear so the information can be easily understood by people of various technology competencies.
>
> Be comprehensive in scope and cover all the major categories discussed in this chapter.
>
> Be as generic as possible, i.e., make no reference by name or any other means by which people can be uniquely identified.

Another helpful summary tool that can prove extremely useful during the planning phases is a "big picture technology analysis" (see figure 2-5). This is a quick and easy way to identify the strengths, weaknesses, opportunities, and challenges posed by technology at your library, as based on your findings so far. Simply follow the instructions on the grid and fill in the boxes accordingly.

FIGURE 2-5
Big Picture Technology Analysis

	Current Strengths Cite the most positive aspects of technology and technology services at the library.	**Current Weaknesses** Cite the weaknesses related to technology and technology services at the library.
INTERNAL		
EXTERNAL		
	Future Opportunities List the best opportunities for future excellence related to technology within the library.	**Future Challenges** List possible challenges/dilemmas the library will face with deploying new and improved technology.
INTERNAL		
EXTERNAL		

TIMELINE

The time a library takes to develop and implement a technology assessment can vary tremendously and depends on a number of factors, including:

- the size of the library
- the size of the planning team and the extent of involvement from other staff and stakeholders
- the scope of the assessment effort (e.g., how many tools will be utilized, how much needs to be inventoried, how in-depth will qualitative assessment be)
- the amount of time and effort a library is able and willing to devote to the assessment

Generally a well-planned, thorough assessment for a small or medium-sized library should take three to six months to complete. Data collection is the most time-consuming part of the job and is usually spread out over a period of several months. Team members should plan on meeting at least once a month (if not more) so they can get acquainted with the process and begin to define goals and objectives (action steps). The first few team meetings may extend three or more hours, but as the assessment goes on, meetings become shorter and are generally used to check progress and coordinate efforts.

DO YOU KNOW IT?

Assessment is vital. Without an assessment, how do you know where to begin and how to move forward?

Teamwork is the key. No person can do or know it all. Teams help break up the workload, provide better feedback and overall communication, and help build long-term support for the plan.

Know your stakeholders. Knowing your customers and stakeholders will yield better results during the assessment and will guarantee your efforts are successful.

Inventory and assessment. Collect information in a systematic and practical way and continually update it as you move forward.

Get input. How do you know the answer to a question unless you ask? Engage your customers and learn about how your library is really doing, as well as where it should be headed.

Keeping up with the Joneses. Comparing your library to others isn't the most important way to judge your library, but it certainly provides a good "measuring stick" and can furnish great ideas. It also never hurts at budgeting and funding time.

Summarize your findings. Nobody outside the technology team is going to pore over the vast amount of information collected, so summarize your findings and make everyone's life easier. Once you have pulled it all together, you'll notice that the planning and implementation stages will start falling into place.

NOTES

1. Taken in part from Martha Hale, Patti Butcher, and Cindi Hickey, "New Pathways to Planning," Northeast Kansas Library System (2003), http://skyways.lib.ks.us/pathway/.

2. "Frequently asked questions" sheet taken in part from J. Velasco, "University-wide Computer and Telecommunications Inventory," New Jersey City University (2001), http://www.njcu.edu/dept/its/documents/support/InventoryFAQ.pdf.

3. WebJunction is an online community where library staff meet to share ideas, solve problems, take online courses, and more. For additional information, visit http://webjunction.org.

Know IT 3

The next step to realizing your library's technology potential is to build confidence by becoming familiar with the subject matter: technology. With familiarity comes knowledge, and with knowledge comes success. Once the assessment is under way, the technology team should begin researching potential technologies. Remember, you can't plan unless you know what to plan for. This chapter is all about discovering what your options are so you can move forward into the planning process—it is not meant to be an exhaustive technology course. Instead, consider it as a primer that will help you get a handle on the jargon, outline the most basic concepts, and provide you with some pointers and advice on where to go to learn more about the technology your library needs.

Developing a solid understanding of technology can be quite a liberating experience; the insights it provides result in improved decision-making and better implementation of solutions suited to your library's patrons and staff. Unfortunately, this stage is also where intimidation generally sets in. Many people get nervous, believing they will not be able to understand the concepts or "get it." Don't be afraid! Technology does not have to be rocket science. You don't have to know how to configure a router in order to speak knowledgeably to a technology person who does have this skill. Technology experts may try to intimidate you with jargon and complex-sounding topics, but remember that the basics of technology are just that—basics. So don't let fear overwhelm you. Learn the basics, begin to assimilate the jargon, and most of all, don't be afraid to question or even challenge the so-called technology experts. It is important not to let them abuse their power or use their expertise to derail the goals and objectives of the library. Defend the technological needs of your library and its customers as vigorously as you would defend your patrons' privacy. Don't back down, and when you don't understand something, research it, study it, and ask questions.

The alternative to this sort of collaborative learning is to put technology decision-making in the hands of one or a few "technology experts" (whether on the library staff, employed by the local town or city government, or a hired consultant). This is rarely in the best interest of the library or the community, so having an educated technology team of decision-makers as well as a knowledgeable staff is essential. Keep in mind, it's not about understanding the details of every technology out there, it's about getting a grasp on the basics, and even more important, understanding the language and jargon. It's also about feeling confident, knowing what questions to ask, and knowing where to go to find answers. As overwhelming as the task may seem, you must learn to keep up-to-date and to continually educate yourself about technology. This involves finding the answers to questions such as, What options are out there? and How do I effectively work with all of the information and make good decisions? The purpose of this chapter is to provide you with a solid framework for what you and your team need to learn about technology.

A key concept when looking at and evaluating technology is to separate the available technologies into at least four categories. In this book, information technology is separated into the following groups:

Must Have. These are the items you should already have at your library. If you don't have these technologies, you are probably behind where you should be. Focus on learning these areas first. Have these basic elements in place before moving on to the next category.

Must Get. These are typically technologies that have generated "buzz" for a while, and many libraries have most likely already implemented them, or are currently doing so. These technologies are just shifting into the Must Have category from either the More Is Better or Technology Thriller categories.

More Is Better. If a piece of chocolate is good, then a bar of chocolate is better. These technologies often have elements that are Must Have, but the more of them you can offer the better. They will typically have a fairly wide and growing appeal to your customers. These technologies should definitely be under consideration for your technology plan if they fit your library's mission.

Technology Thrillers. These items might very well "make someone's day," whether it is patrons or staff. However, they are often limited in their breadth of appeal and would most likely not be missed by the vast majority of your internal and external customers. These types of technologies have the potential of setting your library apart as a technology leader, but their implementation must be weighed against the long-term interests and priorities of the library and the community.

This kind of categorical approach is adapted from commercial product development and marketing concepts, but it applies well to technology planning and assessment because it helps you better analyze what your library needs and what it can live without. This model is particularly relevant when attempting to sort out what you "have to know" and "have to have" versus what you "might want to learn" and "may want to implement" now or in the future.

In order to best highlight the various technologies and concepts surveyed in this chapter, we have organized them into the four categories set out above, which best define their current status in the library world. These four classifications may change over time, so it is important to understand the basic assessment of why a specific technology belongs in one category versus another and how some technologies may cross categories. The technologies covered under these headings in this chapter are not an exhaustive list, nor should this chapter be considered the repository of all you need to know about technology. Fortunately, by using the Internet, everyone, including the amateur, can quickly and easily find information on a variety of topics. Credible resources for the details of any technology can be found on the Web, as well as in texts that are probably already in your library's collection. For additional information, please refer to the section on this chapter in appendix B, as well as the resource libraries in appendix C, where you can find numerous references to helpful resources.

MUST HAVE

The Must Have category includes those core technologies that are essential for the small and medium library and that must be considered the highest priority as you move into the needs assessment and planning stages.

A Solid Network

A solid network infrastructure is the backbone of any library. It won't matter what other technologies you have if your network is unreliable. The network is absolutely and without question the most important aspect of your library's overall system, so do not skimp: buy best-in-class products and make sure the people (internal or external) who manage the network are knowledgeable, reliable, and good communicators.

So what is a network? Think of a network like you would think of telephones. Basically, a network provides a way for computers and other equipment to talk to each other. Networking is a way to connect to the Internet, other computers, printers, and more. All of the components of a network need to speak the same language, and they all have to be connected to each other. The network infrastructure primarily consists of the components that help connect the elements to each other and help connect those elements to the outside world (i.e., the Internet). A network also provides the means for multiple computers to share one Internet connection, one printer, and so on, and to easily transfer files and information between them without the use of a disk, CD, or other storage device. Networking your library is a must. Not only does it increase efficiency, it saves money. There are thousands of good resources for learning more about creating and administering computer networks. Refer to appendix B for further resources.

The essential physical components of a network include wiring, hubs, switches, routers, servers, and workstations. These components work together to form the central nervous system of your network. Without these components properly designed and installed as a system, computers cannot communicate with each other, let alone with the Internet.

A network drawing is useful for gaining an understanding of the library's infrastructure. It is also a useful tool during both the assessment (when documenting your network setup) and planning phases. It can be hand-drawn or generated using software. There are a variety of software applications that can be used to easily generate these types of drawings (Visio, CAD applications). Figure 3-1 is a sample network map from the Guilderland (NY) Public Library.

Wiring and Cabling

In a hardwired network, wire (or cable) is the connection medium. Modern network cabling typically comes in four varieties: Categories 5, 5e, 6, and 7.

> *Cat 5.* This is the base standard for network cabling. It is typically good for 10 megabits and up to 100-megabit networks.

> *Cat 5e.* This is the current standard for new installations. It is basically the same as Cat 5 but has enhancements that make it suitable for systems running up to 1-gigabit network speeds.

> *Cat 6.* This cabling is the same as Cat 5e but is built to a higher standard and therefore should provide better performance at higher data speeds.

FIGURE 3-1
Sample Network Map

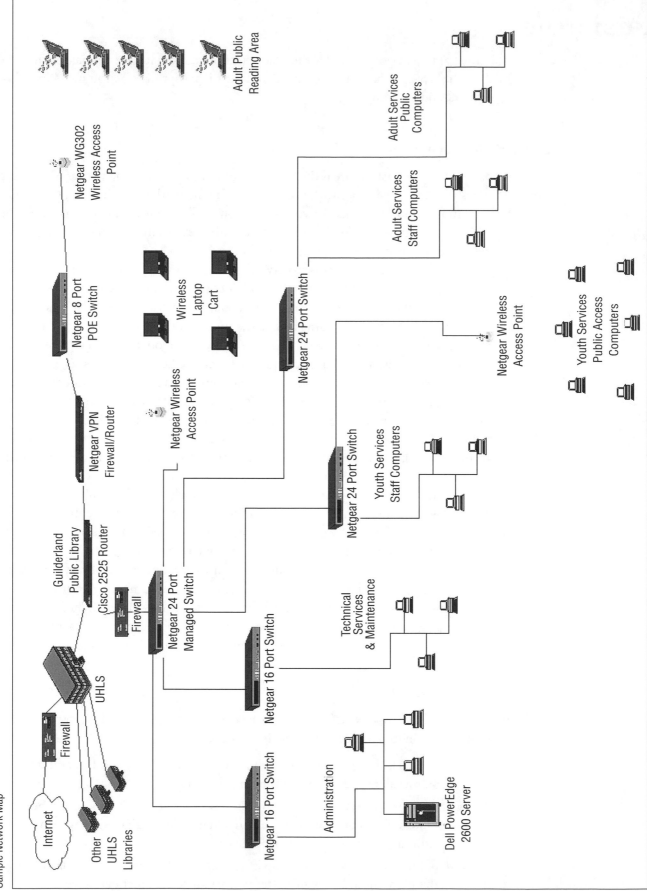

Adapted from Guilderland (NY) Public Library

WIRING

Watch out for sharp bends or frayed wire. Do not run network wire closely along any high-voltage wires. The length of wire from the hub or switch to the computer should not be greater than 295 feet by general Ethernet standards. Distances over that need either intermediate hub/ switch locations or a fiber-optic cable connection. When pulling new cabling, it is often advisable (and most economical in the long run) to pull at least two cables to any one drop location, even if it may not seem necessary at the time.

Cat 7. This standard is still emerging but is another level of enhancement over the preceding standards and should provide even higher performance and higher speeds. It is expected that this standard will have a different connector standard than the current RJ45 that dominates most modern Ethernet networks.

The Internet has great resources on cabling, connectors, panels, standards, and more. A few good examples are listed in the section for this chapter in appendix B.

Hubs and Switches

Hubs and switches connect everything together. They are small, wall- or rack-mounted boxes where network cables are terminated. Switches look nearly identical to hubs, but generally a switch contains more "intelligence," meaning that it has a processor and memory to help optimize network performance. Switches are also a bit more expensive than hubs. Both hubs and switches accomplish the same basic task. However, switches are more efficient at utilizing available network bandwidth and are typically preferred to hubs.

Routers

A router is any device that acts as a gateway between two or more separate networks. It can look similar to a hub or switch but with fewer data ports. Your library's local network is connected to the worldwide network of the Internet via a router. Sticking with the telephone analogy, it is easiest to think of the router as the old-fashioned operator, "routing" calls from one location to another, knowing who is where so it can best route the message in the most efficient way possible.

Servers

Basically, a server is a computer or device on the network that manages resources. The term *server* may refer to both the hardware and software or just the software that performs the service. Servers come in many shapes, sizes, and purposes. A server may have a keyboard, monitor, and mouse directly attached; multiple servers may also share one keyboard, monitor, and mouse via a KVM (keyboard, video, mouse) switch. Servers can focus on a single purpose or they can have several purposes combined into one. The more functions combined onto a single server, the more robust and higher powered that server must be. The following are typical types of servers that might be found in small and medium-sized libraries, based on what purposes they fulfill:

Network servers and file servers. A network server acts as a central repository of data and programs shared by users in a network. It also assists in the operation and security of the network and performs such functions as address and directory services (think of it as the phone book of the network), backup services, security, and so on.

Web servers. Web servers not only house and "serve" out the library's website but often house additional applications that are web-based such as the public catalog interface, indexes such as genealogical records, and calendar and reservation systems. Any computer can be turned into a web server by installing server software and connecting the computer to the Internet.

Catalog servers. This is a server that hosts your library's online catalog system or integrated library system (ILS). In small and medium-sized facilities, this server may be housed locally or, in many instances, at a system or consortium headquarters. Very often, this server is one of the most robust and powerful types, as the catalog system is typically the most mission-critical system in a library. The specifications of this server as well as its operating system and supporting software will be driven by your ILS provider.

E-mail servers. E-mail servers route messages into and out of your organization's network and provide storage for the e-mails that arrive in the system. However, this server's role has recently expanded from that of just a place where mail is routed and stored. It may also provide general file storage, personal and group calendars, and more advanced group file-sharing functionality, as applications like Microsoft Exchange have expanded the functions of e-mail servers within the technology framework.

Other servers. There are a variety of other special and general-purpose servers that your library may have or need. Most support specific applications or functions such as filtering servers, proxy servers, specialty applications, databases, and so on. The needs and requirements of these servers vary widely and will be driven by the purpose or application that they serve.

Workstations. Workstations generally come in the form of personal computers or thin clients (i.e., low-cost computers that rely on a server for many of their capabilities). In a library, workstations are typically dedicated to either staff use or to public use. Libraries use workstations for a variety of purposes, including online catalog access, Internet access, word processing, spreadsheet and database applications, accounting, desktop publishing, and more. Personal computers are typically the most popular option and are divided between PCs and Apple Macintoshes. This book assumes that you have at least a basic understanding of computers and their primary components (computer, monitor, keyboard, and mouse).

PC VS. THIN CLIENT

The "battle" of personal computers versus thin clients goes back almost to the beginning of the personal computer era. Thin clients are very low-cost computer stations that have very few resources of their own and rely on a server to provide the majority of their storage, memory, and processing capability. They are basically a new form of the old-fashioned "dumb terminals." The debate here is between the control and cost control provided by thin client solutions and the capability and flexibility offered by the PC. Though today's thin clients have almost all of the functionality of today's workstation computers, there are still trade-offs—the most important of which is system complexity. There is no magic formula or answer to whether your library should or should not use thin clients. Before taking the plunge, be sure to educate yourself and technology team members about the relative merits of PCs and thin clients. Ask yourself, What will be the up-front demands (e.g., cost of equipment, demands on staff)? What trade-offs, if any, will we face in taking this approach? Do your homework and the math to see which direction is better for your library.

Common and Avoidable Network Mistakes

The following are practical tips for avoiding common mistakes in network operations.

Never turn a server off while it is performing an operation, no matter how harmless that operation might seem. Power a server down only after all programs are completely shut down.

Never power a server down when users are still logged on.

Never delete server files unless it is absolutely clear they are unnecessary.

Never unplug cables from a computer that is turned on.

Never assume a network is backed up and free of viruses. Run constant virus checks.

Always keep good documentation. Write down network configurations and keep them together with warranty information in a safe place.

Never allow network security to lapse.

Always keep backup hand tools, spare media, and extra network computing parts available in case of an emergency.

Never allow any network computer to run in an unventilated or a hot environment or without a UPS (uninterruptible power supply) to protect it in case of power surge or outage.[1]

Network Integrity Tips

The following are commonsense and practical tips related to maintaining and protecting your computer infrastructure.

Have a comprehensive disaster plan in place that covers every type of emergency.

Run daily backups (i.e., a complete copy of the operating system, databases, or files) so the maximum potential loss is only one day's worth of data after any network interruption or malfunction. If your library has a lot of daily data activity, consider scheduling incremental backups throughout the day in order to save information between nightly backups.

Make sure that there is good communication among staff and that network personnel are informed of system shutdowns or problems that may affect the network.

Keep records or logs of important or irreplaceable network information. Make this information available and readily accessible by at least two knowledgeable staff members.

Maintain comprehensive records (maintenance records, licensing agreements, insurance policies, etc.) on all equipment and keep the records in a safe location.

Check the network religiously for viruses and regularly update with virus definitions. (See appendix B for some useful resources regarding computer viruses.)

Cross-train staff; always have at least one reliable second-in-charge who knows or can access network codes, passwords, and rebooting procedures.[2]

A Reliable and Safe Internet Connection

When it comes to Internet connections, there are a variety of options: T1 (and fractional T1), ISDN, DSL, cable, satellite. Usually the decision to be made here is based on what is available and what is most cost-effective given the size and needs of your library. In some cases, multiple connection methods can be used to add additional bandwidth (i.e., how much data you can send through a network) or to diversify the connection methods so a loss of communications on one connection won't leave the library completely disconnected from the Internet and other outside networks.

Along with every Internet connection must be a good, up-to-date firewall solution. A firewall acts as a barrier between computers on a network, constantly monitoring traffic on your network and protecting your library from outside individuals who may try to access, alter, or even destroy files on your servers, workstations, and so on. Just remember that you will eventually get hacked (i.e., someone who isn't authorized will gain some level of access to your system), and undoing the damage without a firewall will cost you far more than purchasing and installing a good firewall at the onset. Firewalls can be configured to define what types of communications can be directed (routed) to each server/computer. Make sure your firewall is configured to allow only minimum access to your system from the outside (the less access the better). Typically, this might only include web-related access to your web server. Frequently, a router and firewall can be purchased as a single solution, which can be a good option for the small or medium library.

Printers and Copiers

Printers and copiers come in various forms: laser, ink-jet, or solid ink; color or black and white; low volume or high volume. Technologies in this area continue to evolve, but the predominant print methods are laser and ink-jet. The key to deciding what is appropriate for you is knowing roughly how many prints per month you expect to make, what type of quality output is needed, and how important color is to your printing needs. Every printer has a rated duty cycle: this is the number of prints per month the printer is designed to produce. Typically, laser printers have a much higher duty cycle than ink-jets and are therefore more appropriate for larger print quantities. A characteristic related to duty cycle is print speed (i.e., the speed at which the printer generates the print and produces it). Speed becomes an issue when demand for a printer is high. Cost per print is another factor to keep in mind. Laser printers will typically have a lower per-print price than ink-jet printers, though they also have a higher initial purchase price. Solid ink solutions typically offer laser quality and duty cycles with easy maintenance and lower long-term costs.

Copiers will continue to be a critical element of any library as long as patrons need to capture information. Many of the same technologies that are used in printers are also used in copiers, and so the issues are also the same. However, copiers typically come in laser format, with the exception of small, office-use, multipurpose ink-jet stations. If your printing and copying demands are high enough, a networked printer/copier might be a good option, because it combines both functions into a single, higher-quality unit, as opposed to two separate units of lesser quality and capability. Leasing printers and copiers can often be an economical way to approach these types of technologies, since a maintenance plan can be bundled with the purchase. Maintenance plans for printers and copiers are usually required for the duty-cycle levels of most libraries and are highly recommended.

Automated Catalog Systems: Integrated Library Systems

This should go without saying, but if you are a small library that hasn't yet taken the plunge, you don't have to make a huge investment to find a decent catalog system that is geared to the needs of your library. The integrated library system (ILS) is involved in every aspect of collection management, from acquisitions to cataloging, circulation, and web-based reserves.[3] There are hundreds of library automation products available on the market today, and several print and online resources are available to help you sift through them all. Refer to the section for this chapter in appendix B for additional resources on this topic.

Office Applications

This is a broad category of software, covering applications for both staff and patrons and including word processing, spreadsheets, desktop publishing, presentation software, financial tools, and e-mail. These are the most common ones and are really just the tip of the iceberg. This book does not attempt to explore each and every application but includes ideas about what to consider when evaluating your options. Microsoft is obviously the giant among the makers of these software applications. Microsoft provides great products, but it is not your only option. Look at where your staff's strengths lie. What are they familiar with? What are your patrons familiar with? What are they asking for?

Open Source Software

If you are so inclined and feel you have the staff to support it, open source software (OSS) may be an alternative option. Open source software has three defining characteristics. First, it can be edited or modified by its users to fill particular needs. Second, while the software is not necessarily available for free, most is generally available at little to no cost. Third, developers are free to redistribute the software. Some examples of open source applications are Apache Web Server, Open Office, Firefox web browser, and the Linux operating system.

What could be better than well-written software available for free and open to modification and customization? That is the lure of open source software, and if initial cost were the only consideration to take into account when implementing a solution, OSS would be the perfect answer for everyone. However, up-front costs should not be the sole deciding factor when it comes to making a technology decision. Be careful here, and always keep an eye on the bottom line. The up-front investment of OSS can be a fraction of the more traditional "mainstream" options. However, the long-term financial investment of supporting OSS could in some cases exceed any initial investment difference with mainstream software. Some other considerations include

> Will the software work for your patrons? Usability is and has been a fundamental issue with OSS.
>
> Who is going to implement it? Open source software is a do-it-yourself solution. The basic supplies (the software itself) are free, but it takes a skilled set of technicians (in the form of programmers) to effectively implement and customize it.
>
> Who's going to maintain it? When purchasing an "out of the box" solution, you can expect the vendor to provide maintenance in the form of support and updates. By contrast, OSS places the burden on the user to solve issues (or at least track down the solution from user groups and discussion threads) and to obtain and install software updates and upgrades.

In the end you'll probably need to pick and choose where open source solutions might be applicable and save you money. The Mount Prospect (IL) Public Library developed a dedicated kiosk-type catalog station that runs Linux and Firefox. The software is all open source and has proven to be a very stable platform for them. It also allows them to use older hardware for catalog stations because Linux and Firefox do not require as much processing power. The Cleveland Heights–University Heights (OH) Public Library suggests using open source technologies like Linux or PHP/MySQL to get great functionality. "In these cases, the only thing you have to worry about is making sure your staff knows how to implement them, rather than needing to maintain expensive licenses," says Catherine Hakala-Ausperk, the library's assistant director.

Ultimately, open source software can be a valuable resource. However, issues with usability and complexity can make implementing and maintaining it difficult. Before deciding on an OSS application, be sure to consider all of the factors beyond just initial cost. For instance, staffing costs will be higher because the pool of OSS experts is smaller than the pool of Microsoft experts. For more information about open source software and related projects, see appendix B.[4]

Online Databases

The selection of reference resources in the form of online or electronic databases is a common practice for libraries of all shapes and sizes. There are numerous choices out there, from online bibliographic and full-text database services to general reference resources and subject databases. Seeing that pretty much all databases these days are web-based, the most common and cost-effective way to purchase one is as a subscription service. This is generally an annual expense—the library renews the subscription each year, although some contracts can stretch over multiple years. Keep in mind that the costs of online databases are as broad as their content. Here are some key questions to consider when looking at purchasing online databases for your library.

How will your patrons and staff use the database?

How often will the product get used? Is the financial investment commensurate with its expected usage?

Does the database enhance the library's collection?

Does the product allow for remote access?

How well does the database cover its subject area(s)?

How accurate and up-to-date is the information?

Is the product or resource easy to use? Is it easily accessible?

Can the information or part of the information be printed? Can search results be sent by e-mail? Is downloading possible?

Is there good customer support available? A toll-free number? An e-mail address? Are those in customer service helpful, knowledgeable, and friendly?

What kind of training is available? Is training free or reasonably priced? Do help and "informal" training extend beyond the "formal" training?

What kind of references does the company have?

Is there print and online documentation available? Is it up-to-date? Is it free? What costs are involved? Are there up-front subscription fees, monthly maintenance costs, annual maintenance costs, or minimum usage charges?

If possible, create a database group or committee from people both within your library and outside of it, including people from neighboring libraries in your county or library district. Such a group is great for brainstorming what products are out there, sharing experiences, collaborating on test trials, and group purchasing.

When it comes to spending money on databases, you will find that their benefits can outweigh their initial cost by saving time and money in the long run. Web-based information resources can help library services in several ways: they provide easier management of resources; they allow for better reference opportunities; and they eliminate storage issues and provide space. For example, a library may decide to move to web-based databases because it is easier to manage a link on the library's website than to run applications on internal servers and PCs. This is also a plus because the software doesn't have to be installed on every computer in the library.[5]

Backup

Backing up your system and the information it contains is an absolutely critical step that must never be skipped. Creating a backup copy of information is more important now than ever before. Viruses, ordinary accidents (i.e., broken pipes, fires), and natural disasters can destroy or impair your active systems and the data stored on them. If you haven't already experienced an "information loss incident," you will undoubtedly encounter such a headache at some point during your career. Computer crashes and accidental file losses are not uncommon, so if you don't have a reliable backup system in place, you will end up regretting it. Most who don't have such a system use the excuses, "I don't have time" or "It's too complicated." The response to this is, Do you have time to rebuild your library's system and information? How complicated and expensive would that be?

Choosing a backup system does not have to be a lengthy or difficult endeavor. There are many options out there. The key is to select something that fits your needs and the risks you face. One solution may not be right for everyone. Sometimes making a simple copy of data from one computer or server to another can be an adequate backup of noncritical information. Other situations may call for a full hard-copy backup with off-site storage and rotation. In recent years, hurricanes alone have proven the need for off-site storage for mission-critical information (i.e., data that cannot easily be rebuilt and that the library cannot live without, such as circulation records, catalog records, etc.). In particular, catalog systems, which are absolutely essential to every library, should have nightly automated backups, with at least a weekly off-site storage rotation. Off-site storage or vaulting is important in cases where a massive information backup is needed in the event of a major catastrophe, and where a locally stored backup may be lost or destroyed. Among the emerging options for off-site storage are online backup or mirroring sites. These services come in various forms and often offer automated backup options to server farms (i.e., large banks of computers) located hundreds or thousands of miles away.

Backup options do not always have to be elaborate. USB drives (external hard drives connected via the USB port), CD/DVDs, and other writable media can be used in the simplest form of backup. The key to using these less sophisticated options is making sure you have a good process in place to ensure that backups are being performed regularly and that some form of off-site storage is occurring. Logs and calendar reminders should be used to keep this process consistent and diligent.

Pest Control

In this day and age, probably the most important application running on your system is the "pest control" software. Pest control covers the gamut from antivirus to anti-spam to anti-spyware. It prevents malicious programs from infiltrating your system, wreaking havoc, and possibly stealing personal information about patrons and staff. No network that is connected to the Internet is totally safe from these pests, but keeping software up-to-date, installing patches on a routine basis, and carefully monitoring a system's "health" can provide a relative level of safety to your systems. However, never assume that your antivirus software is foolproof. Procedures related to e-mail, attachments, and file sharing should be put in place so that your staff do not unwittingly set loose a problem in the network.

Data Storage Options

Data storage options used to be pretty straightforward: hard drives, floppy disks, and CD-ROMs were universal and, with the exception of possible virus contamination, fairly simple to support without a lot of planning. But not in today's world. A flood of storage options now exists, including flash disks and USB drives of every shape and size, MP3 players, web storage, and peer-to-peer networks, not to mention other possibilities on the horizon. And these new storage options all pose issues that libraries have to deal with. Libraries are looking to balance their need for control with their patrons' need to access and store files and information. It is difficult for patrons to make use of public computers if they don't have some way to access and save the files and information they need. We often hear about libraries that don't offer storage options to their patrons because of virus and pest concerns. Unfortunately, this reasoning is misleading. Opening up storage options to patrons does not offer mischief-makers or viruses any easier entry into your network then do general web surfing or e-mail access. As long as strong pest control systems are in place, your network will be adequately protected against any malicious program that might be brought in on a flash memory or a USB stick.

Web Filters

Probably one of the more controversial technologies of the current era is web filtering. The fact that this topic is covered here should not be taken as an endorsement of filtering as a practice. As always, look to your library's mission and balance your community's needs and values against the individual patron's right to access information and content that are not deemed appropriate for everyone. Fortunately for libraries, technologies are emerging that allow filtering to be switched on and off, typically based on a library card number or via password protection controlled by staff members. One complication with filters is funding and compliance with various federal laws. For example, the Children's Internet Protection Act (CIPA) and the Neighborhood Children's Internet Protection Act (NCIPA) base public libraries receiving discounts on Internet access and connections through the E-rate program (i.e., the federal Universal Service Fund for Schools and Libraries). Those libraries receiving federal LSTA funds for Internet access and computers must also take certain steps to comply with the law. When and if possible, avoid making filtering decisions purely based on economics.

When evaluating filters, there are several factors to consider:

> Will you be installing filters on a server or on individual PCs?
>
> What are the terms of licensing them?

How are they available for installation? Online? CD-ROM?

How easy is the product to install and update?

Does the vendor publish a block list? How is it updated, and how often?

Can you adjust or amend the block list? Are there levels of blocking from which you can select?

Does the product track sites visited? Are these logs consistent with your patron privacy policy?

Does the vendor report to you the sites that your patrons visited? Does the vendor sell that information to third parties?

How easy are the filters to turn on and off?

Do the filters work with any security you've already installed on your machines?

You should also ask the vendor for the names of other libraries using the product and check on their experiences with it.[6]

Your Library's Website

In today's library your website is as important as your front door, for it is the library's virtual front door. There is certainly a minimum amount of content and information your website should contain. At the very least, all of your pertinent service information should be listed: library location, directions, hours of operation, holiday closings, staff and board contact information, a brief overview of the library, its mission statement, and a basic summary of the services the library offers. It is also critical to do your best to keep the website fresh and up-to-date. The smaller the library is, the more difficult this becomes, but, as with everything discussed in the book, try to find a balance that works for your library without putting too much strain on your resources.

Telecommunications

Every library has telephones, but it is how those telephones are connected to each other and the outside world that makes up your telecommunications system. Take into account that modern phone systems have a variety of features available, many of which you may not need. Try to be realistic about what options you do need. Break down the feature options into your Must Have, Must Get, More Is Better, and Technology Thriller categories. Look at implementation costs as well as maintenance (both service and hardware) costs. How much could a new phone system streamline current practices? Save the library money in staff time? Increase efficiency? Compare your needs and information to those phone systems available to you, weighing both the short- and long-term costs. And last but not least, always do your research on the variety of systems available. This will lead you to a phone system that works best for your library today and tomorrow and will help you avoid paying for more than you really need.

MUST GET

Wireless Hotspots and Wi-Fi

Wireless or Wi-Fi is a networking option to the traditional "wired" network. It provides interconnectivity between computers, devices, and the library's network via radio signals through the air instead of electrical signals sent through wires. Computers and devices must have Wi-Fi hardware in order to connect to these wireless networks. Wi-Fi is not as fast or as robust as a wired network, but it can be more cost-effective to implement because many computers can be networked together without the costs of cabling installation. The biggest library trend related to wireless is the move toward offering public Wi-Fi, whereby any patron with a Wi-Fi-capable laptop or PDA can access the library's public network and, typically, the library's Internet connection. Lately Wi-Fi access has been shifting from a service implemented by larger, more innovative, or early adopter libraries to an everyday service expected of all community libraries. While larger institutions can now offer a range of features and services with their wireless capabilities, a smaller, budget-conscious library should concentrate on offering the "service" itself and offer basic free Wi-Fi for a relatively low cost. This can be accomplished by creating a single "hotspot"—a small physical area with wireless access. A number of model libraries from this book have successfully implemented free Wi-Fi services, including the St. Joseph County (IN) Public Library and the Delton District (MI) Library.

When adding public Wi-Fi access to your library's service offerings, keep it easy, straightforward, and uncomplicated. Making a library a "hotspot" does not mean the entire library has to be wireless. After all, it's called a hot "spot" for a reason. Start small, get a feel for how the service will work, find out what the patterns of use are, and see if there are locations in (or out of) the library where people are requesting service. By creating a single hotspot, your library can quickly and easily grab attention and get people talking. More important, it will provide an opportunity for constructive, service-building dialogue between the library and its customers. Monitor use (and user comments) and grow the service accordingly. Given that wireless networks are typically quite easy to evolve and adapt and that the technology is changing rapidly, it makes sense to start slow and build accordingly as the demand and technology evolve.

Keep the technology, security, and policies simple. Again, look to the coffee shop and hotel models. Most Wi-Fi users understand they are working in an unsecured environment. Customers have established this expectation based on their "commercial" experiences. Also, begin by forgoing a library card requirement for Wi-Fi use. Take into account that allowing outside users Wi-Fi access will not keep library cardholders off the wireless system. Unless your library becomes inundated with nonresident users or problematic issues arise, don't spend valuable resources fixing a "problem" that may never occur. If demand grows so high that system performance is affected, *then* explore options for locking the system down a bit more. (See the "More Is Better" section in this chapter for information on expanding your library's Wi-Fi capabilities.)

Self-Check

Self-checkout, or self-check, is a way for libraries to offer additional checkout resources without adding staff that the budget cannot support. This is often a controversial service option because it is regarded as a way to eliminate human interaction with patrons. However, self-check should not be implemented to replace people; rather, it should be positioned and promoted as a way to offer self-service options to those patrons who prefer that type of service, or at least to offer patrons a quick way to check out when lines are long. At a time when privacy and anonymity are becoming increasingly important in libraries, self-check offers an improved level of anonymity to patrons. This can be an issue particularly in small communities where the library staff know many, if not all, of the patrons personally. With prices for self-check systems coming down, the financial justification for implementing self-check is becom-

The opponents of self-check solutions will often say they are not appropriate for small and medium libraries. These librarians feel that their bread and butter is in personal interaction and customer service. Because patrons are not waiting in long lines or telling staff they wish they could check themselves out, some librarians conclude that self-check is unnecessary. Although this is a perfectly valid conclusion, other small and medium libraries are finding success in a self-check approach.

At the McMillan (WI) Memorial Library, they purchased two self-check stations and made them available in February 2004. Initially the stations' use was not heavily promoted and some staff members were resistant, but this gave staff and patrons time to get used to the idea. In October of that year, the library eliminated the circulation desk and added a third self-checkout unit. Two of the stations are near the (former) circulation service desk and the other is in the children's room. Semi staffing these stations has helped them keep their patrons from feeling lost or abandoned. By moving staff out from behind desks, the staffers continue to have frequent interaction with patrons while eliminating many low-level clerical tasks. The self-checkout station in the children's room is a blessing. Parents can check out materials while watching their children or during story hour instead of waiting in line with impatient kids. The move to self-check came as part of a remodeling project that increased the library's public space by 25 percent. The library also added a coffee bar, wireless Internet, and Sunday hours. By making self-check one of a series of changes and improvements, the library de-emphasized its potential negative implications. The library also linked the move to self-checkout and the elimination of the circulation desk with the restoration of Sunday hours, which was a major goal of the library board.

ing more apparent, because a self-check unit is now far less expensive in the short term and long term than employing additional library staff to man the checkout counter. However, if your library does not often have long lines at checkout, this may not be the highest-priority offering for you at this time. If you do implement self-check options, try to think outside the box on their placement within the library. Why limit self-check stations to locations near the circulation desk? Why not place them at any spot where patrons can receive assistance if necessary; for example, the children's or adult reference desks? Current opinions on self-check vary widely, so judge for yourself and your situation. (See the "Self-Check Success Story" sidebar for more insight on this topic.)

Assistive and Adaptive Technologies

Though libraries have traditionally prided themselves on being community leaders when it comes to equal access, patrons with disabilities often find libraries to be a challenging place, particularly when it comes to technology. Fortunately, assistive technologies are quickly emerging that help libraries address these patrons' needs cost-effectively and, in some cases, free of charge. A wide range of technologies exists, including screen and text readers, large print, audiobooks, teletype machines, assistive listening devices, and more. Each technology targets a different type of disability, so no one solution will address any and all disabilities. When choosing solutions, first and foremost, look to your service population to assess what disabilities exist in it. Beyond that, take the "low-hanging fruit approach" to assess what other assistive technologies might be implemented to serve other current and potential patrons who have special needs. When making your library open and accessible, consider simple and free improvements such as copier and printer placement and heights, open computer areas for easy wheelchair access, and so on. (See appendix B for more resources on assistive technologies.)

MORE IS BETTER

When it comes to the More Is Better category of technology options, most small and medium libraries tend to struggle. As small organizations with limited resources (people, money, time), they always have tough choices to make. Most libraries will never be able to implement all of these technologies, but that does not mean they should not try to offer some of these solutions. Implementing technologies of this type is a key element in "exceeding" your patrons' expectations.

Expanded Wireless

The best example of a More Is Better technology is public wireless access, which was previously discussed in this chapter as a Must Have technology in the form of a hotspot. Expanding wireless to physically cover your whole library, or, even better, outside the library, moves this technology into the More Is Better classification. You can also think about Wi-Fi as a means to provide new service opportunities.

Wi-Fi is a cost-effective way for your library to deliver Internet and technology access to the community. Libraries want and need to attract "business" (i.e., new customers, community partnerships, increased support), and they need to do it in a creative and cost-effective manner. Why is it that coffee shops, hotels, and even McDonald's are implementing Wi-Fi access? Because it is an economical and creative way to attract customers. Best of all, it attracts customers not only to visit but to stay a while, get comfortable, and explore the library's other services. Such a service attracts customers of all flavors, but it is especially enticing to those patrons that libraries have the greatest difficulty attracting—teenagers and younger adults. Many schools are now on board with Wi-Fi, and most colleges and universities are offering it as well. If a patron in this age group has a laptop, odds are that he or she has Wi-Fi capability. Give your current and potential customers a reason to look to the library for their technology and informational needs. You know they are going to get Wi-Fi access somewhere, so make them think of your library instead of a fast-food restaurant.

The Cedar Park (TX) Public Library purchased wireless cards that can be checked out to patrons for "in library" use on their own laptop computers. The staff at Salem–South Lyon (MI) Public Library use wireless technology to expand reference service. They've had a wireless network for several years and wanted to use the network to push the envelope of customer service, so they implemented Tablet PCs to allow their librarians to stay with the patron throughout the course of the reference interview. Now staff can roam freely around the building with network and Internet access in the palm of their hands. The Salem–South Lyon Library also has eight workstations on mobile carts that can be moved throughout the library. Wireless also provides a great mechanism for expanding computer class offerings in a small library: temporary classrooms can be easily set up in meeting rooms and other library spaces by using portable computers and wireless access. Wi-Fi access in combination with portable computing devices and portable bar code scanners can also streamline collection development and inventory processes, since library staff are no longer chained to a desk to complete these tasks.

One final consideration for smaller libraries faced with space constraints is to look to wireless as a way to provide additional network access points for patrons without taking up valuable space with a computer workstation. Initially this works great for patrons bringing in their own laptops, and it can be expanded so that the library circulates in-house laptops in place of or in addition to stationary desktop computers.

One concern that often comes up with Wi-Fi implementation is that users can access the network from outside the library (i.e., the parking lot). The key questions at hand are

> If the network is robust enough for your customers to use it from the parking lot, why should you be concerned?
>
> These customers are still using the library, right?
>
> Aren't they recognizing the library as a valuable and progressive resource in the community?

You should view Wi-Fi access outside of the library's walls as a positive, not a negative. This type of "out of the box" service helps keep libraries in the forefront of community needs. Turn your concerns into a positive service option that can be marketed and expanded on. This is an opportunity that will ultimately lead to increased users, recognition, and support for the library. Consider this also as an opportunity to look at library statistics in a new way. Purchase a Wi-Fi router that has log options where usage statistics can be gathered. This is the "door count" equivalent for Wi-Fi access. Also, look at public wireless as a means to expand library hours without opening the doors or adding a single staff hour. If the Wi-Fi signal reaches beyond the library walls, so do library services. For an excellent example of Wi-Fi use, see the Twin Bridges (MT) Public Library case study by Bruce Newell, "Make Your Library a Wi-Fi Hotspot" (November 30, 2004), at http://webjunction.org/do/DisplayContent?id=8211.

Looking at Wi-Fi with a fresh and open mind will provide an easy and cost-effective path for providing a new service, so don't be afraid. In the end, free public Wi-Fi access is just one of many technology services your library can offer to raise its profile, offer its customers more, and become a recognized and valuable component of the community.

A Value-Added Website

Most libraries have a basic website that provides the library's location, hours, contact information, and mission statement. The key is to take your site to the next level, adding value and giving customers a reason to come back. Do you link to your online catalog through the website? This is essential. How about including lists of new materials on the site? Do you offer expanded information on services (adult, teen, children, special)? Do patrons have the ability to ask a reference or circulation question online? Can they access policies, procedures, basic circulation information, and the library's annual report? Many libraries now provide online access to forms and information that would traditionally be kept at the reference or circulation desk (e.g., employment applications, donation forms, meeting room applications, information and applications for the Friends of the Library). Do your customers have up-to-date access to program information with online registration when appropriate? How about online readers' advisory? Many of these elements take very little staff time and are very simple to implement. If you have the resources, look at ways to bring personalization and real time information (RSS feeds, weather, etc.) into play on your website. Basically, when it comes to your website's content, there really is never too much you can add to it. The key is to keep the site's content clear and well organized. Information must be up to date, easy to navigate, and easy to find or it won't do your staff and patrons much good.

Solutions That Enhance Your Services

One area of growing popularity is to make various services to patrons accessible via the library's website. By incorporating such services into your library's web page, your library can simultaneously streamline staff processes and improve staff communications, as well as increase customer service options for patrons. Library-specific solutions exist for such things as program calendars, online program and event registration, meeting room scheduling and booking, reading program registration and progress logging, online book clubs, online book and multimedia reviews, and online readers' advisory. These solutions come in a variety of forms from a variety of vendors, but they all help libraries to offer more to their patrons while reducing the demands on staff. For instance, solutions such as online calendars and registration give patrons 24/7 access to information about library programs and sign-up while reducing staff call volume and clerical chores. Solutions such as these also free up staff to provide more hands-on service to those patrons who are looking for that personal touch. Various solutions also allow for the automation of tasks—including automatic e-mail reminders to patrons and staff—which creates better service, increased outreach, and effective marketing without the investment of valuable staff time. (See the "Online Calendar Success Story" sidebar for further insight, and refer to appendix B for more information on vendors and their solutions.)

Print Management

Print management systems have been around for quite a while now but have only recently become more widely accepted and cost-effective due to increased competition and demand. Essentially, a print management system helps you limit and control who can print and what they can print. It can be implemented to manage fees from the patrons who use the library's printers. Print management systems tend to improve printers' usability for patrons and help libraries reduce waste. A variety of approaches exist with server-based and client/server-based solutions, each with their own benefits and drawbacks. Investigate the various options available. In some cases, a solution may be acquired and implemented without any up-front investment by the library. In such instances, a profit-sharing arrangement is made with the vendor wherein the costs of the system are paid out of the proceeds from printing and copying charges. Be wary about entering into such an arrangement that is weighted too heavily in favor of the vendor, however. In most cases, the initial software and installation costs of the system will be paid off within a year or two, after which time the profit-sharing percentages should shift more in favor of the library.

PC Reservation

As computer and Internet usage at public libraries continue to increase, so does demand for those libraries' public computers. Many libraries have turned to PC reservation management solutions in order to limit the frequency and amount of time patrons can spend on the computers, thereby keeping a few individuals from monopolizing them. While this solution can be very effective, be sure to explore all your options. Such systems may be appropriate for a facility that constantly has lines of people waiting for its computers. Just remember that these solutions can be expensive to install and maintain and do not bring a "return on investment" like the print management systems do. Before making an investment in a PC reservation system, consider the cost and service impact of adding more computer workstations instead. If the space allocated to computer stations is limited, would sacrificing a small amount of stack space for more computers be a worthwhile trade-off? Your library should always try to provide a "supply" to meet the "demand" of your customers. Examine all possible solutions to resolve the situation.

Games

Many libraries are hesitant to provide electronic games to their customers, whether in the form of circulating items, through in-house access, or via library programs. Many view such games as entertainment, not education. This is true in many respects, but electronic games also encourage the development of problem-solving and deductive reasoning skills. There are also games on the market with direct educational content. As with any other decision, look at what your child, teen, and adult patrons want and then refer back to your library's mission, while keeping in mind the positive impact of an often misunderstood format. As with other newfangled formats (such as DVDs a few years ago), your library must figure out how to use them to attract a variety of customers. Adding new services like circulating video games in the audiovisual collection and local area network (LAN) gaming programs once a month are great ways to attract male teens and young adults, who are often the most elusive of all the patron segments. LAN gaming can very often be provided on a few computers and allows patrons to compete against each other and sometimes against other "gamers" elsewhere on the Internet. The games and hardware requirements vary widely, but if you have a teen advisory board, tap into their knowledge and see what options your library might be able to provide.

Audiovisual Equipment and Services

As circulating audiovisual collections become more and more important in libraries of all sizes, they are exploring their options for audiovisual equipment, including listening stations and viewing stations for the public. Just as a patron can sit down and read a sample paragraph or chapter of a book before checking it out, consider equal treatment for music, video, and other audiovisual collections. Computer workstations can double as viewing and listening stations, or separate pieces of equipment can be purchased that are specifically designated for these tasks. There are a variety of solutions for libraries of all sizes and budgets. (See appendix B for more information on vendors.) Remember, if your library already houses audiovisual collections, you most likely already have some form of this equipment in your staff area to check for problems and damage. Why not get the most bang for your buck and invest in equipment that can do double duty for the staff and the public?

When it comes to using workstations to satisfy your patrons' audiovisual demands, consider other areas such as digital cameras and digital video cameras. Many patrons may have the equipment to capture pictures and film, but they lack the hardware and software to easily edit and produce their pictures and home movies. By offering a picture/video-editing workstation equipped with hardware and software options, the library can provide a new reason for current and non-library patrons to use the library. Couple this with a training class (see chapter 8) and you have a service offering that will delight those amateur digital photographers and filmmakers.

TECHNOLOGY THRILLERS

Why should a library consider "thrilling" patrons with technology? This is not an easy question to answer, but the bottom line is that these "thrillers" are often the way to get community recognition and support. What about the days when hard work was all that was needed for community approval and praise? Although hard work and the basics behind library service are very important, they aren't necessarily what *sells*. Even though small and medium libraries

TO RFID OR NOT TO RFID

Radio frequency identification (RFID) is a method of providing security and tracking for portable materials of all kinds, including books and videos. It's quite hot in the retail world and is making its way into libraries. By early 2004 about 250 libraries worldwide had implemented RFID systems, so it's very much a cutting-edge technology. And the systems can get pretty expensive. According to the Public Library Association's RFID guidelines, implementing RFID for a 40,000-item library collection would cost around $70,000.[7] In addition to RFID's overall costs, concerns about security of information and patron privacy are also growing. Because of the nature of RFID, it is technically possible (though highly unlikely) for someone within a certain range to scan the books a person has with them to see what they are in possession of. Vendors are working to address these concerns in a number of ways, so just be aware that the issue exists. Technology has a way of evolving to adapt to and address concerns like these. As with any new technology, learn the basics and talk to other libraries and organizations that have implemented RFID (as well as those considering implementation and those that opted against the solution). You could also talk to various vendors and your ILS provider. Analyze the big picture of benefits versus costs and consider both the concrete and intangible costs.

may be limited in their resources, the best ones (including those listed in appendix C) don't let themselves think small just because their staff size and budgets are small.

There is another side to this issue, however. Librarians who are involved with technology can often find themselves suffering from what librarian, technology trainer, and author Michael Stephens calls "technolust"—an irrational love for new technology combined with unrealistic expectations about the solutions it brings. This lust for the latest and greatest technology can often lead to unnecessary headaches, swollen costs, and frazzled staff. As Stephens points out, you must judge your desire for the latest and greatest technology against the backdrop of your library's mission and vision.[8] Keep in mind that many of the past's "techno-thrillers" turned out to be "techno-duds," and the libraries that spent time and money implementing them probably wish they hadn't. The easier, quicker, and cheaper projects should typically be your first priority versus longer, more complicated, and typically more expensive projects. The bottom line is to always balance your technolust with common sense, seek input from your community, and continually evaluate how a new technology relates to your library's mission.

Even though you might not be ready to implement a new technology, it is important that you at least keep up with the latest and greatest technology developments. Things change rather quickly in this area, and though you can never know everything that's out there or every little detail, you can become familiar with the basics, even though many of the ideas and concepts may be new to you. If you have a grasp of the basics of technology, all the new and emerging technologies will be that much easier to follow. Since the techno-thrillers change so rapidly, this book will not attempt to fully educate you on all the ins and outs of them. The following is a quick list of some of today's hot technologies (see appendix B for places to find additional resources).

Blog—a web log of one or more person's thoughts on any subject under the sun

RSS feed—a way for websites (such as your library's home page) to have dynamic links to news and information from around the world

24-hour holds pickup—any of a number of innovative ways for patrons to receive materials being held for them, such as drive-up conveyors, locker storage, delivery, and so on. (See the sidebar "Library Express: Easily Accessible Locker Delivers Holds.")

Remote storage—online storage sites for files, pictures, music, and so on

IP phone system—a phone system that takes advantage of existing networks for both in-house and around-the-world calling needs. Sometimes referred to as voice over IP or VOIP, IP phone systems transmit the voice by sending digital data over local and worldwide networks.

Virtual reference—a reference service initiated electronically via e-mail, chat, or instant messaging in which the patron/customer communicates with library staff without being physically present

Instant messaging (IM) and text messaging—a technology whereby users can communicate via a computer in real time over the Internet, using text-based communication. With text messaging, users send short text messages to a device, such as a cellular phone, PDA, or pager.

Electronic kiosk and digital signage—an electronic bulletin board that can be both interactive and noninteractive

Intranet—an internal-only "internet" that is a one-stop shop for staff information and resources (schedules, policy manuals, product manuals, tools, links, etc.)

MP3 player, iPod, and other online music technology—a wide variety of quickly evolving electronic music and voice recording, listening, and distribution technologies

E-book—an electronic version of a traditional print book that can be read by using a personal computer or an e-book reader. An e-book reader can be a software application for use on a computer, such as Microsoft's free Reader application, or a book-sized computer that is used solely as a reading device.

LIBRARY EXPRESS: EASILY ACCESSIBLE LOCKER DELIVERS HOLDS

Twenty-four-hour holds pickup is an innovative idea in library service because it provides library materials at locations convenient to patrons and allows patrons to pick up those materials according to their own schedules. The Portage County (OH) District Library's Library Express Project provides a solution for patrons who are unable to get to a library branch when it is open or who find that the distance to a branch is problematic. There are fifteen Library Express locations around Portage County. The project provides expanded library service to nearly 46,000 Portage County residents who are currently underserved.

This project was partially funded through an Institute of Museum and Library Services LSTA grant awarded by the State Library of Ohio in 2002. The project required working with a manufacturer to develop the lockers to meet the library's needs, and a locker security system was tailored for the project. The Library Express units are similar to mailbox units seen in condominium developments and mobile home parks and are controlled by an electronic keypad.

Library cardholders can go online at www.portagelibrary .org to search the library's catalog of materials. After browsing the catalog, the patron makes a selection and places holds on items of interest. (Patrons can also place holds by calling or visiting a branch library.) The patron chooses the preferred express location for delivery at the time the holds are placed. The desired items are sent to library headquarters, where they are checked out and delivered to the appropriate Library Express unit. The patron receives a phone call when items are available for pickup.

At the express unit, the patron enters in the last seven digits of his or her library card number into a keypad. The door assigned to the patron automatically opens so the materials can be retrieved. After a few minutes, the library card number is erased from the express unit's memory, and the locker is available to be used for the next delivery. Library materials are delivered five days a week, Monday through Friday. The Library Express units are at outdoor, well-lighted locations and have a book return next to them for convenient return of items.[9]

PDA—a small, handheld "mini-computer" that is typically used for communications and personal information management. PDAs are gradually evolving into general-purpose, yet highly transportable, computers.

RFID—a tagging system that uses radio frequency identification as a replacement for library bar codes. Each wafer-thin, postage stamp–sized RFID tag contains a chip that is both readable and writable, can store a security bit, and can be loaded with information. (See the sidebar "To RFID or Not to RFID" for more information.)

Wiki—a web application that allows users to freely create and edit web content using only a browser. Wikis offer a variety of uses and purposes from sharing information to collaborative content development.

When it comes to cutting-edge technologies and keeping up-to-date, don't limit yourself to what other libraries your size are doing. Don't be afraid to look to larger libraries for inspiration and information. For example, the Kansas City (MO) Public Library provides a great example of a value-added website and integrated RSS feeds, while the Kalamazoo (MI) Public Library offers its patrons digital audiobooks and MP3 players.

SELECTION GUIDELINES FOR NEW TECHNOLOGY

The selection of electronic resources or information technologies demands a new set of standards or criteria. Many of the guidelines that relate to traditional print resources—such as relevance, quality, and pricing—continue to remain important, but the very nature of technology requires looking more closely at the big picture. How will the technology be used? How will it be supported? What will the total costs and benefits to the library be? The following are commonsense tips for evaluating technology and the vendors that supply it.

1. Do your research and educate yourself. Because you work in a library, this should be the easy part. You could consult books, journal articles, electronic discussion lists, and blogs. Network with your colleagues and consider forming a small technology discussion group that meets on a regular basis.

2. Attend vendor demonstrations. These may consist of an in-person visit at a conference or an online or on-site demonstration at your library. Tip: If you can't get a vendor to show up for just your library, offer to host a group session and invite other libraries in your area to help make it worthwhile for the vendor. This could also be an opportunity to enter into a reciprocal agreement. Consider asking for a price break for coordinating this group sales opportunity.

3. Ask questions of the vendors, and more important, check references. Salespeople may tend to gloss over the details of what they're offering. Haven't you heard that saying, "The devil is in the details"? Questions to consider include

   What pricing discounts can be pursued? Most vendors will have plans and programs for consortiums, state discounts, or some kind of group pricing.

   Determine the standards compliance (Z39.50, SIP2, NCIP, etc.) for technologies that need to talk to other systems in your library. For example, if you want your PC reservation system to check for valid library cards, you'll need to make sure the software can talk to your ILS via SIP2 or NCIP.

How does the vendor provide product support? What days and times are support available? Is the support provided direct from the vendor or from somewhere else? What communication or support mechanisms are allowed (phone, e-mail, online/web forms)? What is the typical turnaround time for support? Is support included in the fees? If not, what are the fees for various levels of support?

What is the history (or lack thereof) of the company?

How is the company or its service structured to help you succeed with your technology implementation?

How are maintenance and upgrades handled? What is covered and not covered? Are they included in the price, and if not, what are the costs involved? What elements will need to be upgraded (software and hardware)? Who performs the upgrade, you or the vendor? How long can you expect to be down during the upgrade? Can the upgrade be performed during off-hours so as not to disrupt the staff and patrons? Will fees increase annually? If so, can you get a two- to five-year package that will keep costs down? If hardware fails, what is covered under normal wear and tear? How quickly can you expect hardware to be repaired?

4. Request a free trial of the product. The availability of this will depend on the technology, but explore the options with the vendor.

5. When multiple options (technologies, vendors, products, etc.) are available, consider creating a comparison grid. Assign potential options a numerical rating for various categories that your library has deemed important and relevant.

6. Once you make a decision between competing products, provide feedback to your vendors so they know the outcome of your decision: not only who was chosen, but why. This step, though often difficult and awkward, is crucial if you want better products, pricing, and services in the future.[10]

You should also be aware of any technology standards that may apply to your library and to the technology itself. What are standards, where can you find them, and why should you care about them? There are a variety of national, state, and local standards out there that dictate the types of technology and to what level your library should provide them. Whether you need to pay attention to these standards depends on laws as well as the needs of your library. Many standards are attached to funding and grants; so be judicious but practical, because some standards may cost more to implement and maintain than the funding that goes along with them. As with everything, analyze your library's needs and mission and how the standards relate to them and look at both sides of the equation before proceeding. Keep in mind that hardware and software are in a constant state of flux, and as a result, standards are revised on a regular basis, so factor that into your analysis as well.

KEEP IT FRESH AND PUT IT TO WORK

Bear in mind that the ideas presented in this chapter can be applied and adapted to any technology and technology-related situation, from computer networks to telecommunications to multimedia collections. It is all about the process: where to find information to educate yourself, how to effectively evaluate what you find, and how to incorporate what you have learned into your planning. Keep yourself in the know and talk to others, utilizing blogs, RSS, journal articles, and other resources.

The success and future existence of the small and medium-sized public library in times of limited resources, growing competition, and diminishing appreciation depend on finding additional means of recognition and value in the community. Technology is one such means. Whether it is the technology of yesterday, today, or tomorrow, take what you learn about its capabilities and requirements and apply this to planning technology for your own library. Just remember to keep things simple and not allow yourself to become intimidated, and you will be able to successfully master the process of implementing technology, even if you never become a true technology expert.

DO YOU KNOW IT?

Don't be a technophobe. Technology is less scary if you learn the basics and keep yourself informed.

Keep current. Use acquired knowledge to keep the technology in your library up-to-date and to continually educate yourself and your staff.

Know your Must Have, Must Get, More Is Better, and Technology Thriller items. It is critical to identify technologies in terms of these categories to help determine planning priorities and where to focus your energy and budgets.

Control your technolust. Be disciplined when making decisions about technology for your library and keep your library's mission front and center during evaluation and planning.

NOTES

1. Contribution from Ava Ehde, the branch supervisor of the Manatee County (FL) Public Library–Island Branch. She is also an instructor at the School of Informatics, University at Buffalo (NY). She has worked as a library director, systems coordinator, instruction coordinator, head of reference, and local history librarian.
2. Taken in part from contributions by Ava Ehde.
3. Brian Kenney, "The Future of Integrated Library Systems: An LJ Round Table," *Library Journal* (June 15, 2003), http://www.libraryjournal.com/article/CA302408.html?display=searchResult.
4. Contribution from Daniel Nguyen.
5. Janet Walker Peterson, "Stretch Your Budget! How to Select Web-Based Subscriptions," *Computers in Libraries* 23, no. 2 (February 2003): 20–24.
6. Sara Weissman, "Filters: A Checklist for Product Selection," *Public Libraries* (September/October 2003): 279; also available at http://infotrac.galegroup.com.
7. George Needham, "Hello, Mr. (RFID) Chips" (August 10, 2004), http://webjunction.org/do/DisplayContent?id=7129.
8. Michael Stephens, "Technoplans vs. Technolust," *Library Journal* 129, no. 18 (November 2004): 36–37.
9. Contribution from Pam Hickson-Stevenson, director of the Portage County (OH) District Library.
10. Taken in part from contributions by Ava Ehde.

Plan IT

y now you should have a better understanding of what your library has and what technology options are available on the market. The next steps include processing all the information you've gathered, making some judgments about what your library really needs, and pulling it together into a technology plan. Whether adopting a new technology or enhancing your library's existing technology, you should always have a plan, that is, a series of goals to be accomplished and action steps to be carried out. The process of building a plan (i.e., going from data and analysis to detailed goals and actions) can seem complicated. You have a large number of various inputs: the library's mission and vision, assessment data, big picture assessments, technology knowledge, needs analysis, resources, budgeted dollars, and so on. All this information and input needs to be boiled down into the best, most essential, and most easily accomplished actions. This will result in your final technology plan. This may seem like an overwhelming and agonizing process, but, by keeping it simple, you can accomplish the task efficiently and without undue stress.

Planning is not a linear process but involves making thoughtful and sensible choices from a wide array of needs and solutions. The process is as important as the plan that comes out of it. Bringing the library staff together to work toward a unified vision is crucial to ensuring their ultimate acceptance of the plan. After the initial plan is put to work, the planning process becomes an ongoing cycle, as you receive feedback about the plan, make adjustments, and prepare for the future (see figure 4-1 for an illustration of the planning cycle). It is important to remember that this planning approach may be somewhat different from other mainstream approaches. Just as no two libraries are identical, there is no single cookie-cutter plan or approach to planning. Your plan must be tailored to suit your library.

ESSENTIALS OF PLANNING

Before creating your technology plan it is important to think about why you need a plan, who should be involved in making the plan, and what the plan needs to cover. These considerations will help you as you narrow down your plan to its most essential elements.

FIGURE 4-1
Planning
Cycle
Diagram

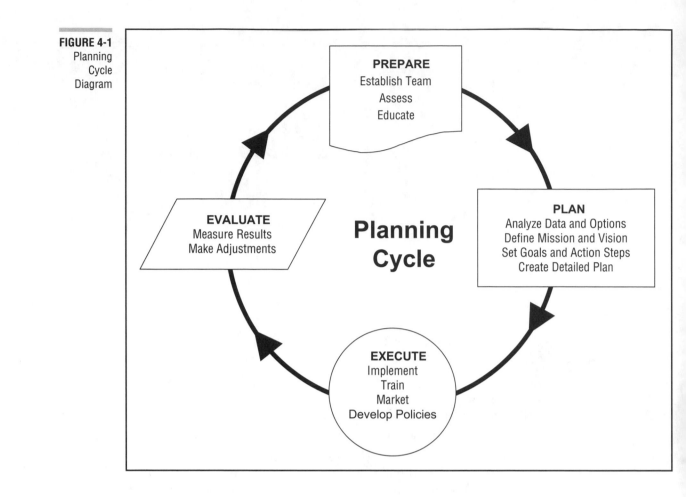

Why

What are the actual benefits of planning? Somewhere along the line you may have heard the phrase, "Failing to plan is planning to fail." These are words to live by when it comes to technology planning. Have you ever heard these excuses before? "We're too small." "It's really no big deal, we just need to get something on paper for the state." "We don't have enough staff or time to create a detailed plan." "Why should we put a lot of effort into something that will never come to fruition?" Attitudes like these are why libraries don't move ahead. Yes, technology planning is involved and takes commitment and time, but it is worth the effort. Through planning, a library will gain a better understanding of technology and, ultimately, make better decisions leading to success—improved services, productivity, and even morale.

Over the years, most small and medium-sized libraries appear to have "gotten by" doing technology planning the old-fashioned way—putting technology into action without much of a formal or well-thought-out plan in place; developing formal plans, but never really doing anything with them once they're created; or viewing plans as nothing more than "official procedure," something required by government. So why all this emphasis on developing high-quality plans if many libraries still "get by" viewing technology plans this way? What is the motivation for changing? In this day and age, it is no longer acceptable for libraries to simply "get by." Libraries of all sizes must look to technology planning to assist them in excelling and becoming the best libraries they can be.

Technology planning is the magic ingredient that will help you to

Obtain funding. Funders will be much more likely to give money for technology if you can show them a technology plan.

Use technology effectively to further your mission. The technology planning process can expand your horizons and help you see new ways in which technology can further your library's mission.

Buy the right equipment. Purchasing hardware, software, and networking equipment can be overwhelming. If you don't plan, it's easy to end up with something that is way too complicated or doesn't do what you need it to do. There's no substitute for thinking through your goals and researching possible solutions.

Save money. You probably don't need the fanciest system on the market. Planning allows you to figure out how to spend less and still meet your needs.

Avoid crises. Bad technology decisions can leave you suffering for years. A faulty system can send your stress level through the roof and make you lose crucial data and capabilities.

Use staff time more effectively. How many hours of staff time have you lost to those niggling technical problems? A technology plan will help you streamline the staff's use of technology and put systems in place that will make technology a useful tool for the staff, not a stumbling block.

Protect yourself from staff turnover. If the person who knows your technology leaves, what will you do? A technology plan can save you by providing documentation of existing systems as well as future plans.[1]

All in all, it's the plan that's the glue. Without a plan and strong leadership to move it along, technology will continue to limp along in smaller libraries. A general rule of thumb for this chapter is, "The more information you are equipped with, the better decisions you will make."

Who

Once you've established why you are creating a plan, think about who is going to be involved in the planning process. Two rules of thumb are

Make sure library staff are actively involved and a key element in the process, from assessment, to planning, to implementation.

Continue with the teamwork approach.

As discussed in chapter 2 on the assessment phase, it is critical to involve your library staff throughout the entire technology planning process. This concept holds true even more during this phase, especially for small and medium-sized libraries where local and municipal government agencies are often responsible for library services. This arrangement can lead to the "parent" entity overseeing library planning with little or no involvement by the staff in their own technology planning and implementation. In order to prevent bad feelings and the creation of an inappropriate or misdirected plan, do not let one person or entity convince you that planning by one person or planning done for you is the right way to go. You should insist on a team approach as led by the library. Don't be intimidated. After all, it's not about how

PARTNERING   Are you short on resources but big on ideas? When it comes time to put your technology plan together, consider partnering with another library or system. Compare needs assessments and look at common goals. How can you work together, complement one another, and pool resources in order to get the things done that will move your libraries out in front? Don't forget about using your state library as a resource.

much you do or don't know about technology; it's about knowing the best approach for your library, where to go for information, and how to put it all together.

When it comes to the teamwork approach, in order to keep things running smoothly, each member of the technology team must become familiar with what the technology is all about. For example, if the team is knowledgeable about hardware specifications, then together the members will be able to develop performance standards for the library's computers, peripheral equipment, and so on. The team will also be better able to analyze the costs and benefits of various hardware models and alternatives. Establishing knowledge of the topic at hand will also give team members insight into the implementation process.[2] In addition, the team should continue to distribute the workload fairly, dividing responsibilities between its various members. Establish timelines and target dates for the various tasks that must be completed. Each member of the technology team must have not only specific duties but a clear idea of the length of time required to prepare the various components of the plan.

As planning continues, the technology team and library administration must be responsible for keeping stakeholders informed and actively involved throughout the process. This is a priority. Broad acceptance of the plan is equally if not more important than the plan itself. Too often technology plans and their resulting projects crash and burn because stakeholders are not adequately brought into the process, in many cases because those in key technology leadership positions appear secretive, domineering, and uncooperative.

What

A plan is a strategy for a course of action to get from where you are now to where you want to be. A technology plan is a document that maps out what and how technology-related systems and services will be implemented to meet your library's mission and goals and best meet the needs of the library and its users. Even more than this, it must be a living document, that is, a document that is never finished but is continuously updated as technology and related requirements and situations change. In order for a technology plan to be truly valuable and not simply another piece of paper, it must

> illustrate how technology is integrated into your library (this part was accomplished by the work that was done during the assessment phase in chapter 2)
>
> provide specific goals and action steps outlining the future direction of technology in your library

be practical and easy to follow so it can actually be implemented instead of sitting on a shelf collecting dust

include an element beyond what is safe and typical

Many planning books might say that the smaller the library is, the smaller and shorter its technology plan should be, since resources are in shorter supply. Although this statement may be true, it does not imply that a shorter plan means an inferior or mediocre one. Small does not have to mean less. It may mean being more imaginative when it comes to budgeting, or extending implementation over a longer period of time, but it never means being less significant. A small library's technology plan can be short in length, but not in content. It should be every bit as detailed, creative, and inspired as a large library's plan.

REVIEW YOUR MISSION AND VISION

Your library's overall mission and vision are also inputs into the planning process, as they will help provide the framework for determining the goals and priorities outlined in your technology plan. A strong, well-thought-out technology plan focuses on technology while also considering the entire library: its overall mission and vision, functional requirements, and characteristics. A mission statement should simply state the overall purpose of the organization; knowing where your library is headed and incorporating this into technology planning is pivotal. On the same note, your library may also have a vision statement, which is a description of the organization as it effectively carries out its operations. In essence, it expresses the destination of the library. What does your library want to become? To help you get started in your analysis, here are a few examples of mission and vision statements from libraries across the country:

Bloomington (IL) Public Library mission. To provide a helpful and friendly place for people of all ages to gain access to and enjoy the world of information; to support lifelong learning; and to be a partner for coping with change.

Liverpool (NY) Public Library mission. The Library responsibly and equitably serves the residents of the Liverpool Central School District. We believe in honoring the public trust bestowed upon the library in a democratic nation by providing free access to information for an informed citizenry. We provide books, videos and other materials to meet the diverse interests and concerns of our community of adults and children. Our materials, programs and technology provide for lifelong learning, cultural experiences and recreation.

Liverpool (NY) Public Library vision. Individuals and groups in the Liverpool Central School District will have their information needs met so that they can fully participate in the life of the community. Community members will utilize library services and resources for enlightenment and entertainment. They will find free, diverse, accessible and up-to-date materials and resources, including electronic technologies. Individuals and groups will be welcomed in a pleasant and safe environment for instructional, informational and entertaining experiences. Community members will be a link in library service, serving as volunteers both with the library and with the Friends of the Library. Community needs will be recognized and services adopted to meet them by ongoing evaluation. The Board of Trustees,

MISSION AND VISION

the staff, and the community members will work together to acquire the resources to fulfill the goals and objectives of the library.

Cleveland Heights–University Heights (OH) Public Library vision. We will know we are succeeding when . . . Our services and facilities appeal to all ages. Our collections, services and staff are outstanding. We have established the library as a Third Place, or "someplace other than work or home where a person can go to . . . feel part of the community." We remain focused on the needs of our customers.

Westlake Porter (OH) Public Library mission. To educate, empower, enlighten, and excite the public by providing access to and instruction in an array of resources in multiple formats on-site and by linking individuals with resources and agencies off-site that meet their information needs.

Baldwin (MI) Public Library mission. We enhance the quality of life and serve as a portal to the world's knowledge.

Delaware County (OH) District Library mission. The Library serves as the public information provider for our community, using traditional and innovative technology to encourage curiosity, free inquiry and lifelong learning in a friendly environment.

Oak Park (IL) Public Library mission. The Library provides superior library materials and services responsive to the evolving informational, educational, vocational, cultural and recreational needs of Oak Park's diverse community.

Now that you've reviewed your library's mission and vision, you can move on to looking at your library's technology needs. Think about how technology relates to the library's overall charge. How does your technology fit with the organizational mission statement? With a good mission statement, this should not be difficult to figure out. If it does prove troublesome, then it's probably time for a revision of the library's mission. It is important to see some relationship to technology within the larger scope of the library. Technology must be a part of the larger picture in order for it and the library to realize their full potential.

UNDERTAKE A NEEDS ANALYSIS

Have you ever tried to order from a restaurant without a menu or from a retailer without a catalog? Probably not—just think how chaotic the process would be. That's what it's like when you try to buy a new computer or set up a new technology service for your library without first making a list of what your library needs and which technologies might help you meet those needs. Without such a list, you may come to conclusions that are premature or in error. Undertaking a needs analysis is a way to jump-start your planning process by helping you create that list. Once needs are clear, then setting goals and action steps will be that much easier.

A needs analysis can be defined as the process of asking critical questions to help you figure out what your library really needs. Brainstorm all the possible options: consider what you want technology to *be* and *do* for your library. By analyzing the assessment data and organizing it into a menu according to the Must Have, Must Get, More Is Better, and Technology Thriller categories, planners will begin to see what areas are lacking and what areas should be developed further. There are several tools you can use to help you analyze your library's needs.

Refer back to the "big picture technology analysis" in chapter 2 (see figure 2-5). Where are your library's strengths and weaknesses?

> If you haven't already done so, complete the analysis sections of the assessment/analysis worksheets in appendix A, answering as many questions as possible. (The assessment sections should have been completed prior to this; see chapter 2.) Looking at your answers in the analysis sections of the worksheets will give you a clear idea of what your library's needs are. Also, ask yourself what, if any, additional questions grew out of the original assessment questions.

> Use the "Technology Brainstorming Worksheet" in appendix A to help identify technologies and services that are beyond the scope of your current services. Open your mind to any and all possibilities. This is where you can really begin thinking outside the box in regard to current services and offerings. When analyzing the results of this exercise, look for consistent patterns or themes. Consider questions such as these:

> > ■ Are you serving one population segment better than others?
> >
> > ■ Are there any obvious or hidden problems or concerns?
> >
> > ■ Are the "where we want to go" answers consistent with the library's mission?
> >
> > ■ How much of a gap is there between where you are and where you want to be?

No matter which tools you use, the goal is to broadly convey what it is you want to accomplish. You can get specific about the needs, but do not get too specific about what you need to buy (that will come later). Remember that you are trying to build your menu, shaping your final options into the Must Have, Must Get, More Is Better, and Technology Thriller categories. From there you will be able to better assign priorities later in the process.

As you proceed through the needs analysis, take time to think about the following types of questions. They will assist you in filtering through all of your needs, helping you make decisions about what you will actually do and in what order you will do it.

> What does the library want and need to do with technology?
>
> Why does the library need a particular technology?
>
> How can technology work for, benefit, and interact with the library as a whole (staff, patrons, procedures, etc.)?
>
> How can technology help staff communicate more effectively and efficiently?

SPREADSHEETS　Consider plugging some of your data from the assessment into a spreadsheet to create graphs and charts. Visual representations of statistics and information can help you better see the big picture. They can also be used in your written plan and can make a great impact when you present the plan to key stakeholders.

How will the library budget for, fund, and implement needed and wanted technology?

What problems may arise with any of the outlined needs?

Will there be new policies or procedures to institute?

What staffing implications may arise?

What will technology do that you can't already do?

Completing a needs analysis is about letting the data lead you to discovering needs and wants. It's a good time to look around at other libraries and organizations to see how to define your needs in relation to what others similar to you are doing. This step will also help justify your decisions and priorities later on. Defining and categorizing your needs will allow you to choose the best, most efficient, and, most important, the most needed solutions for *your* library. Also, bear in mind that while you must define today's needs today, you must also leave room for evolving requirements as new technology becomes available.

CREATE THE PLAN

Now that you and your team have gathered the information about what the library already has (the assessment phase, chapter 2), investigated all the possibilities of what's out there (the research phase, chapter 3), and reviewed the library's mission and completed the needs analysis, it's time to get down to the nitty-gritty of what must be done in order to fulfill the identified needs. This is where critical thinking and analysis are crucial and where the hard choices are made. As you narrow down your choices to create your plan, ask yourself, Which options will best enable my library to meet the needs of its patrons and its staff as supported by the library's mission and vision?

Your primary tool here is the "Technology Planning Worksheet" in appendix A. This worksheet will help you lay out your goals and action steps, identify the value these goals and actions bring to the library, and outline the resources (of people, time, and money) required for implementation. This worksheet will also assist you in prioritizing tasks and delineating potential technology solutions associated with each goal and action.

Goals and Action Steps

Your goals are your desired outcomes and should be stated first. Goals should be directly related to the needs you identified in the needs analysis. Although the goals themselves should be general, they should lead to specific actions or technology solutions. The goals provide direction and focus on the ends rather than the means. Sample goals may include, but are not limited to

Our library will provide its internal and external customers with technologies that enhance patron service options and improve staff efficiency.

Our library will seek funding for technologies that will enhance its services to the community and keep our doors open after hours.

Our library staff will improve internal library practices and communication through the use of technology.

Our library staff will develop sufficient technology literacy to improve customer service and provide quality technology instruction to patrons.

Next come action steps. These are the means and should be developed and written specifically to support each goal. Action steps describe the events that will take place in order to meet desired goals and, in some cases, dictate how the progress toward reaching the goals will be measured. When determining action steps, be specific about what will occur. Make sure goals and actions are realistic, attainable, and measurable. Here are some sample action steps related to the above sample goals (also see the "Sample Technology Planning Worksheet" in figure 4-2).

Implement an online program and event registration system that will allow patrons to view and register for library programs outside of regular library hours.

Create a library intranet to provide a single point of information for staff.

Begin a staff blog to enhance staff intercommunications.

Begin an internal technology training program to educate all staff on how to provide excellent technology assistance.

As your team works through this step, make note of any immediate problems or limitations that come up during your discussions. It is always better to recognize potential roadblocks at the beginning than to be unpleasantly surprised in the middle or at the end of a project. Also, jot down all questions that arise out of the process pertaining to each goal and action step.

Value

For each action step, you should pinpoint the value, or benefit, that step will bring to your library. Values should relate to your library's mission and vision, although broader connections to community needs and the library's budget can also be made. Although it may sound like needless extra work, this simple step will help ensure your success by showing decision-makers the explicit merits of a project. The following are some examples related to the goals and action steps listed above.

Online program registration will make library programs and events more accessible to patrons, which may increase participation in library programming. This service also opens doors for additional collaborations with other organizations in the community. An increase in automated self-service options will ultimately allow staff to concentrate less on paperwork and secretarial duties and more on professional duties that improve the library. Streamlining tasks will ultimately lead to more efficient and cost-effective use of staff.

FIGURE 4-2

Sample Technology Planning Worksheet

Note: The following examples are for illustrative purposes only.

GOALS AND ACTION STEPS	VALUE	TECHNOLOGY SOLUTIONS	RESOURCES			ADDITIONAL QUESTIONS AND COMMENTS	PRIORITY
			People	**Time**	**Money**		
Goal Library staff will improve internal library practices and communication.	Improved internal and external customer service	Utilize existing web and e-mail servers. Evaluate web development tools and possibly purchase a content management system to allow non-HTML experts to manage and add content to the intranet.	1. IT staff to develop intranet 2. IT and individual staff needing accounts will apply for e-mail accounts via the consortium; knowledgeable e-mail staff to train new users	1. 1 week for setup and design 2. 2–4 days for application process and training time 3. 2–4 weeks to gather input and develop guides	1. $0 (use internal web server) 2. $50 per person per year 3. $0 Possible unknown $$ for web development tools or for a content management system	Who will maintain intranet after it's up and running? Will there be a content management system so multiple staff can add information? Review policy for staff e-mail access.	**Goal:** High Priority Actions in Priority Order:
Actions Establish an intranet.	Improved efficiency					What is the training schedule for new e-mail users?	**2**
Expand e-mail access to all clerical and professional staff.	Increased job satisfaction					What is the schedule for training staff on troubleshooting procedures, guides?	**1**
Document basic troubleshooting procedures and tips for all staff.			3. IT staff, with input from other staff, will compile troubleshooting guides and post on intranet			If the number of e-mail accounts and their costs are prohibitive, consider purchasing an e-mail server for the library as a long-term investment. As research ensues for troubleshooting documentation, and if appropriate for the situation, consider a trouble-shooting software solution that would integrate with the intranet for submitting and following up on in-house technology problems and questions.	**3**

A staff intranet, blog, and internal training sessions will assist in improving staff communication, thereby improving morale and customer service. Increased IT support and information sharing will also lead to cost savings for the library as more staff are able to assist patrons and troubleshoot problems without relying on IT staff overtime or calling in outside professionals.

See the "Sample Technology Planning Worksheet" in figure 4-2 for more examples.

Technology Solutions

At this stage in the game you will want to ask yourself, What specific technology solutions might we implement to address these goals and action steps? This is the phase of planning that requires the most technical knowledge, and the planning team should already have a general grasp of what solutions are out there (see chapter 3). Note that the solutions that you come up with at this point might not be the final technologies that you implement, but selecting solutions now will help to firm up the framework of your plan. It will also better assist you in estimating required resources. There may be instances where you don't have enough information to choose a specific technology. Don't put the entire planning process on hold simply because you can't assign a specific technology to an action. Some goals and projects are too complex for technology decisions to be made at this level of planning—you can come back to these later.

Making these decisions may be the most difficult part of the process, especially when it comes to finding solutions that fit within your library's budget. As discussed in chapter 3, available technology options are wide and varied. Do your homework, don't fear the jargon, and learn what you can. Even if you don't understand everything, the process of researching and comparing technologies and solutions will teach you a lot and put you in position to ask the right kinds of questions. Technology specialists at TechSoup.org agree:

> It's important to make sure that all the solutions you pick are compatible . . . Technology is interdependent and there are dozens of options with different price tags for each technology decision, so negotiating your priorities can get very tricky. The important thing is to go back to your original vision of how technology can help you accomplish your mission. What are the key new functions you want technology to fill? Consider price, of course, but don't get locked into an inexpensive technology that won't grow with you and won't work with future technologies.[3]

If you are looking for additional input and opinions beyond the technology team's own expertise and research, look to someone affiliated with the library (board member, volunteer) who has a strong background in computers and related technology. Consider their advice, learn from them what you can, confirm the information, and weigh it against the technology team's findings. And don't be afraid to ask questions. Depending on the situation, this may also be the right time to bring in a consultant. Just remember, these same rules of thumb apply to evaluating information presented by a consultant. (See chapter 5 for more information on hiring and working with consultants.)

The key to finding the right technology solution is to be patient and diligent. Whatever you do, avoid settling on the first option you come across; if it is the right option, a little further investigation and evaluation will confirm that. Consult with other libraries as well as with other organizations and businesses in your community when applicable. There are a vast number of resources out there on the technology options presented in this book, only a small fraction of which are touched on in the resource guide in appendix B. So do your homework, be practical, and simply do your best.

Resources

The plan you create must show what resources are needed to carry out each action step. Primary resources include but are not limited to people, time, and money. Begin this step by estimating how much of each resource will be assigned during implementation of each of your action steps. Keep in mind that this may be subject to change as projects become more specific and the realities of projects come to light. Your initial estimates should be based on staff experiences and input from outside resources.

Because an organization's most important resource is its people, you'll need to think about their roles in the overall plan. Consider questions such as

Who will be in charge of each action/task/project?

What personnel will be assigned to assist with each action/task/project?

Can this be handled by existing staff or will we need to create a new position?

How much staff training will be required?

If you're recommending that new staff (e.g., a full-time or part-time employee, a consultant, etc.) be added, think about how they will be added and what their capabilities and experience should be. (See chapter 5 for more information pertaining to staffing.)

Closely related to people is time. In particular, many decisions will have a significant impact on staff time. Calculate the amount of time you think a project will take (based on an hourly rate) and factor that into your plan. Keep in mind that the number of staff hours allocated to a project or task will not necessarily be an accurate indication of how many calendar days it will take to complete. Equipment delivery times, asynchronous work schedules, and the typical slew of interruptions can impact a timeline. During this step it is also important to ask, What's worth more here—the time or the money? If you're spending time to save money, you may be spending more than you bargained for. Determine what your time (and others' time) is worth and use that information as a way to help decide when to use existing staff, new staff, or outside resources to complete an action or project.

Money tends to be the dominating factor when it comes to considering needs, and it is often the deciding factor in determining what actions and proj-

---

PLANNING TIPS FROM MODEL LIBRARIES

The Newburyport (MA) Public Library has some tips about devising a technology plan: (1) Ask questions! When possible, be cognizant of where your individual library's anticipated technology needs lie within any greater whole, such as a consortium, a community (of borrowers and of residents who are not library users), or the cutting edge internationally. (2) Be inclusive regarding technology planning personnel. Concentrating your efforts among several key staff members who really wish to be involved in the process will spark others and will make training them easier down the line. Also, involve a community member or two and put them "in the know." (3) Make site visits, actually and virtually, to see what other libraries have done. Seeing is believing.

The Yorba Linda (CA) Public Library says:

Get everyone involved. We did a visioning process where everything was on the table, sky's the limit. We're proud to say we accomplished a lot of what many may have thought too grandiose. The staff here believe that Yorba Linda Public Library is the best library in the world, but without the people it would just be a box with books and wires. They want to do new and exciting things; the energy they bring to the library is incredible. It is a pleasure to work at a place where ideas come from the bottom up, top down, and every which way.[4]

ects will be undertaken. So it is essential to consider the financial impact of all aspects of a goal and its related action steps: not only new spending and purchases but also any sunk costs (i.e., nonrecoverable fixed costs such as labor or staff time). Be broad in your thinking, considering costs of hardware, software, shipping and handling, furniture, supplies, maintenance, staffing, and so on. At this level of planning, your numbers will most likely be general estimates, but they will help you to better define the plan and provide additional information for assigning priorities later in the process. (See chapter 6 for additional information on the financial aspects of technology.)

Prioritizing

Once you've established your goals and action steps, determined values, selected potential technologies, and assessed resources, you'll need to start assigning priorities to the goals as well as to the individual action steps. When determining which goals should receive the highest priority, consider this analogy: setting technology goals and priorities is like picking fruit from a huge apple tree. You would never start picking the apples by finding a ladder and climbing to pick the highest fruit first. Instead, as a logical and sensible person, you're going to pick the fruit you can reach from the ground and work your way up the tree. And so it goes with technology planning. Start with the basics, reach what you can first, and then strive for more. This is the low-hanging fruit concept.

As you prioritize keep in mind how your goals and actions fit into the Must Have, Must Get, More Is Better, and Technology Thriller categories as discussed in chapter 3. Evaluate your potential projects by criteria such as these:

Which items represent the library's most pressing needs?

Which items represent the lowest hanging fruit?

Which elements are most critical to the library's mission/vision?

What projects are most in line with meeting the community's expectations?

What projects are mission critical?

What projects can wait a few months?

What goals and tasks need to be accomplished within the year?

What items can wait beyond a year?

What tasks will show the most immediate impact and results?

Which projects are the most cost-effective?

Which projects are the most time-effective?

These and similar questions will help you assign priorities and further establish time allotments to the various goals and action steps. Breaking projects down into categories by priority is important, especially in organizations that are short on resources. Setting priorities will help you fine-tune the plan as well as better organize the work ahead, making it easier to stay on course with your plan. Having a plan with clear priorities also shows funding sources that their money will be spent effectively on projects that will have a definite impact on the library or the community. What better way to build credibility? This credibility guarantees that your efficiency and decisiveness will receive due credit and consideration in the minds of donors and funding sources in the future.

WRITE UP THE PLAN

As a general rule of thumb, a formal technology plan should cover a two-year period. Depending on how technology is used in your library, your plan may cover a shorter or longer period, but it should not exceed three years. Your plan must not only be well documented, it must be easy to follow. Keep in mind that its purpose is to provide written direction for your library. The plan will also become a working document that has the potential of being used in a variety of situations. In particular, it will be used as a guide during the project implementation stages. The final document should come across as well organized, well thought out, proactive, and honest. This can easily be accomplished through a combination of well-researched, team-driven content and clear, concise formatting. When it comes to layout, balance a narrative approach with list-item formats such as bulleted and numbered lists. This approach will encourage stakeholders to read the plan and engage with it rather than filing it away someplace. A well-written plan will serve as an effective informational piece for stakeholders such as staff, board members, and community partners.

As you have seen, a technology plan should document where your library has been, where it is now, what it needs, and the proposed solutions for fulfilling those needs. After covering the basics such as the library's name, library director's name, library address, county, population served, population of county, fiscal years of coverage, and a list of technology team members, a successful technology plan should include the following:

Brief overview. Include a short overview of the library as well as its mission and vision. Describe what the library does and how it's done. Include a summary of the library's technology achievements and their impact. This will set the background for what follows. Then succinctly summarize the plan's recommendations and conclusions. Be sure to show how technology ties into the overall mission and plan of the library.

Assessment. Describe the library's existing technology—equipment, software, and services. Basically, this is your Technology Assessment Summary from chapter 2. (Refer back to the sample summary in appendix A.) This documentation is essential in supporting your statements about the library's needs.

Goals and action steps. This section is the cornerstone of your plan and should dominate both its focus and its length. All items should be both clear and realistic. (Refer back to the Technology Planning Worksheet discussed earlier in this chapter.)

Value. Specifically, how will your plan and specific goals and actions further the mission of the library? What positive impact will the plan have on the library and the community?

Priority. What is the importance of goals and actions? In what order will items be completed?

People resources. What staff, consultants, and external resources are necessary to accomplish your goals and actions? How will they be utilized?

Timeline. Estimate how much time each goal will take and create a basic timetable for the plan, goals, and various action steps. When will you begin implementing the plan, your action steps, and so on? In what order will they occur? For example:

▪ January 15—By this date staff will have researched and ordered XYZ

- March 1–31—XYZ will be installed
- April 1–30—Staff training on XYZ
- May 1—Release to public and public training begins

Costs. How much will this plan cost the library in terms of hardware, software, fees, installation, shipping, labor, and everything else that goes into the cost of each goal and action step? Outline the monetary resources that will be required to complete all parts of the plan. Be particularly careful to create an adequate budget for reaching and maintaining all of your outlined goals (see chapter 6 for further information on budgeting for technology). It is also very helpful to include a copy of the library's budget to show the overall financial commitment to technology by the library.

Training. Outline all training initiatives related to the plan. Internal and external education are vital in ensuring any plan's success. A technology plan is not just about hardware, software, and money; it is also about people. Professional development and training are key components. (See the training sections of chapter 8 for more information.)

Evaluation. Include provisions for evaluating your plan's progress. Answer questions such as, How will the library monitor the progress toward reaching its technology goals and action steps? How will the library measure whether its plan is successful? Make sure you outline how each goal will be evaluated: what method will be used, who will assess, when it will be completed, and so on. For example: "Library staff will measure patron usage of public computers by collecting data from the PC reservation software. Staff will also monitor the increase in public use by tracking the number of people who visit the library." Also, don't forget to include how often the technology plan will be reevaluated. (See chapter 10 for more information on evaluating and monitoring the impact of a project or plan.)

Appendixes. Include additional supportive information such as your technology inventory (put into a simple spreadsheet), other library and community data as appropriate, budget information, significant notes, and so on.

TIE IT ALL TOGETHER

To truly realize the benefits of technology, libraries must try to develop an overall plan for integrating technology into everything they do. An effective technology plan is based on a shared vision that depends on technology to strengthen a library's existing services and procedures. As technology continues to transform society, the question is no longer whether technology will play a role in the library but rather how well libraries will incorporate it to enhance what they are doing for their customers and communities.

Long-Range and Strategic Planning

Technology is now a key element in any library's long-range and strategic planning. As with a library's mission and vision, it is equally important to incorporate technology within the plan that outlines an organization's long-term goals and the ways in which it intends to achieve those goals. The important thing to keep in mind is that a technology plan cannot exist by itself. It must be a part of the larger vision of the library, and this vision is expressed in a long-range plan. Unfortunately, many libraries fail to include technology as a significant part of their overall planning process. The quality and efficiency of services provided by libraries depend greatly on a library's technological motivation, abilities, and competence. How well a library plans for and utilizes technology will be an indicator of its future survival. If your library's long-range plan does not meet these conditions, it is probably time to revisit it. There are numerous books on the market that provide guidance on long-range and strategic planning for libraries.

Space Planning

Often overlooked is the relationship between technology planning and space planning. Although this may seem an obvious connection, it is still a rather new concept to many library stakeholders. As computers and other forms of technology become more prevalent in libraries, so too does the importance of creating adequate space for them. The "Facility Assessment/Analysis Worksheet" in appendix A and the supporting discussion from chapter 2 will help you keep space planning in mind as you approach the process. Be sure to integrate the impact of technology on space planning within the technology plan itself, as well as throughout general library space-related plans and projects. If your library is going through a building renovation or expansion project, once again, be sure to incorporate input from technology stakeholders. All too often architects and designers fail to fully understand the needs of the library. They sometimes bring preconceived notions and boilerplate approaches that don't meet the requirements and aspirations of the modern library.

Replacement Plans

One planning area that is often overlooked is that of phasing out, decommissioning, and replacing hardware. Hardware (particularly computers) has a limited life span, so you should develop a plan for tagging, tracking, and replacing hardware and other technology equipment. Your library should include a reference to this in its policies. Integral to this process is establishing a procedure for inventorying hardware. Think of this procedure just as you would of the bar coding and cataloging of library materials. Not only is this process important for keeping track of equipment, but it is also useful in analyzing the cost-effectiveness of maintaining that equipment. The resulting documentation is also essential in case of disaster. Libraries often fail to collect data like this because they feel they don't have the time, staff, or money, but the reality is that having this documentation readily available helps reduce the total cost of ownership (see chapter 6 for more on this topic). In addition, plan on keeping track of troubleshooting statistics and related support information, because these are helpful in identifying patterns of problems and support needs. These statistics also provide a glimpse into maintenance costs.[5]

Other Plans

Planning occurs in almost all areas of a library on a regular basis. Plans come in a variety of types and sizes; some are detailed, while others are short and sweet; some pertain solely to your library, and others are collaborations between multiple libraries. No matter what plan you are facing, the key is to consider technology's role within that particular plan. Consider disaster planning. A disaster plan documents the policies and procedures that are intended to prepare for disasters and prevent or minimize damage from them. Disaster plans and technology go hand in hand. A good disaster plan covers all technology issues because it is understood that technology is part of the library's backbone. If technology is not adequately considered, then the library will have difficulty recovering from catastrophic events (e.g., hurricanes, floods, fires). (See the section for this chapter in appendix B for some resources on disaster planning.) Other types of plans fall under the "special projects" category and can include such things as program planning, digitization planning, and facilities planning, just to name a few. If your library is part of a bigger system, consortium, or statewide plan (e.g., an automation plan), make sure your library provides input from its point of view, taking into account your library's specific needs and goals as outlined in your technology plan. The key here is to speak up; don't sit back and let others make decisions for you. There are also subprojects that may arise out of your library's overall technology plan. These are projects that need separate plans of their own because of their size and scope. An example of this might be a website development plan.

LIVE WITH THE PLAN

Remember, a technology plan is a living, breathing document that must be capable of modification as new needs and priorities come up. If something does not work out the way you want it to, or if it does not improve library operations as you anticipated, go back, move things around, make adjustments, and rework the plan. Because computer and information technology represent a fundamental change in the way libraries do business, your library must make an ongoing commitment to keep pace with change by reviewing and evaluating (and even revising) its plan each year. This is a must for keeping things on track.

So what are the results of a good technology plan? They should include the following:

a better understanding of how technology can be used to support the library, its mission, and its goals

the establishment of a foundation for technology within the library as a whole

reassurance that the library has addressed its internal and external customers' needs

increased acceptance and support from stakeholders and less opportunity for opposition

the ability to respond efficiently and effectively to new opportunities, thereby gaining credibility and support for the library

a solid approach to future planning for technology and the library as a whole

To be well received a technology plan must be clearly thought out, flexible, and easy to understand. It must describe what you want to do as well as the steps you will take to get to the final product. A strong plan will include proposals for improvements and will quickly move on to explain how these will add value to the library's services and programs. It will also contain information pertaining to the resources (people, money, time) necessary to carry out the plan or its projects. By including each of these elements, you will come up with a solid plan that is both ready to sell and to implement.

DO YOU KNOW IT?

There is no one cookie-cutter planning method. Understand the basic concepts and adapt a planning process that works for your library.

Planning is an ongoing cyclic process. Planning never really ends. It constantly evolves as plans develop, feedback is received, and priorities and technologies change.

Assess your needs. Begin the analysis of what to plan for by assessing your needs as derived from various assessment tools.

Set your goals and action steps. Convert your analysis and needs assessment into goals and actions. These are the cornerstones of the technology plan.

Determine value, solutions, and resources. These are the steps in finalizing which goals will be pursued and the priorities that will be set.

Create a clean, organized, and concise plan. Organize your technology plan in a way that is easy for staff and stakeholders to read and understand.

Live with the plan. Keep your plan handy and live by it. Know that it must evolve with the library and technology.

NOTES

1. Anna Mills, "Why a Technology Plan: Ain't Nothing like the Real Thing, Baby," TechSoup.org (May 4, 2000), http://www.techsoup.org.
2. L. Goddard, "Hardware Renewal Planning," *Feliciter* 50, no. 2 (2004): 46–47.
3. "What's Involved in Technology Planning: Seven Steps to a Better Technology Plan," TechSoup .org (December 5, 2002), http://www.techsoup.org.
4. From the contributions of Nancy K. Alcorn, assistant director of the Newburyport (MA) Public Library, and Danis Kreimeier, director of the Yorba Linda (CA) Public Library.
5. Goddard, "Hardware Renewal Planning."

Staff IT 5

With technology planning comes new services, new resources, and new duties. With new duties come redefined staff roles and titles. Hiring and staffing in public libraries has taken on new meaning, becoming progressively more complex as technology takes on a larger role in day-to-day operations. The roles of library employees are radically changing, with more librarians and library support staff playing a central role in managing and supporting all aspects of technology. As you are well aware, in small and medium sized facilities, it is not uncommon to find staff members who are "jacks of all trades" often stretched to the limit, bearing multiple titles and responsibilities. So how do you successfully operate your library in this sea of change and reorganization? And how do you make things happen (and thrive) when faced with limited resources?

The key to success lies not only in how and what technology you choose but also in how you develop and work with your most valuable resource—people. Kristie Kirkpatrick, director of the Whitman County (WA) Library, says that library is successful because "I trust my staff to do their jobs and excel at them . . . It all goes back to getting good staff—I couldn't have done any of this without my staff!"[1] No matter what your library's size, budget, or demographics, there are a variety of options available when it comes to finding the people to fill technology-related needs and positions. Be creative. Look to new ways to get people on board, encouraging their interest and understanding of technology in the library. Be inventive and mesh successful staffing procedures and techniques from the past with new techniques, fresh thinking, and ideas that have potential right now. This chapter will show you how to find the right person for the job as well as help you develop a more modern library staff. The goal is to bring librarians, paraprofessionals, and "techies" together. Even the smallest of organizations can thrive when it comes to technology if they know how to select and partner with the right people.

LOOKING WITHIN THE LIBRARY

Many libraries already have a wealth of technology knowledge and motivation already on staff. Unfortunately, this talent either goes unrecognized or is ignored. So the first lesson is to learn to make the most of who is already in your organization. Whether conducting a formal technology assessment as outlined in chapter 2 or performing a separate and more focused staff assessment, you must get a grasp of your library's organizational structure and the technology roles and responsibilities defined within that structure. Find out exactly who is working for you and what their skills and interests are. Getting direct staff input is essential, whether using a simple self-assessment tool, a formal review process, or just talking to staff members. Once this information has been gathered, you will be on your way to discovering how you can best utilize your staff members to increase productivity, improve overall service, and keep morale high.

Roles and Responsibilities

Librarians and library staff are assuming expanding roles when it comes to technology. Roles such as technician, troubleshooter, online researcher, trainer, and technology teacher are common for many library staff members whether they are technology experts or not. Full-time and part-time employees alike find themselves with new responsibilities that stretch beyond traditional librarianship. So when it comes to roles and responsibilities, how is your library managing technology? How are responsibilities and duties divided? Is your library practicing a team-based approach? All staff members will have some interaction with technology on a day-to-day basis, but not all will consider it a primary part of their job. This chapter will discuss general staff technology assessment and then focus on how libraries can fill those staff positions that hold primary responsibility for technology-related duties.

Staff Assessment

The realm of staff technology assessment is often dreaded, but it is always well worth the effort. In even the smallest of libraries, there should be staff members responsible for the daily operation of technology—these are people working within the library's walls. Individual libraries must not rely exclusively on outside consultants or systems people at the library system, consortium, or local government level. In today's world any organization that puts all of its technology eggs in one basket will eventually find itself in trouble, as circumstances will inevitably create a situation where problems arise and outside resources are nowhere to be found. The key is to use assessment tools such as self-assessment, interviews, and annual staff reviews to find out who among your staff is most capable to handle the tasks at hand.

TECH TIP

MINIMUM SKILL LEVELS

Staff members need to have a minimum level of skills. At the Whitman County (WA) Rural Library, the director gives staffers autonomy to do their jobs while requiring that every staff member serving customers become tech-savvy. Those staff members who are not willing to climb on board the new program are reassigned to positions behind the scenes at the library.[2] There are several places on the Web where you can find examples of what other libraries define as minimum technology skill levels for various positions. See appendix B for a few resources.

An excellent tool for gathering feedback is the self-assessment. In general terms, a self-assessment is a professional development resource that helps staff members identify their own strengths and weaknesses and chart a course for improvement. Basically, it reflects staff competencies. Self-assessment may be used to determine employee technology skill levels, identifying those staff members best suited to technology-related positions within the library. This process can also help identify areas of technology in which training for the library staff is needed. The areas to be addressed in a technology self-evaluation include basic computer operation, file management, office product use (word processing, spreadsheets, etc.), Internet, e-mail, database use and searching, understanding of technology policies, and multimedia. More advanced subject areas might include network management, cabling, servers, backup systems, wireless networks, and Internet connections.

In order to best devise a staffing plan that is right for your library, have each member of the staff complete the "Staff Self-Assessment Worksheet" in appendix A. The answers they provide on the worksheet will give you a clearer view of where your library stands in terms of your staff and key technology-related duties. Be sure to look for gaps and weaknesses as well as strengths in staff members' abilities. After staff members have completed a self-assessment or have been evaluated in some other manner, categorize them into the various proficiency levels by putting each person's name into the appropriate cell of the "Staff Proficiency Comparison Chart" shown in figure 5-1. The chart lets you see the strengths and weaknesses in the staff's technological competencies.

You are now ready to answer the questions listed below. (Note that more than one individual may be assigned to each of the duties in this list. In fact, this is highly recommended and is emphasized in a team-based approach.)

Who is responsible for planning for technology?

Who is responsible for budgeting for technology or recommending budget items to the director?

Who recommends or creates technology-related policies and procedures?

Who manages the local area network (i.e., oversees the server, computers, peripherals, etc.)?

Is network management broken down by tasks and assigned to various employees? (These tasks include daily and monthly backups, periodic testing and cleaning of equipment, software upgrades, user accounts, e-mail accounts, etc.) If so, who is responsible for these various duties?

Who selects or makes recommendations on software purchases?

Who selects or makes recommendations about online databases?

Who maintains software and database purchases? Does this same person track licensing compliance?

Who troubleshoots technology (hardware, software, audiovisual) on a day-to-day basis?

Who serves as the webmaster, guiding the overall direction of the website, the regular updating of content, and so on?

Who is responsible for overseeing technology skills and training for staff? For the public?

What other duties can you think of?

FIGURE 5-1
Staff Proficiency
Comparison
Chart

AREA OF PROFICIENCY	NOVICE	INTERMEDIATE	ADVANCED
Hardware and Equipment			
Software			
Network Administration			
Technology-Related Instruction to the Public			
Technology-Related Policies			
Technology-Related Collection Development			
Other			

Ask Them

One quick and easy assessment tool is open communication, that is, talking to your employees. Consider holding informal one-on-one conversations or more formal group discussions. Distribute a basic survey to staff asking them to identify overall staffing strengths and weaknesses, library strengths and weaknesses, holes in technology service, technology-related staffing needs, and so on. You might also think about incorporating a comment session or form into annual employee evaluations. Whatever method you choose to use, don't avoid asking just because you're afraid of potential conflict. Many administrators and managers shy away from encouraging people to express opinions about their jobs and the library as a whole. This is unfortunate because it really is a crucial step in staffing your library more effectively. In fact, if you handle things correctly, you might be pleasantly surprised by what you hear from your employees. Be prepared to take the good with the bad, and keep in mind that it's all about improving the library. Some of the negative feedback may be hard to hear, but it often brings hidden and problematic issues to the surface, which can then be examined and potentially revisited. Make sure you have plans for following up on your staffers' input. Asking and then not responding in some way afterward can be more detrimental than never asking at all.

Analyze Your Current Status and Needs

As you attempt to evaluate what staffing options are best for your library, here are a few more key questions to answer:

> Are your current staffing practices and assignment of responsibilities effective and efficient for *your* library? (Don't get hung up on what works for others. Look at what best works for you.)
>
> Do you have people with the right technical skills covering day-to-day operations (e.g., PC troubleshooting, network troubleshooting, etc.)? If not, what can be done differently?
>
> Have you adequately covered responsibilities with the *best* people for the job?
>
> Is there anyone currently involved with technology who isn't correctly matched with their job or duties?

Once you have gathered all your staff assessment data, you can begin to clearly analyze what staffing solutions will work best for your library. After identifying what technology-related duties are critical to your library and what your existing staff's technology capabilities, strengths, and weaknesses are, consider these options:

1. Managing the duties at hand by means of existing staff (by rearranging, reassigning, and promoting them), with possible assistance from volunteers
2. Hiring a new employee (or employees) from outside the library to oversee technology with the support of existing internal personnel
3. Contracting with a consultant or contract IT service provider (again working with internal personnel as much as possible)

The questions to be asked are, Can you meet your needs with option 1? If not, is there enough of a gap to justify option 2? If not, are there good (and affordable) outside resources available to you for option 3? If you go through options 1 through 3 and find yourself back at 1, this is the time to consider collaborative options such as consortiums and ad hoc partnerships with other libraries in your area that have the same or a similar situation. For example, the Whitman County (WA) Rural Library partnered with a neighboring library district to hire and share a qualified computer system administrator, saving them around $25,000 per year.[3]

Evaluating Internal Options

How do you decide if someone on your staff is or is not right for a technology-specific position? In addition to their general attitude (see "The Right Person for the Job" later in this chapter), look for staff members with preexisting skills, aptitudes, and knowledge (refer back to the "Staff Proficiency Comparison Chart" in figure 5-1). Is there anyone currently on staff who isn't responsible for technology who's interested in getting more involved? By the same token, are there any employees currently working with technology who feel overwhelmed by their duties or burned out by their job? The idea is to consider where it may be appropriate to rearrange, divide up, or reassign individual roles and responsibilities. Equally important is to retain internal talent by promoting and rewarding competent, motivated employees. Consider this a sound investment in the library's future. You should also consider collaborative supervision or job-sharing between two or more staff members. How about cross-training more than one part-time staff member to share duties and oversight? For medium-sized facilities, think about pairing a full-time staff member with a part-time one.

There is also the option of creating a team-centered technology environment. A team-based approach to managing technology is gaining in popularity in libraries of all sizes and can be especially beneficial in improving efficiency and reducing stress. The team approach specifically helps to distribute the workload and broaden knowledge of technology throughout the organization, thereby creating more staff who can troubleshoot and answer technology-related questions. Organizational and individual stress are reduced because the staff need not rely on just a single person to solve their technology problems or answer their questions. Response time is better and issues are resolved quicker. This is a new idea to many, and in order for it to work, libraries need to be receptive to changes in traditional people-job relationships. Not only will this approach ultimately save the library money, it will also increase productivity and customer service by empowering more of your staff to solve problems and serve the needs of patrons and their fellow staff members.

THE RIGHT PERSON FOR THE JOB

Have you ever heard the saying, "Hire for attitude, train for skill"? When it comes to promoting and hiring technology personnel, it's not always about finding people with extensive training or experience. Often it's more about finding people with the right attitude. When matching people to technology jobs and duties, look for people who are open, self-motivated, customer service focused, and team oriented. These types of people can be equally if not more effective at overseeing technology than a formally trained technician, especially if these self-starters are also good communicators. Administrators and managers often become consumed with finding someone who has huge amounts of technology experience. Although experience and the right attitude are the ideal combination, getting hung up on experience can become a hindrance, limiting libraries to a very small (and often inappropriate) pool of applicants, who are also probably beyond the library's budget. Frequently the most successful libraries are those whose technology staff learned as they went along; these staffers got involved with technology because they wanted to help people and were willing to learn the skills necessary to support their library's technological needs. For example, the Carrollton (TX) Public Library could not afford a trained systems librarian, so they decided to "grow" their own. They asked a librarian supervisor who seemed to be interested in technology to take on the role and then sent her to as much training as they could afford. This worked well for both the library and the librarian, who now has a great deal more experience.

Communication and leadership are two other important qualities in technology personnel, whether promoted from within or hired from outside. Finding someone who is a good communicator and a natural leader is not easy, but it can be crucial. Lack of communication between the technology personnel and the rest of the staff is probably the most common problem experienced in libraries of all sizes. Breaks in communication often lead to tension, discontent, and, unfortunately at times, misuse of power by those who "know the jargon." Try to hire and partner with technically savvy people who are open communicators, people who don't use their knowledge to overwhelm other staff or make them feel inferior. Look for those people who are willing to openly admit, "I don't know, but I will find the answer." Look for someone who wants to learn as well as share their knowledge with others. Too often IT personnel become consumed with what they believe is "job security," so they are unwilling to admit when they don't know and are afraid to share what they do know with those around them. Whether you are promoting someone on staff to a technology-related position or are hiring a new employee or an outside consultant, here are some important qualities and traits to look for:

good communicator

strong teacher

patient

open to new ideas

can explain things in simple terms without overusing technical jargon

confident enough in their own knowledge that they're not threatened by "educating" others and are willing to share information freely

solid troubleshooting skills beyond basic knowledge (i.e., they can solve problems when the answers aren't obvious)

understands that they are in their position to serve others (patrons and staff), not to "be served"

A common misconception is that leadership is reserved for those in higher-level administrative positions. When it comes to technology and its success, it is just as critical for a part-time clerk in charge of technology to display leadership qualities as it is for a full-time librarian to do so. Leadership is the energetic process of getting other people fully and willingly committed to a course of action and to meet commonly agreed goals or objectives. When it comes to technology, libraries need to lead rather than react, which makes it necessary to have leaders in these positions. Look for someone who has specific ideas about what can be accomplished; someone who can encourage and motivate others; someone who is willing to empower others, share information, and who can energize those around him or her.

HIRING TALENT OUTSIDE YOUR LIBRARY

Sometimes finding the right person for the job means hiring a new employee. This process can be as frustrating as trying to keep up with technology itself. Again, this is where many get hung up searching for that one perfect candidate who has tons of experience but doesn't require the monetary compensation to be found in the private sector. Frustration is inevitable if you go about your search this way. As when reviewing your internal choices, the key to positive results when hiring from outside is to look beyond the candidate's experience to other qualities that make for a strong technology employee. And unlike larger libraries and institutions, the world of small and medium libraries almost certainly means having duties beyond that of technology. For example, you might hire a new clerk who will be responsible for processing library materials as well as overseeing technology, or maybe a full-time librarian with audiovisual and computer oversight who will also assist at the reference desk a few hours a week. In medium-sized libraries, you might have one or more full-time employees exclusively dedicated to technology (although it is recommended that even someone with this job description have some assignment with public service each week). No matter what your situation, these tips apply:

> Take "recruiting" seriously. Advertise openings online as well as by print media and by word of mouth.
>
> Look for people with the same characteristics that your most successful employees have.
>
> Don't just hire to hire.
>
> Avoid hiring someone with the right skills and the wrong attitude.
>
> Select someone who demonstrates a strong team-based and customer-oriented (both internal and external) approach.

This is also a critical time to consider your budget. Do you have the funds to pay for a person with the qualifications you need? Much of this will depend on the job description for the position. Consider what a person with the qualifications you require would currently be earning elsewhere. If you cannot afford to hire the person your library needs, then consider options such as creating an arrangement with another local library in need to share the "right" person, or consider using outside resources for the time being until the right person does become available to you.

Job Descriptions

One potential problem for libraries when it comes to hiring (and promoting) technology staff is the lack of the right tools. An up-to-date, well-composed job description is essential as the starting point for recruiting staff, whether internally or externally. Job descriptions help create a common vision for positions. The better the clarification in the job description, the less time (and money) are wasted on misplaced efforts. Also, the better the job description, the easier it is to assess potential new hires as well as to evaluate the work of existing employees. Libraries cannot afford to waste valuable resources, but unfortunately many do because they don't have good job descriptions to lead the way. There is a scarcity of descriptions for technical positions in the library world, and supervisors and administrators are often unsure about what to include in them because they are either unaware of the actual technology situation in their library or they are unsure about what to look for in a candidate.

Typically, a job description lists the general tasks and responsibilities of a position. When creating a technology-related job description, you should include information on required knowledge and skills as well as personal qualities. It can be extremely helpful to ask existing staff members questions to help you better write new descriptions as well as rework existing ones. Ask the staffers to evaluate what it is they currently do and have them assign percent-

SAMPLE DUTY PERCENTAGES FOR A COMPUTER/TECHNOLOGY ASSISTANT

The following is one example of how a computer/technology assistant's duties may be divided.

60% Under the supervision of the head of Technology/Computer Services, assists with day-to-day operation, maintenance, and routine troubleshooting of the library's computer hardware, software, and audiovisual equipment, maintaining written maintenance logs for work as completed. Also assists in the preparation of specifications for the purchase of computer and audiovisual-related equipment, software, and supplies.

20% Assists the head of Technology/Computer Services in coordinating, scheduling, publicizing, and teaching computer classes for the public and for staff.

15% Assists in providing public service (i.e., reference services) to library users.

5% Assists head of Technology/Computer Services with collection development of circulating audiovisual and technology collections, including movies (DVDs), audio (CDs and audiobooks), MP3 players, and other forthcoming technologies.

ages to the time they spend on each of their duties. You might also ask them how much time would be needed to train someone to do their job or a portion of their job. Avoid using private-sector job descriptions as a cookie-cutter template. You can refer to them as guides, but you should rely mainly on the information about your organization when writing a job description. Use the following guidelines and refer to appendix D for some sample job descriptions from libraries across the United States. Keep in mind that each of the model job descriptions in the appendix should be carefully examined and modified as needed so they fit the specific circumstances and requirements of your library.

Your job descriptions should include the following information:

Job title. Technology-specific job titles include, but are not limited to, network services librarian, information systems librarian, computer support specialist, computer services manager, network manager, computer technician, PC coordinator, PC technician, technology trainer, technology manager, web services librarian, web services assistant, and Internet services librarian. (Note that because of the multifaceted nature of library positions, some organizations continue to use traditional library titles and reflect the technology specifications in the body of the description.)

Summary statement. Briefly describe the basic purpose of the job. Basically, why does the job exist?

Type of supervision received. A generic example might include, "Staff member works independently to prioritize and complete assigned tasks. Assignments are periodically checked for progress by the library director."

Primary duties. List the most important duties and tasks of the job. Use action words such as "perform," "oversee," "manage," and "maintain." Remember, duties can be as varied as job titles.

Additional duties. List all "secondary" responsibilities or tasks.

Abilities. Include the skills, knowledge, qualities, and whatever else is required for the position.

Education and training. This generally includes minimum formal qualifications.

Miscellaneous items. Special requirements, physical demands, work environment, and so on.

Before posting job descriptions, always forward them to appropriate staff members for review and make necessary modifications based on their feedback. Equally important, at some point down the line you should review all your job descriptions, not just those that are technology specific. Reevaluate what you have, making sure the technology duties and responsibilities are up-to-date and are written into all library job descriptions. Update descriptions as often as the jobs change. You should even update the janitorial staff job descriptions, which may include such duties as cleaning computer equipment and accessing meeting room schedules and setup information via a computer.

Searching and Interviewing

In order to find the right people to interview and ultimately to hire, a library, no matter how small, has to seek good candidates. The amount of advertising you do will certainly depend on the type of position you are looking to fill. For best results, consider trying at least two of the following options. Ask strong internal employees for suggestions. Post jobs on the library's website, placing the link prominently on your home page. Place ads via traditional advertising methods such as the classified section of your local newspaper. Look to newspapers that run local as well as regional job postings. You can also use national job websites such as hotjobs .com and monster.com. Local consortiums, library councils, state agencies, and professional association websites offer online posting options and may also be able to make recommendations.[4] Tech-oriented people in particular will use online job listings and sites, so be sure to fully utilize your options there as well.

When you have a strong pool of candidates to select from, it's time for interviews. This is an excellent opportunity for team-building, so be sure to include more than one member of the library in the interviews. You will also end up with a better hire if there is varied input into the decision. Here are just a few quick tips for effectively interviewing candidates for technology-related positions:

Get people to talk about what they've done. If candidates can't talk effectively about their accomplishments, past jobs, and duties, then they probably haven't really done them.

Ask for examples of past projects and how the candidates worked with others on them. For example, if they designed and maintained a web page, how did they work with other employees to get input, ideas, and weekly/monthly updates?

Whether in regard to troubleshooting, supervision, or project work, don't just ask traditional questions; have candidates provide examples of particular situations they faced.

You may also want to ask to see some type of documentation of the candidates' work or some illustration of how they communicate in writing.

Ask candidates to discuss how they personally keep current with technology, as well as how they would assist others on staff in keeping up-to-date.

Look for individuals who display good judgment and strong decision-making and problem-solving skills. Well-thought-out, creative, and customer service–oriented answers to questions are key, and good interpersonal skills are a must. Other qualities to look for include being friendly, helpful, flexible, successful at multi-tasking, and able to work with regular interruptions.

No matter what the position, always take time for small talk at the beginning of the interview. Provide information about the library and always leave time for questions.

CONSULTANTS AND TECHNOLOGY SERVICE PROVIDERS

Consultants and service providers come in many shapes and sizes. They can bring expertise and specialized knowledge that might be lacking in your library. They can also provide supplementary support and knowledge to your staff, and most will do as much or as little as your library is willing to pay for. Their services can range from overseeing a special technology project (e.g., an automation project) to creating or auditing a technology plan, helping evaluate and select hardware and software, overseeing the installation of systems, and troubleshooting and maintenance. Of course, not all consultants or providers do all these things. Many have specialties and focus on project work. Numerous individuals and companies focus specifically on libraries and other nonprofit organizations, while many others are excellent partners for libraries even though they don't specialize in them. Because there are so many options available (with varying levels of expertise and price), it's important to keep an open mind when looking for a person or company to provide assistance. A small or medium-sized library should consider hiring a consultant or service provider if

- its personnel resources are stretched to the limit with existing projects
- a second opinion on a project, assessment, or plan is needed
- a supplemental or higher level of technical assistance is required on an occasional or regular basis
- the library is approaching a new or renovated building project

Kam Hitchcock-Mort, technical service manager at the Carrollton (TX) Public Library, is a big believer in consultants. She states, "I've done it myself at another library and then hired a consultant here. The difference was like night and day. We are positive he saved us more than our fees during the planning and contract negotiation phases. It was all so much easier." Whether choosing a new consultant or evaluating an existing one, think of it much like you would when hiring and assessing an employee. Does the consultant or service provider work well with your staff? Do they listen? Are they responsive? Are they willing to educate staff as they troubleshoot, plan, and so on? Do they offer flexible service and payment options that work with your needs and budget structure? When hiring a consultant or provider, remember that they are not all created equal, and just because they have a "consultant" title doesn't mean they always know what's best for your library. It is important to interview a consultant just as you would a potential employee. This process is an excellent information-gathering opportunity, so take notes and be prepared to learn. Even if you don't end up working with the people you're researching and interviewing, you will certainly gather much potentially valuable and applicable information along the way.

A few good questions can make a world of difference when choosing a vendor or consultant that works well for your organization. The following are some basic tips to remember.

Be prepared. Have a comprehensive idea of what you want to accomplish. Prepare a list of questions about the consultant's experiences, utilizing questions similar to those used in a new employee's interview. By the same token, be prepared to intercept comments and questions from their end. Keep in mind, too, that the more prepared and organized you appear to the consultant, the more aggressive they may be in adjusting their pricing. Knowledge and preparedness are huge factors when negotiating contracts.

Communicate. Be verbally clear in what you are looking for in a partner. Talk candidly about your goals, technology plan, and so on. A good consultant or provider will have many questions and will openly make suggestions along the way. They will take the time to understand the culture of your library (staff composition, comfort levels with technology, needs, workflow, etc.). In addition, make sure any consultants you interview know what your budget range is, and always put things in writing to ensure there is no miscommunication.

Check their past work. Get a history of what they've done. How long have they been in business? What is their training, education, or background? Get references from at least three jobs or current customers. Look at the depth and range of what they've worked on. Do they show creativity and an ability to provide individual attention to your situation, or do they simply regurgitate from past jobs? Was the work done on time? Was written documentation provided to clients? (Ask them to provide samples if possible.) Were they easily and readily accessible? Did they communicate with staff effectively?

Look for professionals who can provide service and budget flexibility. Consider hiring someone on retainer or establishing a service contract. Various contract levels should be available to select from, including professional services and preventative maintenance contracts. Having a choice of levels of support gives you flexibility in finding a package that meets the needs and budget of your library. Do not settle for a company that only offers one option. Most will include a variety of levels based on the services provided and the technicians' training and certifications. When it comes to service contracts, this can be the difference between paying $70 per hour and $150 per hour. Keep in mind that in most cases, a lower-level technician is all that is needed for most emergency and maintenance-related tasks that would be beyond the scope of the personnel in a small library. Before signing any contracts, meet the person who will be doing the actual work and request the use of that one consultant or technician consistently. This will prevent surprises, as well as create uniformity and a greater comfort level for all involved. Make sure you have language in the contract that outlines who will be doing the work and any other specifics discussed in relation to this area. If working with a support contract that involves general or emergency troubleshooting, you will want to get written documentation on response time and costs for weekday, evening, and weekend hours. Also, make sure your contract includes a stipulation for written documentation after each visit and project. Make sure the contract is explicit in defining response times and performance measurements, as well as options for recourse if problems arise (i.e., contract cancellation and refund of unused deposits, payments, etc.). A schedule or timeline is an important part of your contract. Be sure to include what will be done, where it will be done, by whom it will be done, and when it will be done. It is also wise to establish a payment agreement to outside providers based on completed work and a predetermined schedule. For large-scale projects, you might also consider a clause that covers the library when contractual work fails to meet quality and time specifications.

Last but not least, always make sure your contract does not expire. In other words, make sure that hours carry over from one year to the next if they are unused.

VOLUNTEERS

It is funny how small and medium-sized organizations either fully embrace or completely shy away from "free" help. Many libraries cannot exist without the assistance of volunteers. Other libraries may have had a bad experience and are apprehensive that volunteers may make errors or convey incorrect information to staff and patrons. If there is a strong training program and good communication between the paid and the unpaid "staff," using volunteers to implement and support technology can be a rewarding and cost-effective solution.

Look to your board, Friends of the Library, and others within your community (adults, teens, businesses) for volunteers. Every library board should have at least one technically savvy member. Get them involved. Board members should be both supporters of library technology and users of that technology themselves. The Friends of the Library can be a critical resource for supplementary funding for technical projects, as well as providing volunteer personnel resources. The key is to openly communicate with your Friends organization and get them involved in technology. Consider including a list of volunteer activities on your Friends' application form. Aside from traditional tasks such as sorting donated materials for the book sale and supporting the library through letter writing and political advocacy, consider items such as teaching computer classes, computer setup and troubleshooting, and so on.

There can be a wealth of resources and opportunities for collaboration in a community that are not pursued because people don't think of them or there is no communication among organizations. Scan your community with a fresh eye and be proactive in pursuing partnerships with groups and individuals. Look to volunteers from local technology companies and try approaching businesses, not only individuals. You might be able to get a local company to donate so many hours a week of support time from its technology staff (it may be a tax write-off for the company). Collaborate with K–12 schools, looking to high school students as well as teachers and other personnel. You can contact library schools as well as local colleges and technical and trade schools for students who might be looking for hands-on experience to complete an internship or practicum requirement or to build a resume. Many students are very technically savvy and are willing to assist with duties such as inventorying, basic research, computer class instruction, and troubleshooting. Using volunteers in this capacity is often a foreign concept to libraries, but it can be a truly valuable resource if done correctly. As with any other personnel issue, the application and interview process is critical, because you want

TECH TIP

TEEN VOLUNTEERS

If your library is small and lacks the know-how to set up and maintain technology of any kind, consider asking teens for assistance. Teenagers (aka "teen tech assistants") are a great resource for setting up computers, hooking up televisions and VCRs, and maintaining equipment once it's in place. It's always better to seek help rather than do without technology simply because you don't have the knowledge or the time to go about it. Contact a local middle or high school technology specialist to get the names of potential volunteers. You might even have a teenaged page on staff who has a knack for computers and electronics.[5]

to enlist the help of qualified people who fit with your organization. The Webster (NY) Public Library's computer training program was almost entirely staffed by volunteers from the community and from the University at Buffalo's School of Informatics. The library also had great success with internships from various schools and local IT-experienced patrons who volunteered for special hardware and software projects, including inventories, maintenance, and troubleshooting.[6]

DO YOU KNOW IT?

Evaluate. Carefully assess your existing staffing practices as well as the staff members themselves to ensure they have appropriate technology-related roles and responsibilities.

Prepare. Be organized and knowledgeable when interviewing prospective new hires, consultants, service providers, and volunteers.

Focus on attitudes and aptitudes. When hiring, promoting, and contracting people, look beyond their existing skills to their attitude and capacity to learn.

Utilize volunteers effectively. Reevaluate and expand the services provided by volunteers.

NOTES

1. Elizabeth Kellison, "Whitman County Library: The Little Library That Could," WebJunction (March 5, 2004), http://webjunction.org/do/DisplayContent?id=798.
2. Ibid.
3. Ibid.
4. A few examples include the Rochester (NY) Regional Library Council (http://www.rrlc.org), the Kentucky Department of Library and Archives (http://www.kdla.ky.gov/libsupport/jobline.htm), the Nebraska Library Commission (http://www.nlc.state.ne.us/libjob/adjobs.html), and the California State Library Association's Job Mart (http://rsmart.ca/CLA_Members/jobmart.asp).
5. Kimberly Bolan Taney, *Teen Spaces: The Step-by-Step Library Makeover* (Chicago: American Library Association, 2003), 97.
6. For additional information, please contact Kimberly Bolan, former assistant director of the Webster (NY) Public Library.

Pay for IT | 6

Like everything in life, technology takes money. Creating annual budgets, developing project budgets, allocating funds, and negotiating with vendors—all are part and parcel of acquiring, implementing, and maintaining technology. This chapter deals with all of the financial aspects of technology and hopefully will provide new insight and inspiration about how you can better "work the angles" of funding technology for your library. Taking a more business-minded approach to all aspects of operating a library in these days of tight and shrinking budgets is important. What is most important here is to take a look at the financial management of your library. By examining efficiency, total cost of ownership, and return on investment, your library can find ways to do more and get more even if its budget is small. By the same token, expanding your library's technology and its services and applying the principles of this book should also help you begin to increase your funding. The private business sector is full of examples of companies that were able to improve, redirect, and even reinvent themselves when their revenues were dramatically shrinking. Libraries can no longer assume that governmental funding will always be there to finance their operations. It is therefore imperative that libraries try to improve their financial management processes and use analysis tools and unconventional thinking in their efforts to protect and expand their role within the community.

ANNUAL BUDGETS

In general, budgeting is a managerial tool used for planning and decision-making. The purpose of a technology budget is to financially express how your library will achieve its technology-related goals and objectives. A detailed, well-thought-out technology budget will enable you to

> identify and set technology priorities
>
> establish specific planning parameters and guidelines
>
> appropriately allocate and distribute library funds
>
> foster awareness of the financial needs and requirements
> of technology in your library

When it comes to money for technology, start by reviewing your current operating budget and overall financial picture. Is technology a separate line-item category in the budget? If not, it should be. Work with the appropriate people in your organization to address this issue and get the ball rolling. As you analyze your budget, ask such questions as What percentage of our funds is currently dedicated to technology? Does this percentage seem to fit with our library's mission and vision? How do the percentage breakdowns of our library compare to other libraries in our area, particularly those of similar size and demographics? Does our budget follow the generally accepted ratio of 30 percent for hardware and software and 70 percent for training, maintenance, and ongoing support?[1] Budgets are tight for all libraries, which means it generally comes down to priorities. What does your budget say about your library's current priorities? As you work with stakeholders such as board members, administrative staff, and local government officials, work to enlighten them about technology, its relationship to your overall budget, and why it should be a priority. The fundamental concept that you want to convey to your stakeholders is that technology spending is an investment, not just an expense.

As you budget, remember that technology expansion (unlike collection, furniture, and even facility expansion) needs as much funding allocated to ongoing costs as is allocated to initial costs. Training, licensing, replacement, maintenance, and improvements can be expensive ventures, so keep this in mind as you budget. Don't forget to add some squish room (i.e., have a contingency plan) for additional or unexpected costs. It's always wise to break things down into categories in a budget. Being overly specific can hamper your flexibility, but lumping technology into just one or two broad categories isn't always the best course of action either. Those who budget in "broad categorizations" feel it allows for changes in plan and doesn't tie them down to particular purchases. In actuality, if you've done your planning correctly and have already made room for contingencies, then this really shouldn't matter.

When it comes to technology budgeting, make sure you cover all your bases. Potential line items may include

    building, furniture, and equipment purchases and maintenance

    projects (e.g., automation, wireless, etc., as outlined in your plan)

    software purchases, licenses, and so on

    electronic resources (i.e., subscriptions to online materials such as databases and subscription services, online reference service, etc.)

    staff salaries

    staff training

    technology collections (i.e., circulating hardware, audiovisual materials, and so on. These may fall under general collections and not necessarily under the jurisdiction of "technology" but should still be considered.)

    communications (Internet access, telephone, etc.)

For ideas of how you might structure your budget, look at the "Technology Budget Worksheet" in appendix A. Creating a detailed budget can be quite helpful as a way to list and track expenditures. Use the budget worksheet throughout the year to help see where you are and where you need to go monetarily. By using this planning tool as a tracking document, you will also be better able to measure your budget performance. In other words, are you meeting your budget goals throughout the year? Are you overspending or underspending?

The "Savvy Budgeter's Checklist" sidebar is another helpful budgeting tool. It will help make sure you've covered all the bases and are well prepared to defend your budget to those who oversee the library.

Budgeting for Your Vision

Once you establish budget allocations to meet current ongoing costs, allocations must also be made to support the vision of how the library will move forward. New projects are meaningless if money is not budgeted to support them. As you're well aware, library budgets are often stretched to their limits to accommodate a multitude of demands, including that of technological innovation. Formal planning and cost-benefit analysis are essential to ensure that budgets are structured and allocated realistically, and that libraries can effectively manage the total costs associated with the purchase, operation, and staffing of new technology. It is important to have a detailed cost analysis and justification prepared well in advance of the budget cycle. Focus on budgeting for what you need, not just what you can afford. These are the items outlined in your technology plan (see chapter 4). Consider the following advice from Catherine Hakala-Ausperk, assistant director at the Cleveland Heights–University Heights (OH) Public Library:

> Plan for the technologies that will give you the biggest bang for the buck: faster Internet connections, more and newer PCs, faster and more powerful servers, etc. For example, a fast Internet connection that allows people to check their stocks or their e-mail quickly will improve your customer service and image more than having MP3 players around. Even though MP3 players are cool.

To avoid your library's technology from quickly becoming out of date, work to include hardware replacement and software upgrades as ongoing costs in the budget. Again, these are items that should be developed as part of your technology plan. Incorporating items such as these in the annual budget helps level out the peaks of technology investment and ensures an appropriate budget level that keeps technology central to the library's mission. However, when it comes to hardware, keep in mind that you don't have to replace all workstation components every year to have up-to-date technology. A general rule of thumb is to plan for replacement or rollover of computers every three years. Monitors, keyboards, and so on may be retained for longer periods to save money. Look for other ways to help spread out costs. Leasing, for instance, provides an option that can help libraries amortize the costs of equipment and support over a multiyear cycle. This helps to build hardware renewal into operating expenditures rather than the capital budget.[2]

Many small and medium-sized libraries have training funds that are barely adequate to cover conference attendance, much less training. Even more libraries devote little or nothing in their budgets to cover the hours spent by staff in attending training sessions. This is something to try to change. The long-term benefits of staff education far outweigh the initial investment in training costs. Making a broad array of staff knowledgeable about technology can save your library huge investments in support resources. Keeping employees informed and up-to-date translates into happier workers, which means increased efficiency and internal support as well as decreased staff turnover, and this can yield significant savings. Frontline staff who can skillfully troubleshoot and answer patrons' technical questions improve overall customer service, and this means satisfied, happy customers.

ANALYZING WHAT YOU SPEND

In years past, a library would typically approach budgeting as a process of figuring out how to spend what funds it had been allocated. Nowadays most libraries can no longer get by using this method. Tighter fiscal controls, greater accountability, and increased competition for resources all create the need for better analysis of current and future spending. Such analysis takes a variety of forms, including total cost of ownership, return on investment, and staff time versus money. These concepts can assist a library administration in deciding what allocations need to be increased, cut back, or kept at current levels. It isn't enough to use your gut feeling about what you like and don't like or what you think is or is not a good technology or service. Analysis will help lead you to the truth, and the truth will set you free, or at least help justify your funding requests.

Total Cost of Ownership

The price of a piece of hardware or software has never represented the actual or total cost of bringing that particular technology into your library. More and more in libraries and in businesses, the total cost of ownership (TCO) is being examined in order to gauge the true costs involved in implementing and maintaining technology. This concept transforms technology costs from mere line items in a budget to the costs incurred in the broader context of running the library. TCO includes the calculation of costs that may not turn up in a budget but can still have an impact on operations. The following questions will help you in the analysis of the total cost of ownership as it relates to technology:

What was the total cost of purchase, including the technology itself, along with all related equipment, installation charges, employee/consultant time, and miscellaneous charges?

How much staff time was devoted to implementing, training, maintaining, and troubleshooting the technology?

Did a new technology replace an existing technology? If so, what were the cost savings? Increases? What is the difference in the direct investment costs? What is the impact on productivity? Is the new technology taking more time or saving time? Is it increasing the staff's efficiency?

What is the customer impact? Are they satisfied? Is it increasing patrons' efficiency?

What revenues, if any, has the technology brought to the library (i.e., payments for printer services)?

A useful tool in this regard is the Total Cost of Ownership Tracker provided by TechAtlas (see appendix B for details).

Return on Investment

The concept of return on investment (ROI) is basically a ratio:

> ROI *equals* the increase in performance or the savings of time and money *divided by* the total investment in time and money.

When using this formula, any quotient over 1 is good and anything under 1 isn't. However, ROI isn't a fixed number because the return may change over time as more savings are realized. Businesses often try to achieve returns that are above 1 within at least twelve months of implementation. This may be too aggressive for most libraries, but it gives you a point of reference. ROI is gaining popularity with library administrators who have to deal with tighter budgets and demands for greater efficiency from the public and other stakeholders. But for many libraries, ROI is still a foreign concept. It is difficult for many nonprofit organizations to quantify how much return they get on what they spend. However, this concept should be just as important to a library as it is to a Fortune 500 company. Why spend money if you don't gain something from it? The "it" doesn't have to mean profits or revenues. It could mean more patron visits or higher circulation. These types of returns, in addition to "staff time savings," should be the types of things libraries look at when analyzing the return on investment for existing and potential technology projects.

When analyzing the probable ROI for a potential project, you will be forced to make a great number of "guesstimates" and assumptions. These are an expected part of trying to predict ROI. Don't be afraid; you probably will over- or underestimate, but that is expected. Think about how the project will affect different service areas. What extra staff time will be required by it? What time will be saved? In some cases, extra revenue will be realized (e.g., printing costs, room booking fees, computer lab rental fees). These can be more easily added to the equation, although you may be forced to use some guesswork in exactly how much revenue will be generated. Give your best guess and be prepared to show how you arrived at that estimate.

Time vs. Money

Once you've decided which technology projects to take on, you will inevitably be faced with the decision of who will manage and work on those projects. During this process ask yourself, What is the cost impact versus resource allocation for this project? Is it better to pay someone (such as a consultant) to do a task for you, or is it better to have staff take the time to do it? For example, does it pay to have a consultant set up all the new computers while the department head and other staff, who are capable and have the time and knowledge, stand around observing? How about having a consultant work with the staff on two or three computers and then leave the rest for the staff to finish? Will the time savings of a consultant doing it alone outweigh that of the money saved by having the staff do it alone? This is not always the easiest analysis to work out. It is often particularly difficult to analyze the cost of internal staff handling a project. The following are some helpful questions to ask in this process:

> Are current staff fully capable of handling this project? Is there a risk to bringing in outside help?

> If internal staff are assigned to this project, will other resources have to be allocated to handle their other responsibilities?

> Are the projects manageable by outside personnel, or does someone within the organization need to manage the project?

Volunteers can also be great resources when it comes to technology, so try to factor them into this analysis as well. For example, with volunteer computer class instructors, the staff may have to train them initially, but this initial investment of staff time will yield cost savings by the use of volunteer instructors in the future.

FUNDING

Funding methods and structures for libraries are as varied as the libraries themselves. Every state, every county, and virtually every town or school district has its own funding mechanism. Most libraries have a grasp on their base funding and how it is supplied. There a number of sources from which libraries derive their operating funds:

> state, regional, and local taxes, including income, property, intangibles, sales, and excise taxes

> fines and fees

> endowments and other interest on investments

> onetime gifts and bequests

> various grants, both public and private, including LSTA; national endowment grants; and federal, state, and local grants

> grants and gifts from local community groups and charities

> Friends of the Library

> business gifts, grants, and sponsorships

This list is dominated in number, if not magnitude, by non-tax-based funding sources. Though most libraries currently derive the vast majority of their operating funds from taxes, this may not always be possible. Unfortunately, library closings and budget and hours cutbacks are an all-too-common headline due to funding that once existed but was reduced or completely eliminated. Even if your library's current funding situation is good, do not assume that it will always be so. Accordingly, you should look at options for increasing funding and diversifying your income stream. This is one foundation of good general business practice that many libraries overlook or simply avoid.

Prepare yourself. Search for new financial support to supplement existing funding. Be proactive. Look outside the norm. Apply for private or public grants and pursue partnerships with local community groups, businesses, or other libraries in your region. Many funding sources are overlooked because they are not viewed as "typical." For example, many businesses are interested in forming partnerships with nonprofit organizations, yet these opportunities are not pursued because they are "outside the box." Collaborating with local schools can open up a wealth of opportunities for technology grants. Consider setting up an endowment, either in conjunction with or separate from your Friends group. Endowments can help stabilize future funding, providing a steady and predictable cash flow.

One thing that often hurts public libraries seeking additional technology funding within their communities is the traditional stereotype of such libraries as old-fashioned and non-technical. This label certainly has been a detriment when seeking funds to increase technology budgets. Many librarians say they find it difficult to justify spending on technology when they are unable to afford books. Although this argument is well taken, this reasoning can turn into a vicious circle, as libraries are not likely to receive funding to buy technology if they are not using it and are perceived as old-fashioned and nontechnical. If you find yourself stuck in the cycle, your best hope for escape is a well-prepared and well-thought-out technology plan.

Building Big on a Small Budget

If library funds are limited, don't be discouraged. If you are smart about it, you can find the money to fund your technology initiatives. It may mean being creative and maybe putting in a little extra work to find the funds you need. Be sure to consider all funding sources and take a look around the community and within your own library for *free* materials and resources. Another way to help reduce initial costs is to divide projects into phases, distributing the cost over a multiyear period. More ideas on alternative funding options are discussed below.

Grants

Grants are an ever-growing and important part of many libraries' funding makeup. From large foundations like the Bill and Melinda Gates Foundation and federal programs like the LSTA to smaller and regional organizations like the Lilly Endowment, there are grants out there for a variety of projects and initiatives. Some focus specifically on libraries, others specifically on technology. For instance, the Pierce (ID) Free Public Library was able to fund its Technology Center (personal computers, printers, scanners, and more) through the receipt of a $15,000 MIRA (Managing Information with Rural America) grant from the W. K. Kellogg Foundation.[4] The Whitman County (WA) Rural Library is enthusiastic about all kinds of grants. They suggest making sure you cover marketing expenses in the budget of your grant proposal. This shows the grant funding body that you are serious about really making the project a success and not just getting them to pay for something you need. The advice of Mark Pumphrey, director of the Polk County (NC) Public Library, is to never take the first no for an answer. His library was initially turned down for a Gates Foundation grant based on poverty-level criteria. The library appealed; it gathered additional community data showing statistics had changed since the previous census, and the grant was then awarded. Other foundations are also likely to see persistence as an indication of likely project success and be more inclined to fund your project accordingly. For more information on grant funding sources, see the section on this chapter in appendix B.

Raising Funds

Alternative financial sources may include your Friends of the Library group, a library foundation, private donations, and corporate sponsorships. Consider holding a staff brainstorming session to gather ideas on who the library could approach for alternative funding. You might be surprised at the ideas that will come out. Just keep in mind that your enthusiasm for the projects you want funded needs to be well communicated. The more you believe, the more success you will have in getting others to believe. Here are some additional ideas and tips for approaching others for funding support.

- Cultivate relationships with local and regional organizations, foundations, and businesses. Developing a direct personal relationship is the best way to increase your odds of getting funding from private sources. It's a great deal harder to say no to someone you know.
- Develop a standard proposal. Include a cover letter, overview of the services for which funding is being sought, details about the plan and related activities, and contact information for the library. It doesn't hurt to include additional supportive materials about the library and how past funding has been put to good use.
- Offer a menu of options of how technology can be "supported." Items may include direct financial underwriting and support, nonfinancial support in the form of free products and services, donations based on sales (e.g., a portion of all proceeds from a local sandwich shop will be donated to support the local library's technology training program), and company-donated "volunteers" (in other words, the company pays its employees to come help your library with various projects, technology or otherwise).
- Recognize your supporters publicly. Thank-you letters are just a start. Recognition in the form of acknowledgments on library signage, the library website, newsletters, press releases, and verbal acknowledgment at library events are just a few ways to do this. Private-sector funders view this publicity as a return on their donation, which helps them further justify their commitment.
- Share the success of your library's programs with the organizations that support you. Be sure to tell them exactly how their support has helped. Great results from their donation should lead to more donations from that organization.[5]

PROCUREMENT AND PURCHASING

Do you ever feel like a deer in the headlights when it comes to purchasing technology and dealing with technology salesmen? Everyone wants to convince you that their products are just what you need. Some are and some aren't, but how do you find your way through this process? Be patient, be firm, and remember that the devil is in the details, especially when dealing with vendors on pricing and terms.

As you embark on the procurement process, you will discover that the data collected during the assessment phase back in chapter 2 will be needed once again. This information is imperative (and also makes your life easier) when working with vendors, getting cost estimates and quotes, and soliciting bids and estimates from vendors. When soliciting initial estimates, choose one vendor to deal with and draft that request for proposal (RFP) with as much detail as possible. Don't forget to ask for information on miscellaneous (often hidden) charges such as freight, training, maintenance, and extended warranties. Once the vendor returns the estimate, review it for accuracy and completeness. Don't be afraid to make modifications or to send it back for clarification. Use the finalized estimate as a model to draft RFPs to other vendors (see the "Sample Request for Quotation" in appendix A). This way you keep everyone on the same page, and you can compare apples to apples. Avoid phone quotations—it is important to get everything in writing. Attach copies of the estimates to your "Technology Budget Worksheet" (in appendix A) for easy reference. When dealing with vendors, the Guilderland (NY) Public Library suggests:

> Buying in larger quantities sometimes saves money, but whether it is $5 or $5,000, make sure you are treated the same by your vendor. If not, go with a different vendor. Beware of the cheap deals and the quick sales. The money you save can be factored back in with shipping and warranty costs. Find out about all services that the vendor has to offer. Some vendors have specialists that provide free support for technology-related questions. Some include software-licensing specialists, hardware specialists (dealing with storage, computers, and peripherals), and network specialists (dealing with security and bandwidth issues).

Vendor Negotiation

Negotiations are probably the most dreaded activity for librarians. There are certainly many savvy salespeople out there who tend to push their advantage when it comes to negotiations. Dealing with these types can leave you feeling inept. However, it isn't necessary to be the world's best negotiator to get good pricing and terms on technology purchases for your library. Regardless of how smooth or confident the salesperson is, with a little determination, some information, and persistence, you will be able to negotiate a good deal. Try not to focus exclusively on price when working with vendors. Generally this leads to an inadequate deal. Purchasing technology is not like purchasing books. There are simply too many factors involved for you to go on price alone. Two vendors may be offering packages at very different price levels, but a closer look may reveal that the cheaper option is not necessarily the better deal. Look at such factors as exact scope, specifications, warranties, maintenance fees, software licensing terms and lengths, and integration issues and then base your decision on the overall value, not just the initial price. When it comes to changing your orders, be sure the process for submitting and approving them is very specific and well documented. Lack of attention to this detail typically ends up in cost overruns for a library because many vendors will nickel-and-dime you when there is any deviation from the original contract. Here are a few additional tips for negotiating contracts, pricing, terms, and conditions:

> Know the vendors you are working with. Know their history with your organization and learn their history with other organizations (i.e., contact their references). Consider working with small vendors when possible, because they will typically offer you more flexibility and lower overall costs (assuming they are capable of meeting your needs).
>
> Involve management (and possibly even a board member, when applicable) in the negotiation process. When the higher-ups are involved, vendors typically respond with more aggressive pricing and terms.

Clearly define what your library's expectations are for the vendor.

Negotiate detailed pricing for each key deliverable (i.e., what you're getting: service, product, etc.). The more detailed your negotiations and arguments are, the more likely you are to get the best deal. Don't forget to cover licensing agreement details here.

Be prepared for conflict, but remember that you're the one sitting in the driver's seat.

In the contract itself you need to:

> Spell out everything. There can never be too much detail in a contract.
>
> Know when deliverables are due.
>
> Define how the contract can be terminated; include the mechanism as well as the conditions for termination.
>
> Detail the implications (financial or otherwise) for missing deliverables.

When the contract is drawn up, have all technology team members review it; the more eyes, the better.

Matt Gullet, the manager of information technology services at the Bloomington (IL) Public Library, offers this advice:

> There may be certain situations in which you may need to reveal the amount of funds you can use to complete a project with them [the vendor], but as a rule of thumb . . . keep your cards close to your chest and don't give them your budget for a particular project. Once they know your budget, many [vendors] will bill up to that amount . . . Always get several bids or estimates from consultants for your project. Trust is key, so if you find [a vendor] who is reliable and trustworthy, do all that you can to keep them in your library and working on your projects, assuming their costs are reasonably in line.

Licensing

Software licensing can be a can of worms if not managed effectively. The key here is the effective management of licenses (i.e., organizing and tracking them) in order to reduce the cost of ownership as well as proactively plan software and hardware upgrades. In general, you'll be dealing with licenses that fall into two categories:

> Applications that are licensed indefinitely (operating systems, office applications, etc.). You pay for them in your initial purchase and never pay again until you choose to upgrade or change the software.
>
> Subscription applications (reference databases, antivirus software, productivity solutions, etc.) that are typically renewed and paid for annually.

In order to reduce hassles and keep your library in compliance with software licensing requirements, be sure to maintain a software license inventory (this is part of your assessment as outlined in chapter 2). This process can be completed manually by going from computer to computer, or it can be done electronically. There are several cost-effective software solutions out there for those with smaller networks who want to conduct an electronic inventory (see appendix B for some resources). Once you've established your inventory, compare your *count* of the licenses in use to the *actual number* of licenses purchased by your library for each application. Don't let this process overwhelm you. Tackle one application or license at a time, making any necessary purchases to bring your library up to legal compliance.

JOINING FORCES TO GET MORE FOR LESS

In July 1998 ten Indiana libraries joined forces and redefined how they approached technology. The vision was to work cooperatively to hire one computer support provider to address the technology needs of member libraries of all sizes and levels of experience. That vision led to what is now called the Northern Indiana Computer Consortium, which now has forty-seven members in twenty-one counties. Each library was looking for affordable computer support to help guide the implementation of technology. While the needs varied from one library to the next, there were common issues. Many of the libraries were paying $75 to $125 per hour for computer support. Most of the libraries were also working with a computer support company or individual that only had one library as a client. Moreover, many of the libraries were researching and paying for solutions to the same or similar needs or directions and were often competing for the same grant dollars.

The benefits to each library that joined the consortium can be summarized in three words: affordability, flexibility, and experience.

Affordability

- The group agreement rates charged by the computer support provider are significantly discounted to a flat $60 per hour rate.
- Each library pays only for actual hours of computer support used or scheduled.
- The employee benefits and payroll taxes associated with maintaining in-house staff positions for computer support were eliminated.
- Libraries can budget for the service time of the support provider.

Group purchasing can give the member libraries competitive discounts on items ranging from software and hardware to professional services and online resources.

Flexibility

- Hours of computer support service are used on an "as needed" basis or can be on prearranged as "scheduled" or "routed" visits (weekly, biweekly, monthly).
- The service time is "flexible function" in that hours can be used for repairs, support, consultation, networking, and programming to meet the needs of each individual library regardless of its size, level of technology, or expertise.

Experience

- The computer support provider has an experienced, well-trained group of technicians.
- A staff of employees (the current provider has seven) spends a combined three hundred hours per week working with library clients, often on issues specific to particular member libraries.
- The knowledge gained from individual projects benefits the entire consortium group.
- Standardization between member libraries, though not required, increases productivity through familiarity.
- Customized training is offered in a classroom setting at the provider's site or through individual or group training at the library.[6]

When purchasing software and licenses, keep in mind that various vendors may use similar licensing "terms," but these may mean completely different things. Because pricing and subsequent terms can be very application specific, it is important to educate yourself about specific terms and purchase plans. Don't hesitate to comparison shop. If possible, work with a vendor that has a state or local contract; in most instances, libraries qualify for "educational pricing," so don't forget to ask for it. But don't assume that those companies on state contract or the ones offering educational pricing have the best offer available. As with hardware, you will generally get larger discounts by pursuing volume licensing programs when applicable. These programs reduce the costs associated with software acquisitions, upgrades, and management.

Be sure to organize all your licensing information in some way (preferably in a spreadsheet or database), so it is easily accessible for planning and budgeting. Keep this process from becoming confusing by creating a license tracking document to supplement your software inventory. (See the "License Tracking Worksheet" in appendix A for an example.) If possible, it is also recommended that you try to work with just one or two licensing vendors. There are good vendors out there that have salespeople who are extremely proficient at licensing. Their expertise can save you money and time by assisting with procurement, purchase tracking, licensing compliance reports, and more.

PARTNERSHIPS AND CONSORTIUMS

One of the best ways to save money and thus help your library afford more technology is to form partnerships and or join consortiums. Sixty-six percent of public libraries in the United States are part of a consortium, system, or some other formal group partnership.[7] By joining forces, sharing resources, and negotiating in groups, libraries can get much more for their money. The libraries in a partnership may sacrifice some of their independence and flexibility because decisions have to be made for the good of the group, not just the good of a single library. However, most libraries find this trade-off isn't a hard one to make, and the limitations that might come from a group approach are not all that problematic. If there isn't already a group, system, or consortium serving your area, why not partner with other libraries near you on purchases, staffing, computer support, and other services? Linda Yoder, director of the Nappanee (IN) Public Library, claims:

> The greatest benefit of partnering with other libraries when hiring a service provider is getting more affordable service while also cultivating an expert in library IT environments. The experience they gain from working in one library setting is carried over to other libraries' projects. Often a standardization in software and hardware solutions occurs from one library to the next. This standardization increases the technician's efficiency in installing and implementing a solution, thereby further reducing the cost of the project to the library.

The experiences of a group of libraries in northern Indiana are also instructive. See the sidebar "Joining Forces to Get More for Less."

DO YOU KNOW IT?

Budget appropriately. Create technology-specific line items and detailed technology budgets.

Analyze what you spend. Evaluate your spending in terms of the total cost of investment, return on investment, and time versus money.

Seek funding. Look beyond traditional sources of revenue to grants and outside partnerships and fund-raising.

Purchase wisely. Be thorough and prepared as you deal with vendors and make sure that any contract is detailed, specific, and comprehensive

Look to partnerships and consortiums. Libraries that collaborate with each other and with outside organizations can open up a wealth of opportunities and financial savings.

NOTES

1. *Staying Connected* (Seattle, WA: Bill and Melinda Gates Foundation, 2002); also available at http://www.gatesfoundation.org.
2. L. Goddard, "Hardware Renewal Planning," *Feliciter* 50, no. 2 (2004): 46–47.
3. Adapted from Doug Johnson, "Budgeting for Mean, Lean Times" (2005), http://www.doug-johnson.com/handouts/budget.pdf.
4. For more information, visit the Pierce (ID) Free Public Library website at http://www.lili.org/clearwater/Pierce/TechCtr.html.
5. *Staying Connected.*
6. From the contributions of Linda Yoder, director of the Nappanee (IN) Public Library.
7. Adrienne Chute and Elaine Kroe, *Public Libraries in the United States: Fiscal Year 2001* (Washington, DC: National Center for Education Statistics, 2003); also available at http://nces.ed.gov/pubs2003/2003399.pdf.

Implement IT 7

This chapter covers everything from project management to support, maintenance, trouble-shooting, and marketing. Most of these areas have been touched upon in previous chapters, beginning with the assessment phase in chapter 2. These next steps are crucial, however. Without successful implementation from start to finish, technology projects and ideas can be difficult if not impossible to carry out.

IMPLEMENTATION

If you've gotten this far, it most likely means you've finished planning, gotten approval and funding, and are ready to implement a technology solution. Implementation is carrying out your plan. It encompasses all the processes involved in getting technology operating properly. Because no two situations or projects are the same, the focus here is to provide information on fundamental activities critical to a successful technology implementation. No matter what specifics you are dealing with, treat the implementation phase as a project unto itself. All too often technology projects stall or fail during the implementation process. Money, time, and even people's attitudes can sometime take an unexpected turn, and even the most well-thought-out plans can get sidetracked, so have all your ducks in a row and be prepared.

Some general considerations to take into account when implementing technology include

> *Give your staff a reason to use the technology.* Promote what you're doing with the new project and provide practical information and ways for staffers to apply that technology to meet their particular needs. Let them know how the technology will help them and make their jobs easier in the long run, even if there is a learning curve.

> *Schedule site visits.* If you haven't done this already, schedule in-person visits or online "webinars" with libraries or other sites that are already utilizing your new technology. It's easier to envision the technology in your own environment if you (and your staff) can see it in action ahead of time. Ask the other sites plenty of questions and be prepared to learn something about what you will face in your own library's project.

Offer ample initial training. Conduct initial training sessions well in advance of the release of the technology. Don't wait until the last minute; this is the kiss of death. Also, provide the staff with opportunities for questions and discussion and for identifying potential problems as they learn to use the new technology. No plan can anticipate every issue or problem that may arise in this regard. Use training to help flush these problems out. (See chapter 8 for more information on staff training.)

Be patient. It is fair to expect staff to need time to experiment and adapt to change, so allow for an adequate learning curve and time frame. The amount of time needed will, of course, vary depending on the scale and complexity of the project and the aptitude and attitude of your staff.

Provide ongoing information and support. Don't stop training and encouraging the staff once a technology or service is up and running. Provide a mechanism for staff to communicate to "technology implementers" as well as to one another about their struggles and successes.

Make administrative support known. Be sure that the library administration (director, board of trustees, etc.) outwardly shows their support and involvement. The staff will more readily support a solution or project that is clearly and unequivocally endorsed by those in charge.

Enthusiasm is contagious. Don't underestimate the effect that your (and your team's) energy level and commitment have on others. Enthusiasm should filter its way throughout the entire organization.

Each of these essentials will increase the staff's commitment to the new technology, assist in increasing their overall technology use and knowledge, and improve the overall coordination and outcome of the project at hand. Throughout this process, keep in mind the psychological impact of new technology on your staff. How will new technology shape and change the work your staff does, and how will this affect their attitudes and morale? Product rollouts, deadlines, learning something new, and change in general can cause stress and anxiety in an organization, so take this into account as you plan.

Project Management

The key to successful technology implementation is strong project management. Otherwise promising projects can fail because the people behind their implementation lack basic project management skills and methodology. Effective management is about understanding what needs to be done from both a technical point of view and from a "people" perspective. Successful project management is about careful planning, effective leadership, teamwork, a workable timeline, ongoing support, and continued evaluation. It is also about finding a balance between your goals and objectives and what is actually possible. It is a universal rule that in any project you really cannot have it all. In the engineering and project management world, this is referred to as the "two out of three" rule. For delivering any project, there are three parameters that define the ideals:

1. Low cost / under budget
2. Fast implementation / on time
3. Highest quality / no errors

The "two out of three" rule states that you can usually attain two out of three of these parameters for a project, but you can never have all three. For example, if your project must be very cost-effective, you will either have to sacrifice how fast you can implement the project or the quality of what you deliver. Ideally, since you can never have all three, you work to find a balance so that no element is sacrificed too much. This is the premise of good project management.

Many managers fail to realize that it is often just as important to understand how a new project will be rolled out as it is to understand the technical intricacies of what is being implemented. If you are faced with a sizable or complicated project, you might consider purchasing a basic project management software tool to assist you along the way. There are several generic and affordable solutions out there that give you the ability to brainstorm, manage project phases, create timelines and schedules, create and adjust budgets, and more. If nothing else, use a spreadsheet or old-fashioned paper to outline the project plan, timeline, milestones, and objectives clearly.

Rollout

One critical component of implementation is rollout—the installation and introduction of a new technology product, service, or policy. All too often organizations put a ton of effort into their plan only to reach the rollout stage exhausted and uninspired. Project implementations can lose momentum because not enough support has been garnered along the way, or because there simply hasn't been enough attention given to rollout and support strategies. For these reasons, it is essential to pay attention to all aspects of implementation throughout the planning process and to fine-tune everything once it is in place and ready to go. Whenever possible, and especially when implementing larger projects, work in phases or incorporate pilot projects as a first step. This type of approach is often less threatening and overwhelming. Potential bugs can be worked out and solutions tested in advance, and these successes on a small scale can help build the project's credibility and therefore build better long-term acceptance by the staff.

Teamwork and Support

Once again the emphasis is on teamwork, whether you're in the installation, training, or support phase. Look to your technology team as the leaders during implementation. You may decide to vary the team's participants based on how things unfolded over the course of the planning process. There may very well be new key players that have emerged. Don't be afraid to allow your team to evolve as the process unfolds. Various members may have different strengths throughout the process, so be cognizant that your best planners may not always be your best implementers. Continued teamwork and good leadership are among the key reasons for implementation success. It is the people behind the technology, not the technology itself, who keep the process moving forward and inspire and coax the plan through both good times and bad. The active and continued promotion of the new technology to staff and patrons alike is essential in making everyone feel fully prepared and supported. It's about working as a library team, not just as a technology team.

Schedules and Timelines

Be flexible, but also stick to the timetable or schedule as outlined in your plan. Keep in mind that a schedule is only effective if its milestones and deadlines are reachable. If your deadlines are unrealistic you will surely miss some of them, and this may decrease the credibility of the technology and effectiveness of the implementation. Don't allow preferred deadlines to override the actual time necessary for a task to be completed. In most instances, a general rule of thumb is to estimate the amount of time you think it will take to implement a technology and then double it. And if you do happen to miss a deadline or slip behind a bit, remember that it's usually worse to try to hide it. Expect changes along the way and make adjustments as necessary. Closely monitor your delays, progress, successes, and failures. Getting regular feedback is essential here.

SUPPORT, MAINTENANCE, AND TROUBLESHOOTING

Now that your library's new technology is up and running, everything is fantastic and everyone can finally take a well-deserved break. Well, maybe not quite yet. Unfortunately, successful technology implementation is never-ending because technology needs to be supported indefinitely. This means proper and up-to-date maintenance of the network, equipment, and software. It also means timely and effective solutions to hiccups and problems along the way. For these reasons, it is important to keep the technology team intact. It is also important to have a separate plan and well-organized procedure for maintenance, support, and troubleshooting. Implementation will surely bring about new issues and challenges, people will continue to have questions and need support, and plans will need adjustment (and eventual revision) as technology changes.

Support

By establishing an effective support system, you will ensure technology is not only maintained but also used properly. Good support systems can come in all shapes and sizes and can be adapted to any library environment. In trying to establish a system that works best for your library, ask yourself

> How will the library maintain the technology (general maintenance as well as upgrades, hardware replacements, etc.)?
>
> How will the library provide ongoing user support (troubleshooting, training, etc.)?
>
> How will the library measure technology usage and effectiveness (successes and failures)?

Once you have addressed these questions, next consider key elements such as

> implementing clear-cut, easy-to-use troubleshooting procedures
>
> developing a user-friendly and effective problem-reporting system with good status-tracking mechanisms
>
> cross-training staff at various levels
>
> scheduling and allocating maintenance and troubleshooting duties to more than one staff member; again, a team approach
>
> establishing ongoing training and assistance for all users—staff and public

Maintenance

For the purposes of this section, *maintenance* means taking care of and supporting the *physical* aspects of technology. The idea is to get your money's worth, making sure that whatever technology you've chosen lasts its life span and operates and performs to its fullest potential. Most of what will be done involves preventive maintenance (i.e., avoiding problems before they occur). Maintenance schedules, cross-training on various tasks, and job-sharing responsibilities are vital. Basic computer maintenance tasks include the following ones:

Hardware cleaning. See figure 7-1 for some quick computer cleaning tips.

Computer file maintenance. This includes cleaning computer caches, deleting temporary Internet and Windows files, hidden files, cookies, and registry cleaning.

Hard disk space maintenance, space optimization, and defragmentation. These speed up the computer by putting all of the pieces of files together and putting the files you access most where the system can most easily get to them.

System and file backup diagnostics. Occasionally running diagnostic programs can head off small problems before they become big ones.

Pest control. This involves running programs to protect against and get rid of viruses, spyware, and adware. Most of these applications can be scheduled to run full scans on a regular basis.

General network maintenance. This includes eliminating old user accounts, regularly expiring and updating passwords, and cleaning out junk e-mail.

Software upgrades. This involves keeping software updated as necessary.

FIGURE 7-1
Computer
Cleaning
Tips

HARDWARE	SUPPLIES	FREQUENCY
Mouse	Alcohol, tweezers, lint-free cloth	Monthly
Keyboard	Vacuum, damp cloth, cleaning swabs, compressed air	Monthly
Monitor (case and screen)	Soft damp cloth, mini-vacuum (for case); lint-free cloth, antistatic cleaner or solution of water and alcohol (for monitor) *Note: Using the wrong cleaner can damage a monitor screen. Never use an abrasive and never spray cleaning solution directly onto the screen. Always spray onto the cloth first.*	Monthly
Computer box / case	Damp cloth, compressed air	Every 2–3 months (libraries are dusty places)
Printers	Lint-free, damp cloth (for exterior case) *Note: Cleaning of the internal mechanisms will vary depending on the type of printer. See your printer manual for instructions.*	Every 2–4 months

Many small and medium-sized libraries enter into a maintenance contract with a consultant or technology service provider for emergency services or periodic hardware maintenance that are above and beyond the scope of the staff. When entering into a maintenance contract, analyze cost. You should also consider the expertise of your staff. Is it feasible to have staff do 100 percent, 90 percent, or 50 percent of the maintenance? Analyze staff time and materials versus maintenance contract costs. Do you have the staff time and expertise to provide weekly and monthly maintenance, handle minor and major repairs, and so on? (For more information on choosing a consultant or service provider, see chapter 5.)

Software maintenance generally means keeping things up-to-date, whether installing upgrades or implementing patches. Most software comes with a maintenance agreement, but if it doesn't, make sure you negotiate one at the time of purchase. Such agreements generally cover troubleshooting errors and problems as well as new releases or upgrades. Be sure to note whether upgrades are excluded or included in the initial purchase price. You will also need to consider whether upgrades will require changes to other elements such as the operating system, hardware, or network.

Whether hardware or software is involved, it is important to be organized when it comes to maintenance. Consider what types of maintenance need to be performed and who will perform them. Create a checklist and a schedule. These don't have to be elaborate, but even the smallest of libraries cannot afford to lag behind in this area.

Troubleshooting

The first order of business here is to create in-house procedures for troubleshooting (a "help desk" model). How will the staff solve day-to-day problems? What is the chain of command when it comes to small issues? What about bigger, more involved troubleshooting? How will information be disseminated and communicated to staff? Train employees on all levels to break down problems into steps (problem-solving 101) and teach them to look for the obvious first solution (connections, on/off switches, etc.). Train them to ask key questions such as, When does this problem occur? and What else is happening at that time? Are there any coincidences, etc.? See if the problem can be isolated to hardware or software. Troubleshooting is often an exercise in "what isn't wrong" versus "what is wrong." In other words, rule out possible problems to help narrow the search down to the real problem.

There are common guidelines you can provide to general staff when it comes to basic troubleshooting. Educating the staff about these issues will empower them as well as save the library valuable time and money and offer better customer service. Provide staff with written documentation (shared online via a network drive, intranet, etc.). How-to guides and troubleshooting manuals can include opening and closing technology-related procedures, information on your ILS (both the staff side and the OPAC), and general information on computers, printers, audiovisual equipment, software, and the network.

When putting together a troubleshooting guide, state the topic and how-to basics. For instance:

> *Problem*: The computer, monitor, printer will not turn on.
> *Solution*: Is everything plugged in? If not, plug it in. If yes, move on to checking other connections. Secure all connections and reboot the computer and see if that solves the problem.

**OUT
OF
ORDER!**

When it comes to "out of order" signs, create a generic sign that is laminated and can be written on with a dry-erase marker. Leave a space in the bottom-right corner for reporting staff to include their initials and the date the equipment went out of order. That way, all staff know who to ask if there are questions, and they know the problem is being taken care of.

Problem: The monitor appears to be on, but there isn't a picture.

Solution: Is the power light on? Is everything connected? Have the brightness or contrast settings been adjusted?

Problem: The computer is just not responding.

Solution: When all else fails, reboot the machine. First, attempt a "warm boot" (ctrl + alt + del). If that does not work, try a "cold" boot (turn off the power switch, wait ten to twenty seconds, and then turn on again).

Problem: The mouse is not working.

Solution: If you don't see any signs of "mouse life," check to see if it's plugged in. Even if it appears to be plugged in correctly, try reconnecting it and rebooting the computer. If the mouse is partially working but just acting funny, it probably needs cleaning. Take it apart and clean the ball with rubbing alcohol.

Problem: New software was loaded, but I cannot see the updates.

Solution: Did you reboot the computer? Most times, you won't see a change until after you reboot the machine.

Although such tools can take some time to generate and their initial development might seem daunting, think about all the time and money you will save in the long run. Look to other libraries and organizations for previously developed materials that you can use or adapt for your own library. Most of them would be willing to share their materials with you. Or how about a partnership opportunity? You could pool resources with area libraries to develop these guides for all of the library partners.

Whatever you do, keep it simple. Provide basic guidelines for general staff and more detailed information for upper-level employees. Encourage higher-level technology staff to consult user's manuals and online tech support guides, whether vendor specific or generic. (See appendix B for some suggested resources.)

By putting a few simple guidelines and procedures in place, openly communicating with staff, and teaching them to be more self-sufficient, you will be able to streamline day-to-day troubleshooting and ultimately make the library run more smoothly. All too often in smaller libraries, the person responsible for technology receives phone calls during off-duty times (nights, weekends, and even when on vacation). Even though dedicated employees are willing to do this, it is really inappropriate and can damage an organization's morale and cohesiveness. Not only is this an inefficient way to troubleshoot, but it can be costly for an organization if

FIGURE 7-2
Staff Troubleshooting Form

TROUBLESHOOTING FORM

What type of problem is this? (*check one*)

Computer Hardware _____ Software _____ Internet _____

Other Network Issue _____ Printing _____

AV Equipment _____ Other _____

Description of Problem (*please be specific*)

Action Taken

What troubleshooting actions have been taken?

Did you consult with any other staff, etc.?

Reporting Staff Member: _____

Date/Time Submitted: _____

(Use this space to include notes or additional procedural instructions [i.e., fill this form out completely and tape it to _____'s door, put it in _____'s in-box, etc.]. If dealing with hardware, complete an out of order sign and tape it to equipment.)

overtime, consultants, or technology service providers are involved.

Getting the staff involved in troubleshooting procedures not only empowers them but is quite cost-effective for the library. Even if the staff cannot fix the problem, it will still save the library time and money because they can begin the process and eliminate certain possibilities for the technology staff or outside consultant. A basic troubleshooting instruction sheet is quite helpful for those on the front lines (especially for those working nights and weekends). You will be amazed at how a simple tool like this can improve overall customer service and foster communication and rapport between the general staff and the technology staff. The instructions in the sheet should include

> What steps should be taken by on-duty staff before calling in off-duty staff for assistance? Be specific. This is where you can go through the various problem/solution procedures described above.

> If such elementary steps are taken and the problem isn't resolved, what should happen next?

> Who should staff call for first-level support? Is there a chain of command (i.e., contact this person first, this person second, etc.)?

> If no technology-specific staff are available, then what? Is there a help desk for your library system or consortium?

> When is it appropriate to call in outside help such as a consultant or technology service provider? If the library has someone of this nature on contract, when should they be called in? Who should call them in? What other procedures must then be followed?

It is very helpful to include a categorized list of emergency versus nonemergency situations (i.e., what can't wait until tomorrow and what can wait). This way there is no confusion about what is and isn't considered an "emergency." And last but not least, include appropriate contact information so it is readily available and staff do not have to search elsewhere.

Other useful tools include troubleshooting forms (see figure 7-2 for a sample form) and problem report/troubleshooting logs (see the sample form in appendix A). You might also want to consider automating these tools, using e-mail or your library's web page or intranet. If your library is a larger facility, you might think about an alternative online software solution for reporting difficulties and communicating with one another. (See the section for this chapter in appendix B for additional resources.) Be sure to track and document all troubleshooting and help desk requests. This information is vital for keeping a history of your equipment, and it will also shed valuable light on how employees are handling problems, which can be useful in planning staff training. The information is also useful when attempting to gain support for new technology, more staff, and additional funding.

MARKETING

Now that you've planned, purchased, installed, and trained, your work is finally done. Well, maybe not quite yet. The critical step now is advertising what you have. Libraries must learn to be more assertive and learn how to build their skills in the area of marketing and promotion. This is traditionally something that is unfamiliar to most in the profession, but it doesn't have to be. It's simply about telling others what your library is doing and why you're doing it. It's about being proud, proactive, and inspired. So publicize your technological achievements and use them to help gain support and further involvement in the library. Coach your staff to be knowledgeable and upbeat, promoting new technologies and services. After all, they are your frontline "sales force." Good customer service can be as simple as having staff lead the way in introducing new technology to the public by projecting a positive attitude. As Linda Yoder says, "We strongly discourage language that implies any perceived problems are 'a computer glitch.'"

With any library service, technology related or otherwise, marketing is a major key to success. *Marketing* can be defined as identifying the particular wants and needs of a target market of customers and then going about satisfying those customers better than your competitors. It is a combination of communicating, advertising, and sales. Marketing involves market research: analyzing customer needs and then making strategic decisions about product design, pricing, placement, and promotion. At this point, it's all about what to say and how to say it.

Strategies

The first step is a quick and easy approach that allows you to decide on a marketing strategy and devise a simple yet effective plan. You can use the "Marketing Technology Worksheet" in appendix A to identify key information related to product design, placement, pricing, and promotion. Begin by answering the question, What is our library's market segment? A market segment is a group of people with similar wants, needs, and desires whom the library wants and needs to serve. You should be able to identify key market segments within your community. Market segments are identifiable, uniform, measurable, and reachable. Next, answer the question, Why do we want to reach this market segment? Lastly, complete the "Marketing Technology Worksheet" for each of your market segments, filling in product design, pricing, placing, and promotion.

When marketing your library's technology-related services, you want to make sure you're connecting with the right segment of your market. For example, when the Ogden (NY) Farmers' Library bought new PCs, the machines came equipped with USB ports. At first the library wasn't sure what the ports would be used for, until the library director was approached by someone carrying a keychain smart drive. A light dawned! She immediately had the library's network technician tweak the library's security software to allow users to download to the keychain drives. But how was she to market such a feature? Her usual route was to submit an article to local newspapers, but she wasn't sure that would connect with the right people. Instead, she asked herself, "Who are the people I see with these drives?" High school and college students and teachers are the primary users, so she printed up a bunch of brightly colored posters and distributed them to area high schools and colleges. She also sent a news release to those same colleges' and high schools' newspapers.

Among the fundamental promotional tools your library can use to market its technology-related services are the following ones:

Word of mouth. This is always the cheapest and most effective advertising mechanism available.

Your library's website.

Press releases. (See the "Sample Press Release" in appendix E.)

Flyers and brochures. (See examples of these from the Brownsburg [IN] Public Library and the Morrisson-Reeves [IN] Public Library in appendix E.)

Paper or electronic newsletters. These usually contain updates and information and can be sent to existing and future patrons, community groups, businesses, and so on. "The most common way we promote our new services is by featuring them in our newsletters," says Anita Woods, assistant director for support services at Westlake Porter (OH) Public Library. (See a sample of their newsletter in appendix E.)

E-notification of upcoming events and classes.

Cross-promotion. This technique incorporates information about what the library is doing into computer class curriculums and general library programming.

Interest columns or small "ads." Write these for local newspapers and school newsletters. The Whitman (WA) County Library even puts information in the community water bills.

MARKETING WI-FI

Wi-Fi is currently one of the best ways to raise your library's technology image and attract new customers. Simple, hassle-free Wi-Fi services will provide your library with a cost-effective way to gain positive PR and marketing. Basically, it all boils down to, "If you aren't going to tell people about it, why do it?" So consider carefully how to promote your library's Wi-Fi access. Get the word out and promote Wi-Fi in the media, newsletters, e-mails, signage, local billboards, and direct mail, always keeping in mind your audience—technology users who may not be your typical library patrons. Think about the types of marketing they are likely to respond to and what media outlets they are likely to pay attention to. The ultimate goal is to become synonymous with technology's power to provide access to information for the community.

You can advertise Wi-Fi on your library's home page and, if possible, on the "home page" of your OPAC. If a technology user is likely to have a casual interaction with your library, it is most likely to occur on the home page, so make it prominent there. Ask community groups and companies to help advertise, promoting the library's services and offerings to *their* members, employees, and customers And always remember to register the library as a free Wi-Fi location on local and national free Wi-Fi locator sites (see the section for this chapter in appendix B for examples).

FIGURE 7-3
St. Joseph County Public Library Bookmark

Signage, bookmarks, and other visual clues. Think about how products and services are being displayed and advertised within the library walls. (See figure 7-3 for a promotional bookmark from the St. Joseph County [IN] Public Library.)

Knowledgeable and proactive staff.

News media. News coverage in local newspapers and on local television and radio programs can be very useful.

Community events. Opportunities to market your library exist in local fairs and parades.

Public presentations and open houses. Demonstrate and showcase your technologies outside the library as well as in the library itself.

Annual reports. Creatively post these to advertise your successes (these include paper reports as well as postings on your library's website).

Billboards, television/radio ads, movie theater ads, shirts. You'd be surprised at how effective these can be, especially if you partner with other local libraries to cost-share some of the higher-end ideas. The Mooresville (IN) Public Library leased a billboard to advertise its new e-mail notification system for upcoming events and new materials. The Yorba Linda (CA) Public Library created television ads for homework help.

The Hennessey (OK) Public Library has a formula for success: "What You Have + What You'll Give + Changed Image = Get What You Want." Director Mary Haney claims there are two keys to her library's success. The first is her own willingness to plunge in and do what it takes to make sure the library provides real value to the community. The second key is to focus on the library's image; once that changes, people begin to believe they have a special library—and then they make it special because they believe it's special.[1] The Kent District (MI) Public Library incorporates new technologies into its annual marketing plan. For example, to inform patrons about its new self-check units, the library used print ads, in-house promotion (signage, bookmarks, posters, flyers, training brochures), radio interviews, and newspaper articles. They also plan to have their Friends groups and volunteers involved as greeters when they introduce self-check to their patrons.

Putting It into Words

An often difficult area of marketing is to put it all into words. Keep in mind that marketing is an advertising function. It's about informing and reminding your community about the technology products and services available to them, including equipment, materials, assistance, and programs. You're looking to gain the public's attention by clearly identifying your "products" and providing brief, concise, enticing information about them. There are many ways to articulate your library's value. The key is once again to be creative. Think about the benefits that the technology at your library brings to the community. Think about what is important to your users and funders. If you don't tell anyone about what your library has, no one will know it's there. However, you have to keep your message concise, as few people are able to take more than one or two things away from any one advertisement. You want to inform and excite, and then call to action; you want customers to go do something—register for a class or use the library's Wi-Fi. If you're excited about something, others will be excited too. This is a departure from the way libraries traditionally work. Basically, it is a change in library culture. The key is to realize that people won't just walk through the library's doors and know all the exciting things you are doing unless you guide them there.

How do you get the staff to support the library's marketing efforts? First, educate them about the purpose and importance of marketing. Once that is understood, it is important to keep them up-to-date and informed about all aspects of the library's marketing initiatives. Only then can staff effectively assist in getting the library's message out to the community through excellent customer service and positive word of mouth.

Customer Service

As mentioned earlier, word of mouth is the easiest and most cost-effective method of marketing your library to the public. Positive word-of-mouth advertising is dependent on outstanding customer service. A staff that is warm, welcoming, helpful, and knowledgeable is key. It's this attitude that will keep your patrons coming back and get them talking about the library in the community. The Whitman County (WA) Rural Library prides itself on offering "caring and friendly small-town service." They have a good rapport with customers, know them by name, and are genuinely concerned about each other and their community. But that's where the "small town" ends! The library features modern technologies, quality products, and innovative services that are usually reserved for larger, wealthier, or more urban systems. The library focuses its attention on staff and customer service. They set the expectation that customer service is their first priority and that they are going to be the best they can be. Their new image is one of energy and a positive, can-do attitude.[2]

PARTNERSHIPS MAKE A DIFFERENCE

Many successful technology programs are built on a foundation of effective partnerships and strong ties with the community. In order to move forward with technology, your library should try to find a solid foundation of outside support. Thriving technology requires community backing and involvement, whether it comes in the shape of money, volunteer services, training, or promotion. Libraries such as the Polk County (NC) Public Library, Whitman County (WA) Rural Library, and the Bloomington (IL) Public Library know the value of partnerships.

Polk County Public Library

In the year 2000, when the Gates Foundation came to North Carolina, the Polk County Public Library had to do some serious planning and creative partnering to raise the money needed to support a project in the library's Saluda branch.

First, they got the telephone company to agree to wire the building for free. Then they went to the Polk County commissioners, who agreed to transfer $5,000 in contingency funds to the library's budget to support the Internet connection in Saluda for the remainder of the

DEVELOPING PARTNERSHIPS

Right alongside of technology changes must be the building of external relationships. Libraries must network with others in the community who have similar goals and interests and develop partnerships with these organizations. Collaborate with schools to do training programs, small conferences, or mentoring programs and team up with businesses to support library programming that pertains to their business models. For example, develop a Mac users group with the local Apple vendor, seeking sponsors for prizes at your video/computer game competition, or work with your local movie theater to show student-made videos and films. This list could go on and on.

Maintain your library's position as a potential partner in the community with technology. Don't cower to businesses or larger organizations. Instead, look at technology as an opportunity to connect with people as a community partner and also as a resource for future activities, purchases, and so on. All too often libraries approach their "community of opportunities" with their hands out. Instead, try taking a more aggressive approach, stating what you and the library *can offer them*. This does not necessarily advocate "selling products"; it merely means that, as a public institution, libraries have a historical position in the minds of the public that can provide them with a considerable amount of leverage. You just have to figure out what that particular leverage is in your community and use it to the library's advantage.

This is also a game of endurance, for persistence is the way to success. If potential partners say no, don't worry about it.

Ask if you can come back in a year. If they don't follow through, don't write them off. Just keep going back. Once a partner is on board, make sure they know how the particular program ended up and what the future plan is. Ask if they are interested in future planning and collaboration. Be sure your attendees know who is supporting your effort. For instance, the Bloomington (IL) Public Library has held several GameFests for teens. The staff always mention to participating teens that the prizes were donated by EB Games, Best Buy, and Acme Comics. The staff also ask the teens to thank the sponsors for their prizes and participation next time they're in their store. And you know what? It works. The kids go to the stores, thank the sponsors, and the library hears back from the sponsors.

Another good example of successful partnerships is the Educational Alliance. The Bloomington Public Library is in a community comprising Bloomington and Normal. The combined populations are about 100,000. Within the community is the Educational Alliance made up of the local school districts, a local community college, Illinois State University, corporations such as State Farm Insurance, and other organizations such as the Bloomington Public Library. As an active member of the alliance's technology group over the past six years, the library has become a leader for the organization, coordinating and hosting the Student Technology Conference (www.sitcon ference.org) and the Bloomington-Normal Film Festival (www .bnfilmfest.org).[3]

2000–2001 fiscal year. Then they accepted an offer from the telephone company to knock off $500 from each monthly bill for their Internet connection, in exchange for agreeing to allow telephone company customers to pay their telephone bills through a drop box provided by the telephone company at the branch library. Finally, they went to the mayor and the town council of Saluda to get them to agree to pay half of the remaining monthly charges for the Internet connection in Saluda.

Whitman County Rural Library

The Whitman County (WA) Rural Library District quickly learned that success in partnerships was the path to achieving all they desired. The following is just a sampling of what they've accomplished.

The Friends of Whitman County Library give the library around $10,000 annually, along with countless hours of volunteer service. Cooperation with a neighboring library district allowed the libraries to hire and share a qualified computer system administrator, saving them around $25,000 per year and providing them with quality technology support—something they had been missing. Volunteers from the county jail provide the Whitman County Library with hundreds of hours in free labor. The program focuses on job training and mentoring, and the approximate annual savings to the library is $9,000. Regional newspapers, newsletters, and local radio also recognize the value their library brings to the community. They've rewarded the library with frequent coverage, regular columns, booklist space, and more.

A sample list of the Whitman County Library's partners on technology projects and programming include Internet service providers and other businesses; numerous colleges and universities; neighboring public, academic, and school libraries; service learning groups; all fourteen schools in the county; area hospitals; a local YMCA; the Washington State Department of Social and Health Services; the American Legion; the Senior Assistance Fund of Washington; the Boy Scouts; and numerous local agencies such as the Council on Aging, the Community Action Center, the Parks and Recreation Department, the Health Department, Early Learning Services, County Extension services, Community Mobilization Against Substance Abuse, the Whitman County Hospice, and the Chamber of Commerce.[4]

DO YOU KNOW IT?

Manage your projects, don't let them manage you. Follow your plan, manage your time, and document what you do.

Create a support strategy. Devise processes and procedures for keeping your library's technology running and your staff informed.

Empower your staff. Train your staff on troubleshooting techniques and encourage them to be problem-solvers.

Tell the world (or at least your community). Why bother implementing technology if nobody knows about it?

NOTES

1. Joseph Anderson, "The Puss-in-Boots Formula for Success," WebJunction (March 5, 2004), http://webjunction.org/do/DisplayContent?id=1233.

2. Contribution from the Whitman County (WA) Rural Library District. For additional information about this library, see appendix C and Elizabeth Kellison's article "Whitman County Library: The Little Library That Could," WebJunction (March 5, 2004), http://webjunction.org/do/DisplayContent?id=798.

3. Sidebar contributed by Matt Gullet, manager of information technology services at the Bloomington (IL) Public Library.

4. Contribution from the Whitman County (WA) Rural Library District.

Teach IT 8

To *teach* means to educate, to train, to make proficient with specialized instruction and practice. Quality, ongoing training for staff and the public is a critical component to putting any technology into successful practice, yet in many public libraries training is overlooked, underplanned, and is viewed as insignificant. Providing people with technology knowledge, skills, and expertise can mean the difference between a library's success and failure. The education of staff and the public begin back in chapter 2 during the assessment phase. Involving and educating staff and patrons during the initial stages of planning begins the "buy-in" process that ultimately enables key stakeholders to accept, support, and implement the results—new technology and services. The key questions related to training include

> Who should be trained?
>
> What should they be trained in?
>
> How should they be trained?

STAFF TRAINING

Providing technology training to staff and volunteers is essential, because it teaches them the skills that your library needs to succeed. Successful training means that those being trained can demonstrate that they have mastered the material, can apply the skills, and show improved performance that benefits the library.

Training staff at *all levels*—not just those directly responsible for technology—is critical. Equally important is training employees in a *variety of areas* of technology. The idea is not to turn everyone on the staff into experts but to make sure they're informed and have a basic competency level. Establishing a solid, broad-based training program will surely increase your library's efficiency and improve both employee confidence and customer service. "Constant updates, upgrades, and changes require continual learning. At no point can staff coast," says Edward Elsner, director of the Delton District (MI) Library. The common excuses for a weak technology training program include "It's too expensive," "My library can't afford to send too many people," "Staff don't have the time," and "We can't afford to give up the desk time." Actually, your library can't afford not to have a well-trained and prepared staff. Those libraries with strong staff training programs know the importance of strong customer service through increased staff self-sufficiency.

Any technology training program should begin by educating staff (and volunteers) about how technology fits in with the library's mission. Actively incorporating technology into the daily activities of the library (i.e., active learning) is also imperative. This process is about learning by doing and demonstrating how technology can work for the staff in their daily activities, whether circulation, reference, collection development, bill paying, or materials processing. Next comes "formal" training. Formal training options include

Training classes. These can consist of in-house sessions, classes in your library system or regional or state library, continuing education, or college courses. Remember that one staff member can attend the training and then teach others the material.

Independent learning. Online tutorials and instructional books (in the library's collection) can enable staff to train themselves without pressure. Of course, this method of training will depend on the learning ability and motivation level of individual staff members. You will also want to establish goals and deadlines for completion so everyone stays on the same page.

Electronic discussion lists, blogs. These are good ways to keep abreast of what's going on outside your library's walls. (Ask questions and get answers. See appendix B for some good examples.)[1]

Ongoing support. This includes written and verbal communication, manuals, tip sheets, and information and demonstrations provided one-on-one or at staff meetings.

One common thread here is the importance of technology literacy for the entire staff—teaching everyone the basics. Once this has been achieved, it's time to consider the various levels of staff and their skills and knowledge. Here you can refer to the results of your assessment of staff proficiencies from chapter 5. When considering who and what to teach, cross-training staff is highly encouraged. Cross-training means educating and assigning employees tasks outside of their normal job responsibilities, enabling personnel to learn duties associated with more than one job. This results in qualified, on-site backup when the primary staff member is unavailable. In addition, it means that no one person is the sole technology "expert," and the "technology fate" of the library doesn't lie in just one or two people's hands. Ultimately, this all translates into better customer service: shorter downtime, fewer "emergency" phone calls to off-duty staff, a more efficient and cost-effective library, and employees with a broader understanding and appreciation of technology—and ones who are less likely to resist change and improvement because these are less likely to be perceived as a threat to their job security. According to Scott Childers,

> A computer-literate library staff is a necessity. With the continuing increase of reliance on computers and networks, library staff of all levels need to be able to adapt to this ever-changing technology instead of being locked into a certain skill set based on a rote memorization of steps that will become obsolete when hardware is updated or the next version of software is introduced. This does not mean, however, that all library staff

members have to become system managers. Achieving the target level of computer literacy is not a hard goal to accomplish if you commit to it. The level of computer proficiency that a person needs to be computer literate in the early days of this millennium is still relatively low. Achieving library-wide baseline literacy is only the beginning; continuous training at higher proficiency levels helps create a more adaptable workforce.[2]

When deciding what topics to train on, again refer back to your staff assessment as outlined in chapter 5. What technical skills do the staff possess? What's lacking? What are the staff's overall strengths and weaknesses? What types of training would improve knowledge and efficiency and help the staff feel comfortable with technology? What do employees *need* to know about? What do staff *want* to learn about? What are your cross-training needs?

To help you answer these questions, create a list of all the training areas that come to mind. Next, compare these with your "Staff Proficiency Comparison Chart" (refer back to figure 5-1 in chapter 5). You should immediately see where your biggest needs are. Start from there and prioritize.

Public libraries across the country are beginning to understand that technology will have no direct benefit to their customers unless there is a vision to perceive the technology's possibilities and opportunities. Many also realize the importance of a strong staff development program to unlock the potential of their employees, focusing energy and creativity upon the mission, goals, and objectives of the library. The Deschutes (OR) Public Library's staff development goals include

> Each staff member understands and "owns" the mission, goals, objectives, and structure of the library system.
>
> Each staff member has mastered the knowledge, skills, and techniques relevant to his/her area of responsibility.
>
> Each staff member understands the significance and importance of his/her duties in the context of the "bigger picture."
>
> Each professional and management-level staff member is aware of regional and national developments relevant to his/her assigned duties and is engaged in an ongoing review of local operations.
>
> Each staff member actively shares information with fellow employees.[3]

Content

Technology training at libraries ranges from the basics to advanced instruction. It may include fundamental skills such as searching the Web, e-mail use, file saving, and word processing and spreadsheet programs. It may also mean intermediate and advanced sessions that focus on target audiences and teach database searching, more advanced Internet searching, network troubleshooting, and network administration and maintenance. Technology training is not limited to teaching skills and techniques. You can train staff on new policies and procedures, customer service, and marketing as well. Training also means establishing ongoing support in the form of helpful tools and open communication and teaching how to deal with new situations that arise. When developing content or selecting training options, be sure to account for your staff's various learning styles (e.g., learning by hearing, learning by doing, or learning by seeing or writing). (See the sample staff memo from the Howard County (MD) Library in appendix E.)

When developing course content for your training program, look to outside organizations and other libraries for sample classes, curricula, and general ideas. Borrow and modify their materials. Talk to others who are running successful training programs and find out what's worked for them and what hasn't. If you want to train staff outside the library's walls, take advantage of continuing education opportunities that are available locally and regionally. What are private training companies offering? See this book's companion website at http://www.ala.org/editions/extras/Bolan09205/ for sample curricula of basic training programs for staff and the public. See appendix B for more training ideas and resources.

Who?

Once course content is decided on, you need to decide who will perform the training. Will staff perform the training, or will you enlist the help of someone outside the organization (i.e., a hired trainer, consultant, a training center, local consortium, regional library group, or your

---

TIPS FOR TECHNOLOGY TRAINING

Training people in the use of technology presents some special challenges. The trainer needs to be sensitive to the fact that while some learners are comfortable with technology and change, others may struggle to find a level of comfort. The non-judgmental support of the trainer is especially critical for these learners. Here is some practical advice about creating a comfortable learning environment for technology training.

- Avoid using complex language and technical jargon, and don't talk down to students. These approaches don't make you look smarter; they only serve to intimidate, confuse, and offend those you are trying to teach.

- Use positive body language. Be approachable, friendly, and don't loom over students. When working one on one, sit at their level.

- Validate student comprehension. Stay away from yes-or-no questions. Instead use open-ended questions to encourage discussion. You'll end up getting more feedback by interacting this way.

- Be practical. Use everyday examples so students can relate technology to their common experience. For instance, saving files on a computer is similar to filing a letter away in a filing cabinet.

- Set prerequisites for formal training classes so students are on the same level. If someone lags behind, don't hold back the entire class. Keep moving forward and encourage the student having difficulties to sign up

for the class a second time (or maybe even go back a level).

- Don't automatically blame a student if something goes wrong. Instead, focus the issue on the shortcomings of the hardware, software, and so on. Be positive, encourage students, and let them know they can't break it!

- Don't take over for a student if you feel something is taking too long (i.e., don't type or mouse for them). Instead, work through students to solve the problem. Remember the proverb, "Give a man a fish and you feed him for a day. Teach a man to fish and you feed him for a lifetime."

- Provide a few minutes for practice and questions at the end of training sessions. Don't rush students out the door.

- Make yourself available for questions. Let students know you and others at the library are there to support their technology needs.

- Provide some kind of take-home literature for future reference and include training information and materials on your library's website.

- Get a formal (brief) written evaluation from students to find out the positives and negatives about the training. Ask for their ideas about future training.

---

state library)? An outside trainer may be able to customize a workshop to your library's specific staff, technology needs, time frame, and budget. Just keep in mind that creative solutions such as developing partnerships and enlisting the help of volunteers can provide many options for even the smallest budget. A very effective and cost-saving training method is to "train the trainer"—investing time and money training one or two staff members in a specific subject area (so they become the experts) and then having them train the rest of the staff. This type of training involves not only teaching the subject matter at hand but also educating staff how to be good instructors. Other options to consider are organizations such as WebJunction, which has a wide selection of online course offerings. They offer, for example, a series of courses on managing public-access computers, including software updates and upgrades and computer troubleshooting. Further information on WebJunction and other training resources is found in appendix B.

Where and When?

Will training be held in the library or off-site via a computer training facility? Does your library have a training lab? If not, does it have a place that can be set aside for small group sessions? If you're without a formal training facility and want to hold a large group session, make arrangements with another library that has a training area, or even your state library or regional council or system to utilize their lab. Virtual training is also an option when outside trainers or companies offer webinars and online demonstrations. Many large training facilities and numerous technology vendors are willing to do free or low-cost training in this manner. Oftentimes, in rural situations, resources are limited and libraries serve a large geographic area. Collaboration, online training options, training software, and "training the trainer" work well in this situation. The St. Louis County (MO) Library transformed a bookmobile into a cybermobile to train its remote staff in the mechanics of their new integrated library system. The South Central Regional (NY) Library Council constructed a mobile lab for computer and network training.[4]

No matter what type of training you're doing, make sure you allow for adequate time frames. Offer the training related to new technology implementation *before* rollout so people have time to adapt, there are no surprises, questions can be asked and answered, and kinks can be worked out. Many troublesome implementations are due to insufficient training beforehand. Aside from training specifically associated with a particular technology project or product rollout, you should make instruction a regular, ongoing part of week-to-week staff development. Consider holding short (fifteen- to twenty-minute), weekly technology briefing sessions that include tips, trends, updates, and so on. A sample schedule might look as follows:

> Week 1: The USB Drive—What Is It and How to Use It
>
> Week 2: E-Mail Techniques
>
> Week 3: Information about the Server Upgrade
>
> Weeks 4, 5, 6: Microsoft Word, Excel, and PowerPoint Tips
>
> Week 7: Web Browser Tips
>
> Week 8: Technology Marketing Tips

For more in-depth topics, hold a longer session once a month. Keep the staff abreast of happenings, updates, and additional training items via postings on an intranet or even on a bulletin board. Consider creating a blog for meeting minutes, discussion points, and so on. Evaluation of the library's staff training program is also important, so be sure to get feedback, whether in the form of one-on-one informal interviews, staff surveys, or evaluation forms. (See the public survey in figure 8-1 later in this chapter, which you can adapt to your staff classes.)

Effective technology training means more than having staff complete classes or workshops, however. Training is ongoing and never-ending. Ongoing education can take the form of open communications, product update memos and demonstrations, and simple how-to guides. Once staff members have been formally trained on a topic, it is equally important to keep them up-to-date so that the information is fresh in their minds and their skills remain sharp.

Training Procedures for New Staff

By creating standards and guides for new staff members (and new volunteers), you make their transition into their new jobs easier, but you should also clearly define who will provide training to the new staff members. Incorporate technology training into your orientation and training program for new employees. At the Mount Prospect (IL) Public Library, training is mandatory for all new hires and includes instruction in e-mail use and ILS searching. The staff are also offered training on all products the library uses in its day-to-day business. These sessions cover word processing, spreadsheets, presentation skills, advanced searching techniques on the ILS as well as subscription databases, and advanced Internet search skills.

You can make training a team effort by assigning different staff members to different areas of training. Utilize simple techniques such as shadowing, manuals (paper and online), and one-on-one or small group instruction. Include a "Basic Introduction to Technology" guide that new hires can take home with them or view online. This guide can cover ILS basics (both staff-side and the OPAC), your library's web page, library software instruction, basic hardware information, and troubleshooting guidelines and tips. Don't overlook vital information for new hires such as technology expectations, efficiency tips, copies of policies and procedures, and tips on customer service. Emphasizing technology right from the start—whether at the interview, when touring the library, or during training—will get everyone off to a good start.

TRAINING THE PUBLIC

Offering computer classes to the public can bring benefits that go beyond simply increasing your library's program statistics (although this is a huge plus to those libraries that know the value of a good public training program and implement it successfully). Technology programs for patrons not only offer a way to extend traditional library programming into the twenty-first century, they provide a way for libraries to demonstrate that they are a vital resource for technology information and knowledge. These programs are probably the most important way a library can raise its profile as a technology leader in the community. The community needs to be educated to use technology, but its members must also be made aware that of the library as an indispensable source of this information. Technology training for the public can come in many forms, whether informal one-on-one instruction, formal computer classes and how-to-sessions, or recreational programs.

Content

When it comes to your external customers or patrons, useful information can be gathered from your community assessment from chapter 2. Look at the demographics of your service population. What do people want to learn about? What would you like to teach them about? What do you think they need to know that they are likely unaware of? What's hot and popular and would attract current and new patrons? Recognize that different users have different technology needs, and that it is important to offer different services to different people. There are many model programs out there from which to obtain great ideas and borrow information. Look to the model libraries listed in appendix C and mentioned elsewhere in this book for ideas. The St. Joseph County (IN) Public Library has an excellent computer education program, for example. The Bloomington (IL) Public Library has had great success with its after-school computer club for teens, its "Prime Time" computer club for seniors, and its GameFest program. Other technology programs for the public could include digital filmmaking, animation and modeling, and digital scrapbooking, just to name a few. Get ideas from other libraries and adapt them to your situation; the idea here is to not waste precious time and resources creating something from scratch when there are good foundations already out there.

Ideas for Public Computer Classes

To get you started, here are a few ideas for computer classes from small and medium-sized libraries across the United States.

> *Library catalog.* How to use the library's catalog (to search for, reserve, and renew materials; to view your account; and to place a hold, reserve, or interlibrary loan request). An online catalog class might not seem very "sexy," yet it is the foundation of public training. This is the core technology of the library. It is an opportunity to show users what the library is all about. It is also an opportunity to be creative and to publicize. Consider making it a required class for your other classes. You might not have people banging down your doors like they do for the other classes, but if your library is creative about the class content and publicity, you'll come out ahead. Many people claim to know everything about a library's catalog system, yet they are pleasantly surprised by the tips and tricks they learn in a class.
>
> *Other library-specific classes.* These may include instruction on finding magazine articles online and database searching. Include a basic how-to class as well as an intermediate-level class for these and other topics.
>
> *Keyboarding and mousing.* This is geared to the computer novice who needs to practice the most basic computer skills.
>
> *Basic computers (i.e., "computers made easy").* A class for beginner computer users with little or no computer knowledge, covering computer terminology, turning a computer on and off, and using a mouse.
>
> *Internet.* Basic-level class covers how to navigate and search the Internet. Intermediate and advanced classes may cover in-depth searching, website evaluation, and specialized subject areas such as travel and vacation planning, genealogy, health information, business, investing, job searching, popular culture (movies, music, etc.), car buying, and consumer information.

E-mail. Beginning-level class covers how to read, compose, and send e-mail; how to create an e-mail address book; and how to attach files and pictures to e-mail. Intermediate-level class covers file attachments, organizing messages into folders, and so on.

Application software such as Microsoft (Word, Excel, PowerPoint, Access). Beginning-level class would cover the basics of word processing, spreadsheets, presentation, and database software use. Many libraries also offer intermediate and advanced-level classes. This class can also be done with open source software products.

Other specialized how-to classes. These can include buying a computer, selecting technology for personal use, scanners, digital cameras, digital photography, web design, HTML basics, desktop publishing (making greeting cards, business cards, etc.), chatting on the Web, audio and video on the Internet (MP3 players, etc.), downloading and installing software, pest control (backups, antivirus protection, privacy), Windows basics (moving, resizing, and arranging windows, useful keyboard shortcuts and tips), basic file management and organization, and introduction to networks.

Targeted sessions. These would focus on your senior population, parenting population, homeschoolers, or other specialized user groups.

See the section for this chapter in appendix B for more training resources and refer to this book's companion website at http://www.ala.org/editions/extras/Bolan09205/ for sample computer class training curricula.

Computer Class Planning Basics

Scheduling computer classes can be a tricky thing for a library with a small staff and a limited budget. The scheduling of classes will generally evolve as your training program grows. You might start by offering particular classes on a specific day of the week or once a month, but you will soon find that your schedule demands quickly change as your program develops and the word gets out. The key is to be flexible. When the Webster (NY) Public Library began its program in 1999, the library held a total of 105 classes, training 328 patrons. By the end of 2003 the program had grown to 156 classes training 982 patrons; this was a 49 percent increase in the number of classes and a 200 percent increase in attendance.[5] With the rise in popularity of the classes came the scheduling of more class sessions (both in frequency and in type), the training of new volunteer and staff instructors, and the building of a computer lab that was deemed vital to the library as part of its new building project in 2002. The reasons for the library's success included

the staff's dedication to publicizing and teaching

a flexible schedule that worked to meet the demands of the public

an open-minded approach to who could be a technology instructor, including librarians, support staff, MLS graduate students, and volunteers with technology backgrounds

an interviewing, training, and support mechanism for instructors, including strong communication between staff and volunteers

takeaway training packets for the public

evaluation forms that were distributed at every class, compiled monthly, and used to develop future classes and services

strong customer service and support after the classes

At the Wood County (OH) District Public Library, the reference staff take turns teaching technology classes, and tech lab monitors (pages) cover the evening and weekend shifts. The Whitman County (WA) Public Library offers Technology Tuesdays on which the staff work one-on-one with customers, teaching them computer skills and assisting with specific projects. According to the library,

> This cooperative program with the Department of Health and Social Services brought computers to our library, as well as much-needed training and support to job-seekers in navigating employment-related databases and assistance with resumes. Outreach presentations and demonstrations of library resources, Internet navigation, research techniques, troubleshooting, and more also followed.[6]

Evaluating Classes

It is just as important to evaluate training classes for the public as it is those for library staff, so be sure to get feedback from class participants through the use of surveys and evaluation forms. When creating training surveys and evaluation forms, consider these tips:

Be brief and to the point. Stick to asking questions that will help you assess the program and gain feedback for the future.

Make the majority of the questions close ended. This includes yes/no, scaled (i.e., on a scale of 1–5), and multiple-choice questions.

Always include a "thank you" at the end of the survey or evaluation.

Have the trainers encourage patrons to fill out the forms. Make sure trainers collect them at the end of class. If using an online survey, set aside a few minutes at the end of class for time to complete it.

Include a "for staff use only" section at the bottom of the form, allowing you to gather trainer information (i.e., who taught the class, their comments, etc.).

Compile statistics monthly and use feedback to keep your programming in line with patron needs and wants.

Sample survey question might include

Had you ever used _____ before today's class?   Yes __   No __

Did the presenter appear knowledgeable about the topic?   Yes __   No __

Was the instruction booklet helpful?   Mostly __   Partly __   Will be __   No __

Do you feel the level of the class was: Just right __   Too advanced __   Too basic __

What other computer classes would you like to see at _____ Public Library?

Your age? (optional)   12–19 __   20–29 __   30–49 __   50–69 __   70+ __

Additional comments or suggestions:

(See figure 8-1 for another example of a class survey.)

FIGURE 8-1
Computer Class Survey

St. Joseph County Public Library
Computer Class Survey

Name of Instructor: _____

Class Location: _____

Class Title (*please circle one*):

Beginning Internet   E-mail Basics

Advanced Internet   Seniors' Class   Other: _____

Was the instructor knowledgeable and responsive to questions?

Yes   No   Somewhat

Was the class what you thought it would be?   Yes   No

Comments: _____

How would you rate this class overall?   Excellent   Good   Fair   Poor

What would you like to see added as future computer classes or topics for classes? _____

_____

When is the best time for you to attend library programs? (*circle all that apply*)

Monday:	Morning	Afternoon	Evening
Tuesday:	Morning	Afternoon	Evening
Wednesday:	Morning	Afternoon	Evening
Thursday:	Morning	Afternoon	Evening
Friday:	Morning	Afternoon	
Saturday:	Morning	Afternoon	

Thank you for taking the time to fill out this evaluation!

Please return to any SJCPL public service desk.

Training Facilities

In an ideal world, every library would have its own computer training lab or computer center. Computer labs are not only wonderful for staff and public training; they also open up opportunities for quiet study, hosting regional library workshops and meetings, and one-on-one instruction when classes aren't in session. Such computer facilities should be designed to be multipurpose and flexible. To help offset costs and keep your lab fully utilized, consider "renting" out your space to local businesses and other organizations that need space to do training. You'd be surprised at the organizations in need of such spaces. This is also a great fund-raising opportunity that can offset your library's training expenses, and it is great public relations and a way to demonstrate the library's dedication to technology. The Nappanee (IN) Public Library currently has an arrangement with a nonprofit organization that provides instructors and laptop labs to conduct computer classes for both staff and the public in one of the three meeting room areas in the library. The Nappanee library also received a grant to purchase ten laptops that will remain on-site for classroom training and individual use in quiet study areas throughout the library via a wireless connection. The library plans to check out the laptop "lab" to other organizations in the community that want to train at their own location. So don't let your lab sit idle when classes aren't in session!

Successful training facilities can come in all shapes and sizes. The Guilderland (NY) Public Library has a very small, four-computer room that they close off for small group training, while the Bloomington (IL) Public Library has a dedicated sixteen-seat technology room for public and staff programs that is equipped with the latest software, hardware, smart board technology, and a high-end sound system. The Pierce (ID) Free Public Library's technology center enables residents to access computer technology, the Internet, and cost-effective computer courses. The center's computers are equipped with software for a number of uses, including typing a letter, resume writing, creating an invoice database, and designing flyers, business plan templates, and personal and business legal forms. All software loaded on the computers can be used at any time, and there is never a fee for their use.[8]

DO YOU KNOW IT?

Train your staff. Educate the staff about how to get the most from technology as well as how to effectively instruct patrons and provide good customer service.

Teach the public. Provide a variety of computer class levels and topics to the public.

Be creative with programming. Technology programming is one of the best ways to draw in users and non-users alike.

NOTES

1. See *Staying Connected* (Seattle, WA: Bill and Melinda Gates Foundation, 2002), 21; also available at http://www.gatesfoundation.org.

2. Scott Childers, "Computer Literacy: Necessity or Buzzword?" *Information Technology and Libraries* 22, no. 3 (September 2003): 100–104.

3. Michael K. Gaston, "Unlocking Potential Staff Development at Deschutes Public Library District," *OLA Quarterly* 5, no. 4 (Winter 2000); also available at http://www.olaweb.org/quarterly/quar5-4/gaston.shtml.

4. Eric Lease Morgan, "A Different Type of Distance Education," *Computers in Libraries* 19, no. 2 (February 1999): 35.

5. Computer class statistics from the Webster (NY) Public Library. For additional information, contact Kimberly Bolan (former assistant director of the library).

6. Contributions from the Wood County (OH) District Public Library and the Whitman County (WA) Public Library.

7. Enid Costley, "Creating Lesson Plans for Teaching the Public," WebJunction (March 1, 2004), http://webjunction.org/do/DisplayContent?id=1243.

8. For a list of computer class offerings and more information on the Pierce (ID) Free Public Library, visit http://www.lili.org/clearwater/Piercepl.html.

Regulate IT 9

Policy is about choice. Policies are conscious choices or decisions that guide actions and influence end results. Libraries typically establish policies to guide their service priorities (collection development, personnel, access and circulation). Such policies are the basis for procedures, are broadly stated, and provide official guidelines for actions and decisions that support the library's operations. Producing policies is a commitment, as it takes time and thought to develop useful and relevant documents, yet the process doesn't have to be a dreaded or painful experience. The exploration of policies can often lead to new insights about your library, your staff, and your patrons.

Policies provide a point of reference or direction for library personnel, allowing for better decisions and consistency in service. They also serve as a source of backup or support when there is a problem. Policies give staff the information to do their jobs effectively; support the plans, goals, and objectives of the library; and protect the rights and fair treatment of library staff and patrons. Policies are not meant to "rule" over patrons; rather, well-written and well-implemented policies provide a means for customers to know what to expect from the library. A good library technology policy should reflect the needs of the community, because policy decisions generally have the most impact on patrons. Policies also need to agree with local, state, and other relevant laws.

POLICIES, PROCEDURES, AND GUIDELINES

The focus of this chapter is on the basics of technology policies. Many of the tips and suggestions provided here apply not just to the use of technology but to all areas of the library and its services. Just as with technology itself, the key here is to understand the policy basics and where to go for additional information. A policy is different from a procedure or a guideline. *Policy* is "the generic term used for a policy statement and the potential regulations, procedures, and guidelines that apply to it."[1] A *procedure* is a written, step-by-step description of how staff will carry out a policy, and a *guideline* is a description of best practices that offers suggestions for staff on implementing policies and procedures (although guidelines also refer to steps for patrons to follow). (For more in-depth information on this topic, refer to *Creating Policies for Results* by Sandra Nelson and June Garcia.) The idea for the small or medium library here is to have a strong understanding of the technology your library is implementing and to recognize what policies are needed to equip your library with the appropriate guidance to successfully put the technology into practice.

General Policy Guidelines

The goal for the small or medium-sized library is to efficiently create well-thought-out, solid policy documents that can be easily followed and understood by both staff and patrons. To begin this process, you will need to address

> the implications of new technologies on existing policies and laws
>
> the need for revision of library policies or for the creation of new, independent policies

Questions to consider include the following: Are the library's technology projects and implementations in compliance with existing library policies? Do existing policies need to be modified as a result of new technology implementations and practices? Can an existing library policy be modified to include information on new technology (e.g., adding electronic resources procedures and guidelines to an existing collection development policy), or will a new policy need to be developed that is specifically focused on the technology issue at hand (e.g., an Internet use policy)? Are there any other outside local, state, or federal policies or laws that come into play during this process?

Having a grasp on existing technology-related policies and practices is important, since you can't move forward if you don't know where you're starting from. The assessment of such policies should have been started during the assessment phase. CompuMentor's "Policies Checklist" (see figure 9-1) is a useful tool to get you started. Of course, it can be adapted as your library sees fit.

Although not every small or medium-sized library's list of policies is identical, the overall guidelines are very much the same. Whether starting from scratch or revising existing policies, keep the following in mind.

> *Work in a team.* Form a committee or team consisting of board members, the library director, technology team member(s), and patron representatives, with the specific responsibility to develop policies in a particular area or areas. As with the technology planning process, technology-related policies have implications for the entire library, so it is important to actively involve and consult the technology team members (and other key staff) throughout the policy process.

FIGURE 9-1

CompuMentor's Policies Checklist

POLICY AREA	APPLICABLE	IN USE	WRITTEN
Statement of technology skills required for each position	Yes / No		
Information access, usage, and distribution (data privacy)	Yes / No		
File sharing and organization	Yes / No		
E-mail and Internet usage policy	Yes / No		
Password security policies	Yes / No		
Licensing and copying software	Yes / No		
Remote access policy	Yes / No		
Lab usage guidelines	Yes / No		
Document (file) retention	Yes / No		
Treatment of laptops and other mobile technology	Yes / No		
Personal use of organizational computer resources	Yes / No		
Volunteer access to computers and network	Yes / No		
Public or client accesss to computers and network	Yes / No		
Other (please provide details):			

Keep it simple. Even though policies are designed to be a variety of things, it doesn't mean they have to be long and wordy to be of high quality. The small or medium library does not have time for long-winded legalese. Besides, the longer and more complex your policies are, the less likely your patrons are to read them and follow them. Policies should be succinct and easy to understand.

Think carefully. Consider the statements presented in your library's policies and how they will be perceived by patrons and community members. Keep in mind that a policy can be a public relations tool as well as a means of guidance and protection. More specifically, when policies are seen as too restrictive or authoritarian, patrons may develop negative feelings about the library.

Research. Find out what others are doing. Survey other libraries within and outside your state. Gather sample policies, examine them, and adapt their content to your library's own needs and requirements.

Review and approve. Have staff and legal counsel review policies and then get them approved by your board.

Don't forget about implementation. Integrate policies into your library's daily procedures, bringing staff up to speed. Work with the staff and gain their support. After all, they are the people who are expected to enforce and follow the policies.

Revise as needed. Refer to the section on reviewing and updating policies later in this chapter.

Create a manual. Record all policies in a handbook or manual and make it readily available. Two copies are ideal: one for the office and one for behind a service desk. If you have an intranet, make an electronic version available there as well.

Core Policies

The following information relates to those technology-related policies that are central to most small and medium libraries. For examples of best practices in policy development, and for a wide range of sample policies and additional policy development resources, refer to the section for this chapter in appendix B as well as to several of the model libraries listed in appendix C, including the Westlake Porter (OH) Public Library and St. Joseph County (IN) Public Library.

Computer Use Policy and Guidelines

Any library with computers should have a computer use policy and guidelines—a document that outlines the acceptable use of a library's computer hardware, software, network, Internet access, copiers, and printers. This policy comes in many shapes and forms and is often called a computer use policy or an acceptable use policy (a policy that a user must agree to follow in order have access to library technology resources and information). Though some libraries will have other names for this policy, the key here is not in the name, but in the content. A strong policy will allow your library to offer the highest level of service to its patrons as well as help your staff best manage computer and related resources. The questions to consider when developing this policy include, Are you restricting use of applications? Will you block computer usage due to fines? Will there be time limits on public computer use? If so, how will you monitor time limits? Will there be a sign-up procedure for computer use? If so, how will that be handled? Additional topics commonly addressed in a computer use policy include

Internet use

e-mail and chat

storage devices (floppy disks, CDs, zip and USB drives)

downloading

individual versus group use

printer and printing issues

copier and copying issues

wireless access

laptop use (if applicable)

headphone use

Once the overall content and scope of the document have been determined, the structure of a computer use policy should include

a disclaimer

confidentiality

rights and responsibilities of the users

general rules of use and conduct, or usage guidelines (what will
and won't be allowed, parental permission, etc.)

sign-up and time limit guidelines (if applicable)

Again, keep in mind that policies are not meant to rule over patrons. For example, when it comes to computer and Internet use, think about the consequences of limiting patrons to a very narrow window of time per day. How will this affect abusers? Legitimate users? What is the benefit to the library if computers sit empty without any patrons using them? What is the impact of customers leaving unhappy? It is also common for computer use policies to include references to other library policies and related resources, including a code of conduct/behavior, an Internet use policy (if this is a separate policy), and so on. See the Westlake Porter (OH) Public Library's website for a wealth of policy examples, including its "Public Internet Access and Computer Use Policy."

Internet Policy and Guidelines

Closely tied and often presented in one policy are computer use and Internet use. Some libraries have a computer use *or* an Internet use policy, while others combine the two and still others create two separate policies. No matter how it is handled, when tackling an Internet policy, besides many of the issues mentioned previously under computer use, the policy should consider topics related to choosing and evaluating sources, access by minors, users' security and confidentiality, filtering, and copyright. Some believe an Internet access policy shouldn't be any different from a policy on access to other types of library materials and that in fact a separate Internet policy is unnecessary. The Internet trainer Michael Sauers thinks that a well-written behavior policy will encompass most of what needs to be addressed when it comes to the Internet:

> In many libraries today, policies regarding Internet access by patrons have been over-analyzed and over-thought. The result of this has been to turn library staff into a police force, reducing the time available to perform many other important tasks. In these cases the computer is being treated differently than other library resources. By removing the computer from the equation, most libraries will realize that they already have a policy on library behavior that can be applied to computer and Internet access-related problems. This policy method removes the need for library staff to be police and gives that staff additional flexibility to deal with problems as they arise.[2]

For many small and medium-sized libraries, this may be the answer. However, every library must judge for itself what strategy will best help meet its mission and vision.

Wi-Fi

Again, most likely, your library will address this issue in its computer use policy, but Wi-Fi is sometimes set aside as a completely separate policy. The contents should include a general introduction, technical requirements, and a disclaimer. When discussing Wi-Fi technical requirements, it's important that the instructions or guidelines be accurate but not too detailed. According to Sauers,

> Since there are any number of combinations of devices (laptops, PDAs, cell phones) and operating systems (Windows Me/XP/2000, Mac, PalmOS) with which a patron might

TECH TIP

DISASTER PLANNING

All libraries small or large should have a policy related to disaster planning. This is one area that is often overlooked, especially in smaller facilities. For more information on disaster plans and policy, see chapter 4 and the resources in appendix B.

want to use your connection, you do not want to include detailed instructions. You may, however, wish to create these instructions as separate handouts, but they do not belong as part of your library's policy.

Sauers also recommends addressing limitations in the service as well as security issues:

> Since the layout and the materials used in the construction of your building will have an effect on the ability of a patron to connect (and more importantly the number of hotspots you placed within your building), you should make a point to mention that not every location in the building may have access at any particular time. Next, your policy should mention security issues. Public WiFi access is not secure—it isn't designed to be. Unfortunately, not all WiFi users realize this. Therefore you should explicitly mention this. Lastly, as with data-related disclaimers in standard Internet access policies, you will want to disavow responsibility for patron data, and in these cases, patron hardware.[3]

Refer to the Arapahoe (CO) Library District, Mount Prospect (IL) Public Library, McMillan (WI) Memorial Library, and Kalamazoo (MI) Public Library for specific examples of Wi-Fi policies (see appendixes B and C for these libraries' websites and additional information).

Computer Security Policy

Most small library facilities do not have a computer security policy. In actuality, much of this information can be covered in a general computer use policy, but a medium-sized facility may want to consider developing a separate security policy, because having more staff and more users can open up more potential issues. Overall, a computer security policy should include information related to Internet access and also consider theft, damage, viruses, and vandalism. It should state what hardware and software the library should protect, how it should be protected, how to respond to security threats, and who should be involved in that response.

Computer Lab or Computer Center and Multimedia Room Use

Most likely, issues related to computer labs and centers and multimedia rooms will be included in your library's meeting room, computer use, or Internet use policies. Whatever direction you head in, be sure that one of your policies addresses all or most of these issues:

> hours and availability
> closing procedures
> intended audience (including access rules for those under eighteen)
> age validation (library card or a valid ID)
> group and individual use (e.g., maximum number of people
>> per workstation, maximum number of people in the room)

time limits (if any)

printing guidelines

disciplinary actions related to violation of policy

Be sure to also think about procedural questions such as, Will we need someone in our computer lab at all times? Can a volunteer fulfill our computer staffing needs? For an example of a computer lab policy, see the Peoria (AZ) Public Library website. (See the resource libraries in appendix C and this book's website, http://www.ala.org/editions/extras/Bolan09205/.)

Other Policies

Miscellaneous library equipment and its use (whether in-house or circulating) may also come into play during policy consideration and development. Items may include MP3 players, e-book readers, games equipment, and fax machines, just to name a few. Generally, the policy relating to such equipment will appear as part of a broader policy, such as a borrowing policy or a public use of library equipment policy. Some libraries, however, choose to have separate policies for such equipment, including faxing policies. On a different note, but still related to technology, is the use of cell phones in libraries. Although this is more a behavior or conduct policy issue, there may also be information technology implications. Other general policies that might come into play when it comes to technology include collection development, procurement, fixed asset disposal (i.e., getting rid of furniture and equipment that is no longer functional or useful), personnel, and disaster recovery.

Sometimes forgotten is the issue of staff policies as they relate to equipment, Internet use, security, and e-mail. Just keep in mind that although guidelines provide equal treatment and protection for staff, policies that are too restrictive or authoritarian will impact morale and job satisfaction.

Review and Update

No policy can be considered cast in stone. Once it is written, a periodic (yearly, at a minimum) review and update is necessary. Though you may be content with your existing policies and no issues may arise, rapidly changing technological and legal environments demand that your technology policies be living documents, adapting with change. Technology, situations, and needs will transform over time and will influence policy.

MAKE PEOPLE AWARE

Because policies are intended to be a point of reference for patrons, it is important that they be made readily available for the public's information. If people can't read or find the rules, it is hard to expect them to know or follow them. The creation of a policy handbook or manual is one way to make policies available. Whether in print or electronic format, the manual should be easy to use, up-to-date, and consistent. Many libraries, including the Salem–South Lyon District (MI) Library and the St. Joseph County (IN) Public Library, provide policy manuals on their website for easy access by patrons. (See appendix C for more information on these and other model libraries.) If your library has its policies on the website, be sure that they can easily be found. You should post critical policies and guidelines such as those on computer use near computer workstations or key service areas as appropriate. Make signage attractive. If you want people to read a policy, you have to be creative. Consider making the information into an eye-catching screen saver on public computers. Policy awareness is also about making your staff familiar with policies and their content. By educating the staff, you are better educating your public. This also helps avoid issues that may arise from misunderstanding policies.

User Guidelines

Even the best-written policies sometimes need a little user-friendly assistance in the form of user guidelines or tip sheets. Guidelines help fill in the blanks between what is allowed and acceptable and how to actually use the library's resources. The relationship between policies and guidelines is important because you want to "guide" users in a direction that leads to policy compliance. Ideas for sample user guides or instruction sheets include

> using the public catalog
>
> reserving a PC
>
> wireless access and computer setup
>
> finding programs on the library web calendar and signing up online
>
> booking a meeting room online
>
> using laptops in the library

DO YOU KNOW IT?

Understand the true meaning. Policies are not meant to "rule" over patrons. Instead they should clearly explain the expectations of the library for patrons and staff.

Don't get carried away. Policies cover many areas, so decide what mix and coverage of policies are right for your library and then work to craft only those relevant policies.

Keep policies simple. The main goal is to create thoughtful and succinct policy documents that can be easily followed and understood by both patrons and staff.

Create basic staff policies. Communicating clear expectations to staff can be as important as setting policies for the public.

Review polices on a regular *basis.* Frequently review and revise your policies with public and staff input.

Advertise your policies. Make your policies public and "market" them via signage, your website, and handouts.

NOTES

1. Sandra Nelson and June Garcia, *Creating Policies for Results* (Chicago: American Library Association, 2003).
2. Michael Sauers, "Don't Doesn't Work," WebJunction (August 20, 2004), http://webjunction.org/do/DisplayContent?id=7202.
3. Michael Sauers, "A Library Policy for Public Wireless Internet Access," WebJunction (July 1, 2005), http://webjunction.org/do/DisplayContent?id=11033.

Evaluate IT 10

No matter how good your assessment, your plan, your implementation, and your training, if you're not getting *results* from technology, it doesn't matter. How do you know technology is "working" in your library? Are you getting the results you expected when you planned the project? How do you know that you are delivering what best meets your users' needs and the library's needs? Is what was once a great and needed solution still meeting the library's needs and vision? The answers to all of these questions can only be determined one way . . . evaluate it . . . again and again and again. In this context, *evaluation* means examining the performance of technology and related programs and services in your library. The evaluative process exists to assist you in making decisions about what is working and what needs improvement. Evaluation is also critical in helping your library "tell its story" so you can increase support and position your library as a necessary and valuable part of the community.

Evaluation is an ongoing process, like everything else covered in this book. It is one continuous loop that never really ends; it just continues to evolve and move forward—assess, plan, implement, evaluate. This is the cycle to commit to for the long-term success of the library. Evaluation is typically the weakest component, however, because it has the least follow-through. People are often discouraged or dissuaded by the simple mention of the word *evaluation*. This generally results in libraries gathering the bare minimum of statistics and quantitative information necessary for state and local reporting. The key is to know what to gather and how to effectively collect and present the resulting information. Without such data all you really have is a gut feeling of how you are doing; unfortunately, gut feelings are generally not enough to influence decision-makers and funding sources.

By establishing clear goals and objectives and by incorporating evaluation methods into the technology plan (see chapter 4), you will be able to successfully evaluate the results, performance, and impact of technology. Ask yourself these questions: Have goals been fulfilled? Are the staff happy? Are the patrons happy? Is additional training (staff or public) needed? Were there any unanticipated costs (hardware, software, training, other)? Were there any places where money was saved? As discussed in chapter 4, your goals and action steps must be able to be quantified and qualified. The challenge here is to create realistic mechanisms for the evaluation of technology's impact on your library. In order to do this you will need to take the following steps:

1. Identify data collection methods and tools.
2. Establish how the data and information will be collected (procedures, etc.).
3. Collect the data.
4. Examine the results.
5. Compile and report the results.

The ideal approach is to start this process during the assessment phase as outlined in chapter 2. By incorporating these steps during the early stages, you will already have done much of the work when you begin evaluating the impact of what you have implemented. And by collecting similar statistics from before and after your implementation, you will have a much clearer view of technology's *impact* on the library. A lack of statistics and data about technology and its effects can make it extremely difficult to draw conclusions, gain support, and move forward.

WHAT TO EVALUATE

Begin the process by deciding *what* it is you need to evaluate. First of all, you will want to assess your technology plan. This includes the planning process itself as well as the plan's results. Look at the overall successes and failures of the plan. Did you keep to time frames? Is the technology doing what it is supposed to do? Is it following what was laid out in the technology plan? Was the money well spent? What was the outcome of the technology projects that stemmed from the plan? Were there implementation issues? Did the vendors deliver what was promised? Was work done on time and at the prices they quoted? How well are services and policies being implemented? Technology team members should be playing a role throughout this process. There should also be some type of evaluation of the team's own effectiveness, as well as the effectiveness of the overall technology planning process.

Two key areas to concentrate on during evaluation are

Specific technologies. Evaluate the performance and impact of specific equipment and resources. Is the technology making a difference to its users (public and staff)? What effect is it having on library statistics—overall use, computer use, and so on?

Technology services. What impact is the service having on the community? This includes public training, programs, and user support services. Include in-house support and troubleshooting services for employees, as well as training and staff development.

No matter what you are evaluating, look at what is necessary for improvement to occur. What lessons have you learned? What specific factors contributed to successes and failures? What impeded or facilitated progress and results?

TOOLS AND METHODS

The next step in the process is to figure out how you will go about evaluating each of the areas significant to your library. Many of the assessment tools discussed in chapter 2 may be used to continuously measure progress, uncovering areas that have excelled and those in need of improvement. Most of the tools and processes established during your first assessment will make any future evaluations that much faster and easier. Continued evaluation will tell you exactly have far you've come and how far you have to go.

Evaluation data can be quantitative (i.e., statistical information coming from surveys, counts, etc.) or qualitative (i.e., descriptive rather than numerical information, such as inspirational anecdotes, personal interviews, patron and staff comments, general observations, focus groups comments, etc.). Many evaluations will make use of both types of data. In order to decide what kind of evaluative information you need for each area, ask yourself, What data are necessary in order to assess where we are? What level of detail is necessary? Let's review some of the basic mechanisms for getting data:

Traditional library statistics. These include circulation, door counts, reference stats, program attendance, and so on. These statistics are important, but you should not focus exclusively on them.

Non-traditional statistics. These include computer usage, catalog searches, website hits, Wi-Fi connections, and so on. You may not have the historical data for these measurements, but capturing them is important as you move forward.

Surveys results from patrons and staff. This information is crucial for finding out the "whys" behind the data. Question: Why have internal holds and circulation counts dropped? Answer: Because the holds system on the library's new ILS is too difficult to use.

General comments from patrons and staff. These include suggestion box comments, online suggestions, personal observations, and discussions with patrons. Again, these are all useful for finding out the "whys" and assessing the needs and wants of your users. Patricia Uttaro, director of the Ogden (NY) Farmers' Library, suggests spending time out on the floor of the library, watching people and talking to them.

Comments from non-users or future patrons. Do you ask the people you currently don't serve questions about how they view the library and technology? Why don't they come in to the library? What technology and related services can you offer that might entice them to come? What does the library need to do better?

Library comparisons. Those libraries you compare with your own library are hopefully improving too, so be sure to update your comparison data.

Staff evaluations. How have new initiatives impacted the staff? Have their competencies improved? Are staff fully utilizing new technology to maximize productivity and customer service? What are staff members' thoughts and impressions about technology-related problems and issues? Whether through formal performance appraisals, informal discussions, self-assessment, or a combination of these, make sure you keep abreast of how staff members are performing and how technology is performing for them.

Quantifying Impact

Keep in mind that it is not enough simply to list vague, unsubstantiated benefits that your library provides. Try to find undeniable and tangible ways to quantify this impact. WebJunction offers a wealth of tools and links that can help libraries effectively use statistics, outcome-based evaluations, and even anecdotal evidence to substantiate the impact of the library on the community. For example: How many people did your staff teach to use the Internet effectively? How many patrons successfully learned how to create a resume and then found employment as a result? How many new patrons did the library attract because of technology rather than traditional library materials (books and magazines)? How many of your patrons use the public computers? Did patrons come in to use the Wi-Fi connection, only to check out a book they had always meant to read but never thought to get at the library? These types of results and outcomes are what will have the greatest long-term impact on how stakeholders and the community as a whole view your library and its inherent value.

WHERE DO YOU GO FROM HERE?

This book has covered a great deal of information about how technology affects libraries. The key concepts of keeping it simple, picking the low-hanging fruit, being persistent, and continually evaluating, planning, implementing, and evaluating are important not only to technology but to any service area in your library. If you can keep these basic principles in mind, you will be able to achieve success in almost any situation. Challenges will occur, but rising to challenges is one of those intangible things that makes life interesting.

Whatever confronts your library in the future, you can find a way to make it work. It isn't always about having perfect answers; it is about trying to perfect the answers you have. Moving forward means never saying, "We've always done it this way" or "We don't have the time or the money." Moving forward means constantly asking yourself, What can we do better? What can we do that we aren't doing now? This thinking is what will move your library into the future; it will save libraries of all sizes from irrelevance or, even worse, extinction. Do not be afraid. Opportunities for greatness are out there. Just look at so many of the model libraries mentioned in this book. Libraries have been an integral part of human history almost since writing began. If libraries are willing to adapt and embrace the changes that society, culture, and technology inevitably bring, they will stay vital for the foreseeable future.

Worksheets A

Hardware Inventory Worksheet

Item / Description	General Category	Date of Purchase or Age	Type of Use	Under Warranty	Support Contract Current	Obsolescence Rating	Upgradable (Y/N)	Serial Number	Approx. Cost	Other Notes

Possible Inventory General Categories

Workstation
Server
Network Infrastructure
Printers
Misc.
A/V Equipment
Utility (Telephone)
Archival Access (Microfilm)
Graphics and Publishing (Scanner, Specialty Printers)

Type of Use

P Public
S Staff
M Mixed
I Infrastructure
C Catalog Only

Obsolescence Rating

1 Current
2 Acceptable
3 Near Obsolete
4 Obsolete

Software Inventory Worksheet

Application / Description	General Category	Number of Licenses	Date of Purchase or Age	Type of Use	Under Warranty	Support Contract Current	Obsolescence Rating	Upgradable (Y/N)	Approx. Cost	Other Notes

Type of Use

P	Public
S	Staff
M	Mixed
I	Infrastructure
C	Catalog Only

Obsolescence Rating

1	Current
2	Acceptable
3	Near Obsolete
4	Obsolete

Possible Inventory General Categories

Server OS
Workstation OS
Office Applications
Other Productivity
Graphics and Publishing
Back Office (Mail, Web, database)
Accounting
Catalog / Circulation
Misc.

Hardware and Software Assessment/Analysis Worksheet

Network Infrastructure and Servers *Assessment*

Servers

Current number of servers
Number of servers per function

File Sharing	
Web Serving	
E-mail	
Software Services	
Network Services	
Circulation	
Other	

Network

Number of Internet lines installed

T1/Frame Relay	
DSL/ISDN/Cable	

Estimated bandwidth percentage used
Is firewall installed and current (purchased within last 24 months)?
Current number of routers
Current number of switches/hubs

10MB	
100MB or higher	

Current number of available ports

10MB	
100MB or higher	

Current number of hardwired ports
Current number of unused hardwired ports
Are all areas where computers may be desired covered by hardwired ports?
Are all of these locations covered by electric power outlets?
Does the entire library have Wi-Fi coverage?
Are there spots with no coverage where coverage may be desirable?
Does your current Wi-Fi equipment support both B and G communication standards?
Do patrons have ample power outlets to plug in their laptops at the most popular hotspots?

Backups

Is backup system utilized and run nightly?
Is off-site storage used for backups?

Monthly	
Daily	

Are all mission-critical systems protected with power backup?

Network Infrastructure and Servers *Analysis*

Servers

Are the current servers adequate to meet the library's needs?
How many servers may need to be added for any of the following functions?

File Sharing	
Web Serving	
E-mail	
Software Services	
Network Services	
Circulation	
Other	

Network

Based on bandwidth usage, is the current Internet connection adequate?
Estimate what level of bandwidth is needed to meet library's peak demands.
What areas of the library's network infrastructure need updating or replacement?

Firewalls	
Routers	
Switches/Hubs	

How many switch/hub ports need to be added to meet the library's needs?

Now	
In 2 years	

How many hardwired drops need to be added to meet the library's needs?

Now	
In 2 years	

How many electrical outlets need to be added to meet the library's needs?

Now	
In 2 years	

How many Wi-Fi nodes need to be added to meet the library's needs?

Now	
In 2 years	

Does the current Wi-Fi equipment need to be upgraded to meet new standards?

Backups

Does the backup system need to be upgraded?
Should off-site storage be implemented?

Monthly	
Daily	

Should power backups be upgraded or expanded to cover additional equipment?
How many power backups are required to cover all critical equipment?

Hardware and Software Assessment/Analysis Worksheet (Cont.)

Public

Workstations *Assessment*
Current number of workstations allocated to patron use

PCs (Windows)	
PCs (Linux)	
Macs	
Laptops (any OS)	

Percentage of day that PC usage is at or near capacity
Current number of special needs computers and equipment (Zoomtext, Braille keyboards, readers)
Current number of specialty work spaces (i.e., listening/viewing stations, literacy kiosks, etc.)

Public

Workstations *Analysis*
Based on capacity sampling, should additional computers be added?

PCs (Windows)	
PCs (Linux)	
Macs	
Laptops (any OS)	

Is the number of special needs computers and equipment adequate?
Is the number of specialty work spaces adequate?

Public

Printers and Copiers *Assessment*
Number of public printers — B & W / Color

Average number of pages printed per month — B & W / Color

Average monthly duty cycle of public printers — B & W / Color

Copiers

Number of public copiers — B & W / Color

Average number of copies per month — B & W / Color

Average monthly duty cycle of public copiers — B & W / Color

Fees

Per-page charge for public printers (if any) — B & W / Color

How are fees handled: honor system, pay to retrieve printouts, print management system?
Total monthly fees collected from public printing and copying
Total monthly spending on printing/copying supplies for public (toner, ink, paper, maintenance, etc.)
 (If supply spending is not broken out public vs. staff, then estimate, using usage statistics if possible.)
If automated, what payment methods are accepted? — Coin Box / Printer/Copier Card / Integrated to ILS User Account

Printers and Copiers *Analysis*
Are any printers exceeding their monthly duty cycle rating?
How many printers should be added to keep printing levels below
 per-printer duty cycles? — B & W / Color
Are any copiers exceeding the monthly duty cycle rating?
How many printers should be added to keep printing levels below
 per-printer duty cycles? — B & W / Color
Are printing and copying fees in line with other areas' libraries and service providers?
Based on customer feedback, is the current printing "process" easy to understand?
Based on customer feedback, is the current print/copy system viewed as fair?
Are collected fees fully covering the library's printing costs?
If no fees are collected or the honor system is used, would a print management system
 pay for itself?
If an automated print system is already in place, should fees be adjusted
 based on cost vs. income?

Hardware and Software Assessment/Analysis Worksheet (Cont.)

Software *Assessment*

Servers

Number of servers running obsolete or near-obsolete operating systems

Number of servers with no or obsolete "antivirus" or "pest control" software

Is current e-mail system adequate for the library's needs?

Does the current e-mail system offer SPAM-blocking options?

Does the library host its own website?

Is it fully protected, patched, and updated?

Are the web development tools easy to use?

Is more than one staff member trained to use the web development tools?

Is content filtering being provided and is it CIPA compliant?

If no, are content filters available for the current system?

If yes, are the content filters frequently updated and adjustable?

Can filters be disabled?

For Staff

For Adult Patrons

Workstations

Number of workstations running obsolete or near-obsolete operating systems

Number of workstations with no "office" software (word processing, spreadsheets, etc.)

Number of workstations with no or obsolete "antivirus" or "pest control" software

Current number of reference databases available

(List, with subscription costs, basic content descriptions, usage statistics, etc., on a separate table/sheet)

Software *Analysis*

Note: Much of this can be listed in a separate table or added to your hardware inventory worksheets.

Servers

What servers need software upgrades to eliminate obsolescence for the next 2 years?

What servers need "antivirus" and "pest control" software installation or upgrades?

Should the e-mail system be expanded, upgraded, or replaced?

Should the library continue with its current web hosting direction?

If the library will start or continue hosting its website, what upgrades are needed?
(web server, Internet connection, security/firewall/anti-pest, development tools, etc.)

Should content filters be installed or upgraded?

Should options for filter disabling be added or removed?

For Staff

For Adult Patrons

Workstations

What workstations need software upgrades to eliminate obsolescence for the next year?

What workstations need "antivirus" and "pest control" software installation or upgrades?

Add to database tables your analysis of cost per use and compare per database.

Do any databases have a per-use cost that is far out of line with others?

Are there databases that seem to have overlap in coverage?

Are there reference areas that seem to lack coverage?

Hardware and Software Assessment/Analysis Worksheet (Cont.)

Phone

Miscellaneous Systems *Assessment*
Does the library have any electronic public displays or kiosks?
Is there an automated phone system in place?
Is the system managed by staff or an outside service?
Does the system have voice mail?
How many patrons call but fail to reach a staff member?
  (Ask your phone service provider for a busy line study to determine phone line usage.)

Circulation

Is there an automated circulation and catalog system?
Current number of public access catalog stations
Current number of self-check stations
Do staff service areas other than circulation assist patrons with checkout?
Are reference staff constantly having to manually type in bar codes?
Does the circulation system have Internet options for   Patron Renewals
                                                                Overdue Notices
                                                                Holds/Reserves
Does the circulation system have telephony solutions for   Patron Renewals
                                                                Overdue Notices
                                                                Holds/Reserves

Phone

Miscellaneous Systems *Analysis*
Would a public kiosk or digital display be beneficial to the library?
Does the phone system adequately handle current needs?
Does the busy line study indicate a need for additional phone lines?
If the library doesn't have voice mail, would adding this option add convience for staff and patrons?

Circulation

Does the current automation system meet the library's needs?
If not, what are the options that exist?
  (new system, join a regional consortium, other)

Are there options on your current catalog/circulation system that aren't implemented that may
  add to your service options or reduce staff workload?

Are telephony solutions likely to be used by your patron base? Particularly with Internet options available?

Patrons, Services, and Policy Assessment/Analysis Worksheet

Patron Overview *Assessment*

Overall population—How many people in your community?

Juvenile (6th grade and under)	
Teens (7th grade–12th grade)	
Adults	
Seniors	

Library's overall population growth over last 5 years

Projected overall population growth over next 5 years (see govt. entities or Chamber of Comm.)

Number of cardholders

Percentage growth of cardholders in last 5 years

Number of daily visitors

Percentage growth of daily visitors in last 5 years

Are library income/budget projections available for the next 5 years?

Current-year reference question counts

Percentage growth of reference question counts in last 5 years

Average yearly increase in reference counts

Library circulation

Percentage growth of circulation over last 5 years

What percentage of daily library users typically have a library card?

What is the age group breakdown of those using technology within the library? (percentage)

Juvenile (6th grade and under)	
Teens (7th grade–12th grade)	
Adults	
Seniors	

What is the typical computer literacy level of patrons per broad-based group?

Rate: 1: No Knowledge, 2: Some Knowledge,
3: Good Knowledge, 4: Technically Savvy

Juvenile	
Teens	
Adults	
Seniors	

Average number of daily programs

Average number of program attendees daily

Average number of meetings by outside groups at the library daily

Average number of outside group meeting attendees

Average yearly reading and book club participants

Stats for the New Century (You may or may not have access to these types of stats.)

Website hits

Which pages are the most frequently visited?

  List:

Average number of online catalog searches (from outside the library if possible)

Average Internet users per day

Average Wi-Fi users per day (if Wi-Fi is in use)

Daily circulation of technology items (i.e., laptops, iPods, A/V equipment)

Average reference counts for technology-specific questions

Average daily technology-related programs (or programs that significantly use technology)

Average daily attendance of technology-related programs

Patrons, Services, and Policy Assessment/Analysis Worksheet (Cont.)

Patron Overview *Analysis*

Compare your population data with your current budget priorities. Are there areas of disconnect?

What future growth trends will the library need to address?

If income/budget projections are available, does it appear that budget growth is going to keep
up with service increases mandated by population growth?

If not, what are the most likely areas of library services where growth can be limited to keep core
services in line with the library's priorities?

What are likely to be the changes brought on by the changing technology literacy of the
patron base?

Will the future call for more or less technology training (e.g., more older patrons want training while
younger patrons are highly computer-savvy and will need less training)?

How can future library programming be shifted to take into account shifting patron needs?

What areas of the library that use manual processes should be considered for more automated solutions
(e.g., program planning and online registration, meeting room booking,
reading programs, media and electonic booking)?

Is the overall design of the library website adequate to serve the patrons?

What do some of the average-use statistics tell you about how patrons are using the library?

What areas of the library besides books seem to be the most popular and highly used?

Policies and Procedures *Assessment*

Is there an Internet policy in place?
Is there a general computer use policy in place?
Are policies and guidelines posted for patrons to see?
Does the library have a procedure for out-of-town/visiting patrons or those without cards?
Is the library complying with the Children's Internet Protection Act (CIPA) and other regulations?
Does the library have a disaster recovery plan?

Policies and Procedures *Analysis*

Are the current Internet and computer-use policies adequate and in line with regional standards?

Are policies and procedures in line with typical policies/procedures from around the country?

If CIPA regulations are not being met, would adherence to them be a "positive" for the library?
For how the library is perceived by the community or in relation to funding?

If a disaster recovery plan is not in place, is a plan being developed to put into place?

Patrons, Services, and Policy Assessment/Analysis Worksheet (Cont.)

Services and Programs *Assessment*

Public Computers

Are computer access services beyond online catalogs offered to the public?
  List: (examples may include Internet, e-mail, other software, databases, etc.)
Does the library require computer users, etc., to have a library card?
Do patrons typically have to wait for access to public PCs at peak times?
Does the library offer sign-up for public PC time?
If yes, is the reservation system available online from outside the library?

Wi-Fi

Does the library use wireless networking (Wi-Fi)?   Internal Only
                                                                                 Public

Is Wi-Fi open to the public or does it require validation (library card, key at reference desk, etc.)?
Does the Wi-Fi coverage extend beyond the walls of the library?

Technology Training (Formal and Informal)

Is brief individual technology instruction available for patrons from on-duty staff?
Are training programs offered to patrons on Internet use?
  List:

Are training programs offered on the online catalog and related items?
  List:

Are other technology-related classes offered to the public?
  List:

Are programs and services in place for bibliographic instruction?   In Person
  List: Via the Library's Website

Are there any remote conferencing options for training available in your area (i.e., local colleges)?

Circulation

Does the library provide a method for placing materials requests, holds, interlibrary loans online?
Does the library give e-mail notification of fines, reserves/holds, programs, room reservations, etc.?
Does the library circulate technology-related collections?
If yes, how many items are "circulated" per week?

                                                                                Software
                                                                                Hardware
                        Audiovisual Materials (DVDs, computer games, music, etc.)
                                        Virtual or "e" Collections (i.e., e-books)
                                                                                   Other

Is virtual or electronic reference offered?
If so, how many reference questions per week?

                                                                            Via E-mail
                                                                             Via Chat
                                                        Via Third-Party Software

Does the library have adaptive technologies for special needs patrons?
If so, typically how many patrons per day require special needs technologies?
List technologies available:

Does the library offer online program calendars and information?
Does the library allow patrons to register online for programs?
Does the library provide online access to meeting room availability?
Does the library allow meeting room use requests to be submitted online?
Does the library offer online services for reading programs or book clubs?

Other:

152

Patrons, Services, and Policy Assessment/Analysis Worksheet (Cont.)

Public Computers	**Services and Programs** *Analysis* What additions and/or changes need to be made in the public computer area to improve service?
Wi-Fi	What additions and/or changes need to be made to Wi-Fi options to improve service?
Technology Training (Formal and Informal)	What additions and/or changes need to be made to technology training services?
Circulation	What additions and/or changes need to be made to circulation services?
	What additions and/or changes need to be made to online/virtual reference services to meet patron needs? What additions and/or changes need to be made to special needs technology services to meet patron needs? What other technology or services should be added to improve services and help better automate staff processes?

Facility Assessment/Analysis Worksheet

Public Workstations Space *Assessment*

Workstations

Current number of public workstations (see Hardware and Software Worksheets)
Space that would typically be allocated to public workstations (65 sq ft per*)   square feet
Current space allocated to public workstations   square feet
Difference in actual versus standard and typical   square feet
Percentage of day that PC usage is at or near capacity

PACs

Current number of public catalog only stations
Space that would typically be allocated to catalog stations (35 sq ft per*)   square feet
Current space allocated to public catalog only stations   square feet
Difference in actual versus standard and typical   square feet
Percentage of day that PC usage is at or near capacity

Printers

Current number of public printers
Space that would typically be allocated to public printers (50 sq ft per*)   square feet
Current space allocated to public printers   square feet
Difference in actual versus standard and typical   square feet
Percentage of day that printer usage is at or near capacity

Copiers

Current number of public copier stations
Space that would typically be allocated to public copiers (50 sq ft per*)   square feet
Current space allocated to public copier stations   square feet
Difference in actual versus standard and typical   square feet
Percentage of day that public copier usage is at or near capacity

Collection

Current amount of space allocated to technology-related collections   Total square feet
Books—square feet
Magazines—square feet
Technology items (e.g., laptops)—square feet

Other:

Public Workstations Space *Analysis*

Does the space assessment indicate problem areas where the library's space allocations are disportionate to standards?

Can reallocation of space help address these problem areas? If so, how?

Does the analysis provide support for expansion of the library? If so, how?

Miscellaneous Facilities *Assessment/Analysis*

Does the current placement of workstations seem logical and work with the library's layout?
Does the current placement of printers and copiers seem logical and work with the library's layout?
Are patrons able to easily find them without asking staff for assistance?
Are they located so staff can easily give assistance and answer questions?
Is the current location of server room/network operation center (NOC) adequate?
Is there space for expansion of the network/equipment if necessary?
Do computer workstations and PACs meet ADA requirements?**
Do the overall technology areas and computer labs meet ADA requirements?**
How much shelf space in your library is dedicated to technology-related topics? (shelves or %)

Books
Magazines
A/V
Other

How does this compare to other collection areas? Is it proportionate?

* Square feet per task area based on experience, as well as research from the following two studies:
Mark Hasskart and James Lothrop, "New York—Spaced Out or Out of Space" (presentation at the New York Library Association's annual conference, 2001); and State of Wisconsin Department of Public Instruction, Anders C. Dahlgren, consultant, "Public Library Space Needs: A Planning Outline" (1998), http://www.dpi.state.wi.us/dlcl/pld/plspace.html.
** See http://www.usdoj.gov/crt/ada/publicat.htm#Anchor-ADA-23240.

Staff Assessment/Analysis Worksheet

General Staff Statistics *Assessment*

Total FTE Librarians

Full-Time Librarians

Part-Time Librarians

Total FTE Paraprofessionals

Full-Time Paraprofessionals

Part-Time Paraprofessionals

Maximum number of staff working at any one time (typical scenario)

Projected staff growth over next 5 years (%)

Librarians

Paraprofessionals

General Staff Statistics *Analysis*

Will the projected growth in staff be adequately handled by current infrastructure?

Is the current allocation of technology-related space capable of handling the projected staff growth?

Staff Hardware and Equipment *Assessment*

Staff

The current number of computers allocated for staff use

PCs

Open Source (Linux)

Mac

Laptops (any OS)

Printers and Copiers

Number of staff-only printers — B & W / Color

Average number of pages printed by staff-only printers per month — B & W / Color

Average monthly duty cycle of staff printers — B & W / Color

Number of staff-only copiers — B & W / Color

Average number of copies per month — B & W / Color

Average monthly duty cycle of staff copiers — B & W / Color

Staff Hardware and Equipment *Analysis*

Staff

Is the current number of staff computers adequate to meet current needs?

As staff grows, what platforms are the best option to meet future needs?

What staff computers need upgrade/replacement in the next 2 years?

What other staff technology equipment needs upgrade/replacement in the next 2 years?

Printers and Copiers

Is the current number of printers/copiers available for staff use adequate?

What printer/copier options for staff would best meet both current and future needs?

Staff Assessment/Analysis Worksheet (Cont.)

Software *Assessment*

Number of staff workstations running obsolete or near-obsolete operating systems
☐

Number of staff workstations with no or obsolete "antivirus" or "pest control" software
☐

Software *Analysis*

What staff workstations need software upgrades to eliminate obsolescence for the next year?

What staff workstations need installation or upgrades to "antivirus" and "pest control" software?

General Staff Technology Proficiency *Assessment*

What is the general state of technology "knowledge" of staff? — Librarians / Paraprofessionals
  Rate: Great, Acceptable, Needs Improvement
Do the least "tech-savvy" staff have basic computer skills to effectively do their jobs? — Librarians / Paraprofessionals
  Rate: Great, Acceptable, Needs Improvement
Are staff expected to assist patrons with computer and technology-related issues? — Librarians / Paraprofessionals

Are there any staff that don't have basic computer skills?
Do most of the staff take advantage of training opportunities to upgrade their technology skills?
Other:

General Staff Technology Proficiency *Analysis*

What training programs and plans are indicated by the assessment (see also next section)?
  Consider both technology team assessment and the staff self-assessment information.

What job responsibility shifts might be indicated by the assessment?
  (For example, who might be shifted to a technology-related job based on previously unknown computer proficiency?)

Staff Training Programs *Assessment*

What programs are in place to train staff in general Internet usage, searching, evaluation, etc.?
  List:

What programs are in place to train staff in general software use?
  List:

What programs are in place to train staff in database and Internet use?
  List:

What programs are in place to train staff on technology maintenance and basic repair issues?
  List:

What programs are in place to help staff improve their customer service skills?
  List:

Are technology programs marketed to staff to encourage their participation?
Other:

Staff Training Programs *Analysis*

Analyze existing programs for overlap and consolidation options.

What programs should be added to address staff weakness (highlighted by the staff assessment)?

What improvements in marketing and communication of staff programs could be made to improve participation?

Staff Assessment/Analysis Worksheet (Cont.)

Technology and Customer Service *Assessment*

Is the general attitude of staff toward patrons positive?

Are staff eager to assist patrons with technology questions unrelated to the library?

Are staff eager to assist patrons with technology-related questions?

Do staff look to technology to assist in serving customers and solving service issues?
Do most staff take advantage of training opportunities to upgrade their customer service skills?

Librarians	
Paraprofessionals	
Librarians	
Paraprofessionals	
Librarians	
Paraprofessionals	

Technology and Customer Service *Analysis*

What kinds of initiatives or training programs might help improve staff customer service skills?

What process automation options might assist in improving customer service within the library?
 (For example, self-service options that save time for those who want the option and reduce lines for those who don't.)

What initiatives might be undertaken to increase communication between the technology department and other library staff?

Technology Policy *Assessment/Analysis*

Do all staff have access to the same software?

Are there staff policies in place regarding Internet use, personal computer use, e-mail, etc.? What are they?
 Are they effective? What revisions might be warranted?

Are there procedures in place for handling technology problems, emergencies, etc.? What are they?

Are staff computers filtered?
 If so, are there options for turning off filters?

Are staff familiar with technology-related policies that are in place for the public (Internet use, computer use, etc.)?
 If not, what actions can be taken to educate/inform them?

Are copies of public policies readily available for staff to refer to, distribute, etc.?

Library Comparison Worksheet

Your Library's Name _____

Section 1: Baseline Comparisons

Library	Population	Expenditures per Capita	Books per Capita	Loans per Capita	Registered Borrowers as % of Population	Hours Open per Week (unduplicated)	Attendance per Capita (persons entering the library)	Reference Transactions per Capita	Staff per 1,000 Population
Your Library									
Library 1									
Library 2									
Library 3									
Library 4									
Library 5									

Section 2: Comparing the Services

Library	# of OPACs	# of Computers for Public Use	# of Computers for Staff Use	Space Allocated to Public Computers (sq ft)	Offers Free Wi-Fi: Hotspot(s) or Full Library Coverage	Website: Hosts Own, ISP, Consortium	Offers Online: Holds, Reserves, Renewals	Offers Virtual Reference	# of Technology Programs
Your Library									
Library 1									
Library 2									
Library 3									
Library 4									
Library 5									

Library	Number of Printers	Number of Copiers	Printing and Copying Fees (B&W/Color)	Printing and Copying Is Automated (Coin-Op vs. Acct / Card Sys.)	Space Allocated to Printers and Copiers (sq ft)	Offers Online Calendar (Dynamic, Registration, Cancellations)	Offers Online Meeting Room Schedules (Searches, Booking)	Offers Online Reading / Book Clubs (Reg., Logging, Reviews)	Space Allocated to Technology Collections (sq ft)
Your Library									
Library 1									
Library 2									
Library 3									
Library 4									
Library 5									

Technology Brainstorming Worksheet

	Where have we been? (In relation to this aspect of technology, what is the library's current and past situation, attitude?)	Where should we be? (How does this aspect of technology relate to the library's mission, service priorities, long-range plan?)	Where are we headed? (Where would we like to see the library headed in regard to this aspect of technology?)
Targeted customers			
Hardware, software, infrastructure			
Services Including, but not limited to, programs, public training classes, special services			
Collection Circulating and non-circulating audiovisual and technology-related collections			
Staffing Including, but not limited to, customer service, internal training, staffing levels, troubleshooting, oversight			
Physical space Location, function, layout, design, etc.			

Sample Technology Assessment Summary

Introduction

(LIBRARY NAME) is located in (TOWN, STATE). It is a member of the (INSERT APPROPRIATE INFORMATION—LIBRARY SYSTEM, CONSORTIUM, ETC.). (LIBRARY NAME) serves a community of (POPULATION).

(LIBRARY NAME) meets all the requirements, as defined by the State Education Department (INSERT OTHER INFORMATION AS APPROPRIATE).

(LIBRARY NAME) has continually demonstrated its commitment to technology by providing an array of resources and related programming to its public and staff, including (DESCRIPTION OF HOW THIS HAS BEEN DEMONSTRATED).

Equipment, Infrastructure, and Services

Equipment/Hardware

The following equipment currently resides in the library:

- Compaq ProLiant ML350 file server running Windows 2000 Server
- Compaq dual processor backup server
- (NUMBER) computers networked to the server
- (NUMBER) laptops
- (NUMBER) 15" flat panel monitors and (NUMBER) 17" flat panel monitors for public use
- (NUMBER) 15" flat panel monitors and (NUMBER) 15" CRT monitors for staff use
- Compaq 20/20 GB external tape backup system
- Compaq UPS R3000 XR battery backup
- (NUMBER) networked printers
- IP phone system running through a 3COM NBX 100

Connections

(LIBRARY NAME) functions in a LAN/WAN environment. It is connected to the WAN via a router and a dedicated Fractional T1 connection at 128 Kbps.

Plenum-rated Category 5 wiring is present throughout the building. Due to the lack of drops provided in the building expansion project, 1 12-port hub, 2 16-port switches, and 6 5-port switches were installed in the central public computing area as well as in the staff area.

All laptops in the Computer Lab are connected via a wireless network. Currently, the library has 1 WL 510 Enterprise access point. The library is investigating the option of a wireless hotspot for (DATE).

Software

- Windows 2003 (server) and Windows XP (workstations)
- Current protocol for the LAN/WAN is TCP/IP
- Internet Explorer 6.0
- Microsoft Office 2003
- Evanced Solutions Events v 4.0 and Room Reserve v 4.0
- Dreamweaver 8.0
- Norton Antivirus Corporate Edition
- Ad-Aware SE Enterprise Edition
- Adobe Acrobat Reader 7.0
- SAM v 8.5 (PC and print management)

Necessary telecommunications software that provides (LIBRARY NAME) with Internet access, e-mail, an online catalog, and various reference databases is provided to (LIBRARY NAME) through (LIBRARY SYSTEM/CONSORTIUM).

Services

Of the (NUMBER) public computers, all have access to the Internet. (NUMBER) of these computers are reserved for "open access" to the Internet with software monitoring the age level of the patron using the machine. "Open access" means patrons can surf freely without restrictions beyond pornography and chat filtering. The remaining machines include (NUMBER) with access to the Online Public Access Catalog only. (NUMBER) computers have limited online database access and (NUMBER) have access to Microsoft Office products.

(LIBRARY NAME) offers a comprehensive website for its patrons and staff at (URL), including access to

- general information about (LIBRARY NAME) and its services
- monthly listings of new library materials
- program information updated daily with the ability for patrons to sign up online
- meeting room information updated daily with the ability for patrons to request a room online

- a variety of links to community, local, and other useful informational Internet resources
- a genealogy and local history database that is updated monthly
- (NUMBER) reference databases, including (LIST RESOURCES IF APPROPRIATE) with remote access to (NUMBER, ETC.)
- the Online Public Access Catalog, which provides access in English and Spanish to collections of all public libraries in (INSERT APPROPRIATE REGIONAL INFORMATION)

(LIBRARY NAME) continues to have one of the most successful public computer training programs in (GEOGRAPHIC REGION). Currently, (LIBRARY NAME) offers (NUMBER) computer classes for the public and staff, including (LIST NAMES OF CLASSES). Customers are trained in the library's wireless training lab. Individuals receive hands-on instruction, each student getting his/her own laptop. (LIBRARY NAME) also owns a multimedia projector that is used for in-house class instruction as well as for community outreach demonstrations. Computer class instructors are paid (DOLLAR AMOUNT) per class. Funding is provided by the Friends of the Library.

Technology Developments

On (DATE), filtering of pornography and chat was enabled at (LIBRARY NAME). This was in response to the 2001 Children's Internet Protection Act (CIPA). Designed to protect children from viewing offensive material on the Internet, the law requires some level of "filtering" of websites. CIPA requires all library computers, including staff machines, to be filtered to some degree. CIPA is tied to E-Rate funding.

On (DATE) the library updated its *Internet Policy* and *Internet Guidelines*, both of which are posted on the library's website at (URL) as well as displayed on all public PCs in the central computing area.

As of (DATE), the library established 2 full-service handicap accessible workstations.

In order to meet the need for increased support of (LIBRARY NAME)'s expanded network, a part-time position of Library Assistant for Technology Services was created in (MONTH/YEAR).

On (DATE), (LIBRARY NAME), in conjunction with the Friends of the Library, purchased online program registration and room reservation software from (COMPANY NAME). Staff members were trained in (MONTH/YEAR) and the programs were advertised and incorporated into the library's website in (MONTH/YEAR). These new services went live to the public on (DATE). Patrons and staff can now view up-to-the-minute program information and register for library events 24 hours a day, 7 days a week. In addition, patrons can also view the library's public meeting room schedules and submit use requests online 24 hours a day, 7 days a week.

In (MONTH/YEAR), (LIBRARY SYSTEM/CONSORTIUM) began researching a new ILS vendor. Several staff members participated in committee work. Various other staff members attended demonstrations provided by three vendor finalists. A final decision was announced on (DATE). It was decided that the (LIBRARY SYSTEM/CONSORTIUM) would enter into negotiations with (COMPANY NAME)

Maintenance and Training

(LIBRARY NAME) currently has 1.5 staff members dedicated to the management of technology in the library, including the provision of network-based services. They are the Technology Services Librarian (full-time), who has 6 years of experience in this area, and the Library Assistant for Technology Services (part-time), who has 3 years of experience in this area.

The majority of the maintenance of the library's network is provided in-house. An additional (DOLLAR AMOUNT) has been budgeted for external network consultation to handle repairs, upgrades, and troubleshooting outside the scope of staff. (COMPANY NAME) will provide these services between (DATE RANGE). This contract will be negotiated annually.

In (YEAR), (LIBRARY NAME) committed (DOLLAR AMOUNT) to technology training for its staff. An additional (DOLLAR AMOUNT) was committed for national and state conferences that cover topics in network services and technology. A similar level of funding is expected for (YEAR).

In-house staff technology meetings will be held monthly, and an annual technology workshop for the entire staff is planned for (DATE).

Technology Planning Worksheet

Goals and Action Steps	Value	Technology Solutions	Resources			Additional Questions and Comments	Priority
			People	Time	Money		
Goal: *Actions:*							
Goal: *Actions:*							
Goal: *Actions:*							
Goal: *Actions:*							

Staff Self-Assessment Worksheet

Name	Dept.	Check One per Question (NS=No Skill, L=Learning, P=Proficient)			How Did You Learn the Skill? (ST=Self-taught, B=Book, L=Library Instruction, FC=Formal Course, O=Other)					Comments (Include any comments, notes, suggestions, etc. pertaining to each question)
		NS	L	P	ST	B	L	FC	O	
Basic Hardware *See appendix B for a few resources that list basic hardware competencies. Modify and integrate them here as appropriate for your library. A few examples are shown.*										
I know what this is and what it does:										
Hard Drive										
USB Drive										
Network Card										
Basic Computer Skills *See appendix B for a few resources that list basic computer skill competencies in the areas of operating systems and file management. Modify and integrate them here as appropriate for your library. A few examples are shown.*										
I know how to….										
Correctly start up and shut down computers										
Correctly start up and shut down printers										
Maximize and minimize a window										
Select, open, move, and close a window										
Resize a window and tile/stack windows										
Scroll up/down, left/right within a window										
Select, open, and move an icon										
Use drop list menus, radio buttons, checkboxes										
Start an application										
Office applications										
ILS application (staff and patron side)										
Other										
Create a new document										
Name a document										
Retrieve a document from floppy disk										
Retrieve a document from hard drive										
Rename a document										

Staff-Self-Assessment Worksheet (Cont.)

Name / Dept.	Check One per Question (NS=No Skill, L=Learning, P=Proficient)			How Did You Learn the Skill? (ST=Self-taught, B=Book, L=Library Instruction, FC=Formal Course, O=Other)					Comments (Include any comments, notes, suggestions, etc. pertaining to each question)
	NS	L	P	ST	B	L	FC	O	
Edit and re-save a document									
Save a document to a hard drive using both Save and Save As commands									
Save a document to a portable device such as a									
CD									
USB Drive									
Create, name, organize folders									
Save, open, organize documents within folders									
Open and work with more than one application at a time									
Open and work with more than one document at a time									
Print documents									
Successfully utilize various printing options (formatting, etc.)									

Computer Maintenance

See appendix B for a few resources that list basic maintenance competencies. Modify and integrate them here as appropriate for your library. A few examples are shown.

I know how to...

	NS	L	P	ST	B	L	FC	O	
Empty the recycle bin									
Keep virus protection updated									

Internet

See appendix B for a few resources that list basic Internet competencies. Modify and integrate them here as appropriate for your library. A few examples are shown.

I know how to...

Navigation:

	NS	L	P	ST	B	L	FC	O	
Type in an address									
Add something to my favorites or bookmark list									
Print									
Find a word or phrase within a page									

Searching:

	NS	L	P	ST	B	L	FC	O	
Subject and keyword search									
Truncate									
Use all the features of [insert search engine of choice]									
Find information about library services on the library's website									

E-mail

See appendix B for a few resources that list basic e-mail competencies. Modify and integrate them here as appropriate for your library. A few examples are shown.

I know how to....

Open a message

Compose and send a message

Use the address book

Open an attachment

Miscellaneous

See appendix B for a few resources that list other technology competencies specifically related to libraries. Modify and integrate them here as appropriate for your library. A few examples are shown.

I know how to use and effectively instruct others on

Online catalog—patron interface

Automation system—staff interface

Full-text periodicals

Online databases

Hardware for people with disabilities

Software for people with disabilities

Intermediate–Advanced Skills

See appendix B for a few resources that list more advanced competencies. You might consider making this a second-level questionnaire once staff have handed in the basic level. Modify questions and include hands-on demonstration as appropriate for your library.

Staff should be able to *demonstrate* these skills:

Install/reinstall and update system software

Install/reinstall and update printer drivers

Basic networking skills:

File sharing

Connecting computer to network

Simplistic troubleshooting

Terms

You might consider including a basic vocabulary section. See appendix B for a few resources that list basic competency technology vocabulary. Modify and integrate them here as appropriate for your library.

I know what this is:

Technology Budget Worksheet

Category	Current Year Budget	Previous Year Budget	Difference (Curr. - Prev.)	% Change (Diff./Prev.)	Notes
Staff	$ -	$ -	$ -	%	
Networks and Infrastructure	$ -	$ -	$ -	%	
Servers	$ -	$ -	$ -	%	
Workstations	$ -	$ -	$ -	%	
Printers/Copiers	$ -	$ -	$ -	%	
Software	$ -	$ -	$ -	%	
Maintenance	$ -	$ -	$ -	%	
Services/Repairs/etc.	$ -	$ -	$ -	%	
Circulating Collections (hardware, software)	$ -	$ -	$ -	%	
Miscellaneous	$ -	$ -	$ -	%	
TOTAL	$ -	$ -	$ -		

Sample Request for Quotation

Request for Quotation for the XXX Public Library

Attention:

Company Name:

Company Address:

Description	Qty	Unit Cost	Total
TOTAL*			

*Please include freight and any miscellaneous charges as applicable.

**Note: XXX Public Library is tax exempt.

Additional Notes:

_____

Signature of Person Preparing Quotation   Date

_____

Please Print Name

Please sign and return via e-mail or fax to XXX Public Library

Library e-mail: Library fax:

License Tracking Worksheet

License Information						Sales Contact Information			Service Contact Information		
Application/ Product	Vendor	Date License Signed/ Purchased	Terms (single user, site license, open license)	# of Lic.	Renewal Date	Name	Phone, E-mail, etc.		Name	Phone, E-mail, etc.	

Problem Report/Troubleshooting Log

Date	Equipment (Name and Description)	Description of Problem	Person Reporting Problem	Date Resolved	Who Fixed the Problem?	What Was the Problem?	How Long Did It Take to Fix? (est. in 15-min. increments)

Marketing Technology Worksheet

Product Design
What materials, services, or programs does this group need from the library? What might we offer?

Pricing
What resources (staff and materials) might be needed to offer these current or new services? Estimate costs in dollars and time.

Placement
Where is the most effective location to provide these services or programs? How can we reach our target group?

Promotion
How will we inform the market segment? Where and how can we attract these people to use the service, technology, etc.?

Resources B

This appendix provides a sampling of resources and tools that you may find helpful. Please note that the inclusion of any specific vendor or product in this list does not indicate the authors' endorsement or recommendation. The intent is to simply make readers aware of potentially helpful and relevant resources.

Chapter 1: General Resources

American Library Association—TechSource
    http://www.techsource.ala.org/
    A unit of the publishing division of the American Library Association, TechSource publishes *Library Technology Reports* and *Smart Libraries Newsletter* (formerly *Library Systems Newsletter*).

Bill and Melinda Gates Foundation   Global Libraries Program
    http://www.gatesfoundation.org/Libraries/
    This foundation began with the mission of connecting libraries to the Internet. Its current challenge is to help public libraries stay connected. The website includes access to *Staying Connected*, a toolkit designed to help libraries engage local communities in their technology programs and enlist their help in sustaining those programs. The toolkit is available at http://www.gatesfoundation .org/Libraries/USLibraryProgram/Stayingconnected/ StayingConnectedToolkit.htm.

Center for the Study of Rural Librarianship
    http://jupiter.clarion.edu/~csrl/csrlhom.htm
    Clarion University's website devoted to the study and assistance of rural libraries across the United States and the globe.

Library and Information Technology Association
    http://www.ala.org/ala/lita/litahome.htm
    The information technology branch of the American Library Association. Their site contains information about trends, publications, resources, and services.

Library Futures Quarterly
    http://www.libraryfutures.com
    A print newsletter for public library administrators, managers, and trustees who want to be well informed about the potential future of public libraries.

NPower
    http://www.npower.org
    A national network of independent nonprofit organizations that provides technology assistance to other nonprofits. Their mission is to ensure that all nonprofits can use technology to better serve their communities.

TechBlog
    http://www.libraryjournal.com/blog/670000067-July-2005.html?starting=11
    Library Journal's TechBlog is a community of library and information professionals who provide information on a variety of technology topics.

WebJunction
    http://webjunction.org
    This is a website with tons of great information. The "Technology Resources" page includes practical tips, tools, and information to help you with computer and Internet issues in your public access computing program. The "Technology Watch List for Small Libraries" is also excellent. This list is updated quarterly and points out the

technologies that will bring your library the most bang for the buck.

Note: Refer to your state library's web page for information on training, new technology, policies, standards, grants and funding, and more. You might also want to take a look at what other state libraries have to offer.

Chapter 2: Assess IT

Belarc
> http://www.belarc.com/free_download.html
> A company that develops and licenses Internet-based products geared to the maintenance of personal computers for both organizations and individual consumers. One product, the Belarc Advisor, builds a detailed profile of installed software and hardware and displays the results in your web browser.

CompuMentor
> http://www.compumentor.org
> A nonprofit organization specializing in technology assistance for community-based organizations. CompuMentor is also the home of TechSoup.org. This resource offers technology planning, implementation, and support services information and sample worksheets for assessment. CompuMentor is a helpful reference relating to multiple chapters in this book.

Google Analytics
> http://www.google.com/analytics/
> Tells you everything you want to know about how your visitors found you on the Web and how they interact with your website.

Hennen's American Public Library Ratings
> http://haplr-index.com/index.html
> A state-by-state index of ratings of the nations' public libraries.

McNamara, Carter. "Basics of Conducting Focus Groups." Management Assistance Program for Nonprofits. February 16, 1988.
> http://www.mapnp.org/library/evaluatn/focusgrp.htm
> Describes the how-tos for preparing, planning, and conducting focus groups.

Northeast Kansas Library System, New Pathways to Planning
> http://skyways.lib.ks.us/pathway/

PublicLibraries.com
> http://www.publiclibraries.com
> Links to libraries in all fifty states, plus state, academic, and national libraries.

Tame the Web
> http://tametheweb.com
> A blog by Michael Stephens.

TechAtlas and TechSurveyor
> http://techatlas.org/tools/features.asp
> Managed by NPower, these resources provide assistance with technology assessment and planning exclusively for nonprofit organizations. There are two types of TechAtlas accounts available. A free "basic account" includes basic technology assessment, planning, and inventory tools for nonprofits. An "enhanced account" provides access to technology planning and asset management tools such as online inventorying, help desk tracking, and special assessments on a subscription basis with specialized content to meet your needs.

U.S. Census Bureau—Demographic Profiles
> http://censtats.census.gov/pub/Profiles.shtml
> Enter your state and city, town, and so on, and quickly find demographic information about your geographic area.

WebTrends
> http://www.webtrends.com
> Resource for web analytics, including the ability to sign up for an all-access pass to free product trials, guides, white papers, and events. This resource and its products are very much business oriented, but they still have some interesting information.

Chapter 3: Know IT

Acqweb—Library and Information Science Resources: Software, OPACs, and Library Systems
> http://acqweb.library.vanderbilt.edu/lis_sys.html
> Directory of various software, OPAC, and library system sites. Includes a guide to automated systems, software, hardware, and consulting companies.

American Locker Security Systems
> http://www.americanlocker.com
> Provides a locker system as utilized by the Portage County (OH) District Library.

Apple
> http://www.apple.com
> Resource for Mac, iPod, and Wi-Fi hardware and software.

Audible.com
> http://www.audible.com
> Provider of downloadable spoken audio. Audible .com is Amazon.com's and the Apple iTunes Music

Store's preeminent provider of spoken word products for downloading or streaming via the Web.

Banerjee, Kyle. "How Much Security Does Your Library Need?" *Computers in Libraries* 23, no. 5 (May 2003): 12–14, 54–56.

How much should you worry about computer security? This article addresses the answer—it depends on what your library does and who your users are.

Bilal, Dania. *Automating Media Centers and Small Libraries: A Microcomputer-Based Approach*. 2nd ed. Portsmouth, NH: Libraries Unlimited, 2002.

Hands-on guide for those automating a library. This second edition is expanded and updated to reflect the many recent changes in automation. Includes information on choosing vendors, collection preparation, installation, and online networking, as well as step-by-step checklists and hands-on exercises.

Blogwithoutalibrary.net

http://www.blogwithoutalibrary.net

A blog about what libraries are doing with blogs, RSS feeds, and other emerging technologies. Includes discussion, helpful links, and a list of blogging libraries.

BookLetters

http://www.bookletters.com

An e-service that enables staff to reach out to patrons with e-newsletters and enhanced web services.

CDW Government

http://www.cdwg.com

A leading provider of technology solutions for government and education. You can create an online account for easy access to hardware and software educational/governmental pricing, easy ordering, and more. Their online Technology Research Center is also quite helpful, providing articles, in-depth reference guides, webinars, and hands-on case studies.

Cisco Systems

http://www.cisco.com/en/US/products/

Provider of network, storage, cabling, and security products.

Cohen, Steven M. *Keeping Current: Advanced Internet Strategies to Meet Librarian and Patron Needs*. Chicago: American Library Association, 2003.

Keeping up with the ever-growing Web, along with professional resources and information, can be an overwhelming challenge for busy librarians. This book includes software and product evaluation that help librarians do their jobs better, easier, and faster.

Cohn, John M., Ann L. Kelsey, and Keith Michael Fiels. *Planning for Integrated Systems and Technologies: A How-to-Do-It Manual for Librarians*. New York: Neal-Schuman, 2001.

A practical guide to planning for automation, whether installing a new system or replacing one. Includes information on selection and implementation, preparing RFPs, evaluating vendor proposals to negotiating contracts, testing, and training. While all the content might not be appropriate for your environment, much of it can still be helpful for the smaller library.

Comprise Technologies, Inc.

http://www.comprisetechnologies.com

Vendor of SAM web-based PC and print management systems.

Computers in Libraries

http://www.infotoday.com/cilmag/default.shtml

Monthly magazine providing coverage of the news and issues in library information technology and focusing on the practical application of technology. Includes special features such as the annual "Buyer's Guide" (also available online), which includes supplier information about hardware and software, online databases, and other products and services.

CybraryN

http://www.cybrarian.com/pages/1/index.htm

Provider of public access control and security software, including print cost recovery, PC reservation, remote computer control, desktop security, and more.

e*vanced solutions, Inc

http://www.e-vancedsolutions.com

Provides web-based solutions for managing library programs and events, registration, meeting and study room reservation, and summer and year-round reading programs. All products are built specifically for libraries and go beyond others of their kind to engage patrons in library services. Geared to libraries of all sizes and budgets.

EngagedPatrons.org

http://www.engagedpatrons.org

Provides website services connecting public libraries and their patrons. Free RSS feed hosting, blog hosting, and online events hosting for non–technology oriented libraries.

EnvisionWare

http://envisionware.com

Provider of PC management solutions, from PC reservation to print management and more.

F-Secure Corporation

http://www.f-secure.com/virus-info/

Resource for security and pest control information, including news, descriptions, tools, and tips.

Freedom Scientific

http://www.freedomscientific.com

Provides assistive and adaptive technology for individuals who are blind or have impaired vision or learning disabilities.

Gibbons, Susan, Thomas A. Peters, and Robin Bryan. *E-Book Functionalities: What Libraries and Their Patrons Want and Expect from Electronic Book Technologies*. Chicago: American Library Association, 2003.

In-depth reviews and research related to e-book functionality. Some guidance is offered on e-book RFPs, license agreements, and purchases.

GoPrint

http://www.goprint.com

A systems integration and management consulting company with strong expertise in networks and printing software solutions.

Hotwired

http://www.hotwired.com

Good online as well as subscription resource for "staying in the know." Includes technology news (and an eight-year archive), crash courses, gadgets and gizmos information, and more. Subscription information for *Wired* magazine is also available on the site. A great resource for both patrons and staff.

Infogrip

http://infogrip.com

Company specializing in providing customers with assistive technology and ergonomic products and training.

Integrated Library System Reports

http://www.ilsr.com/tech.htm

This resource includes information on technology planning and ILS vendors as well as sample plans, RFPs, white papers, and more. While the information may seem to focus on larger libraries and library systems, it is still helpful for smaller libraries to review while deciding on system requirements and preparing for a library automation project.

Kensington

http://www.kensington.com

Supplier of a comprehensive line of computer accessories and products, from mice, trackballs, and keyboards to computer security solutions, iPod accessories, desktop and Mac accessories, computer cleaning supplies, and much more.

Lazzaro, Joe. *Adaptive Technologies for Learning and Work Environments*. 2nd ed. Chicago: American Library Association, 2001.

Discusses the latest advancements in assistive hardware and software, how to implement them, and how to provide vital training and technical support.

The Librarian's Yellow Pages

http://www.librariansyellowpages.com

An online and printed, easy-to-use buyer's guide created by librarians for librarians. It contains thousands of publications, products, and services in listings, and display ads under hundreds of subject headings.

Library Journal—Buyer's Guide and *Automated System Marketplace*

http://www.libraryjournal.com

Available in print via your library's *Library Journal* subscription or online. The *Buyer's Guide* is a helpful place to get information about all types of vendors. The *Marketplace* looks more closely at the business climate, company standings, new products, and trends in the ILS marketplace.

The Library Network—Technology Committee

http://tech.tln.lib.mi.us

The Library Network is a public library cooperative serving sixty-five libraries in southeast Michigan. Its Technology Committee's website is an excellent source for online resources related to technology, including hardware and software, help guides, operating systems, security, and much more.

Library Technology Guides

http://www.librarytechnology.org

This website aims to provide comprehensive and objective information related to the field of library automation, whether you are in the process of selecting a library automation system or just want to keep up with developments in the field. Find out about the companies, which automation products libraries are using, ILS trends, and more. You can also get XML updates. This site has no affiliation with any library automation company.

Library Web Chic

http://librarywebchic.net/wordpress/

Resources for librarians who are interested in the application of web design and web technologies in libraries.

Linksys

http://www.linksys.com

A division of Cisco Systems, a provider of networking hardware and support.

Macworld

http://www.macworld.com

Website and magazine that provides in-depth reporting, news analysis, help, and how-to advice for Macintosh professionals and savvy Mac users. Subscription information for *Macworld* magazine is also available here. A great resource for both patrons and staff.

NetLibrary

http://www.netlibrary.com

A resource for e-books, e-audiobooks, e-journals, subject centers, and collection development resources that help build, manage, and enhance your collection.

Open Source Software

http://www.opensource.org

A nonprofit corporation dedicated to managing and promoting an open source definition.

OverDrive/Digital Library Reserve, Inc.

http://www.overdrive.com

Vendor of digital audiobooks, e-books, e-music, and digital video for download.

PC Magazine

http://www.pcmag.com

A magazine and online resource that delivers reviews, testing information, and buying information related to computing and Internet products. RSS feeds, free newsletters, and subscription information for *PC Magazine* are also available on the website. A great resource for both patrons and staff.

PC World

http://www.pcworld.com

Magazine and online resource full of technology media, research, and company information. *PC World* magazine is targeted to meet the informational needs of tech-savvy managers and includes monthly reviews and rankings, news, how-to articles, features, and special reports. The website is more appropriate for management-level buyers and users and offers product reviews, pricing information, downloads (freeware and shareware, interactive tools) and free e-newsletters. A great resource for both patrons and staff.

Pharos Systems

http://www.pharos.com

Company providing a full suite of products that help you manage printing, PC reservations, and more.

Plymouth Rocket, Inc.

http://www.plymouthrocket.com

A software development company whose mission is to design, develop, and bring to market dynamic web applications that are powerful and easy to use. The company's signature product, EventKeeper, enables organizations to add and update information on upcoming events using a web-based interface.

Primasoft Organizer Pro

http://www.primasoft.com/pro_software/library_catalog_software_1.htm

Library catalog software for the smallest of private, public, or corporate libraries.

PUBLIB-L

http://lists.webjunction.org/publib/

An electronic discussion list for issues relating to public librarianship.

Research Buzz

http://www.researchbuzz.com

This site provides almost daily updates on search engines, new data-managing software, browser technology, and other topics for reference librarians. A weekly newsletter is available, or you're welcome to subscribe to the RSS feed.

SafeNet Inc.

http://www.safenet-inc.com

A company providing information technology security.

Smart, Laura. "Making Sense of RFID." *Library Journal's netConnect* (October 15, 2004).

http://www.libraryjournal.com/article/CA456770.html

Discusses the pros and cons of RFID. Includes a return on investment checklist, helpful lists of questions for colleagues and vendors, and other resources.

Smart Computing—In Plain English

http://www.smartcomputing.com

Their goal is to provide the most complete coverage of computers and consumer electronics. They offer publications for every computer user from novice to advanced, and for every market from consumer to business. Subscribers to any of their publications enjoy access to all the content they produce. Their "Latest Product Reviews"

section is quite helpful and can be found at http://www
.smartcomputing.com/editorial/productreview.asp.

SourceForge.net
http://www.sourceforge.net
Has the largest repository of open source code and
applications available on the Internet and hosts more
open source development products than any other site or
network worldwide.

Superpatron
http://vielmetti.typepad.com/superpatron/
Blog for library patrons on the lookout for great ideas
from libraries around the world.

Tech Notes
http://www.ala.org/ala/pla/plapubs/technotes/technotes
.htm
Short, web-based papers provided by the Public Library
Association for public librarians on technologies such as
filtering, RFID, virtual reference, wireless, and more.

Telus
http://www.telus.com/cgi-ebs/jsp/homepage.jsp
A Canadian telecommunications company providing a
full range of communications products and services.

3Com
http://www.3com.com/index2.html
Company that provides networking and Wi-Fi hardware
and support.

Valinor.ca
http://valinor.ca
This site contains information for librarians and
archivists and contains over 2,000 documents and images,
most to do with librarianship, archives, and computing.

Veicon Technology, Inc.
http://www.veicon.com
Provides turnkey public-access solutions that take
advantage of the inherent security and reliability of thin
client desktops.

VendPrint
http://vendprint.com
Solutions for network printing and document
management.

WebFeat
http://www.webfeat.org
Offers a variety of federated search engine products,
including WebFeat Express, which is geared toward small to
medium-sized libraries looking to maximize e-resources.

Web4Lib
http://lists.webjunction.org/web4lib/
A discussion list for issues related to the creation,
management, and support of library-based web servers,
services, and applications.

Wilson, Paula. "Library Service without Wires: Connectivity
and Content." *Public Libraries* 43, no. 6 (November/December
2004): 328–29.
Presents details on the wireless services implemented by
many libraries.

Wireless Libraries Blog
http://wirelesslibraries.blogspot.com
The purpose of this blog is to advance the use of
wireless local area networks (WLANs) in libraries. A
LibWireless discussion group is also available at http://
people.morrisville.edu/~drewwe/wireless/libwireless.html.

Note: Many larger companies like Microsoft, Hewlett-Packard,
and various ILS vendors have white pages, guides on how to
choose a server, and other resources on their websites.

Chapter 4: Plan IT

Cohn, John M., Ann L. Kelsey, and Keith Michael Fiels.
*Writing and Updating Technology Plans: A Guidebook with
Sample Plans*. New York: Neal-Schuman, 1999.
Even though this resource is aimed at larger libraries
with more detailed instructions, it still provides some
helpful information on creating, implementing, updating,
evaluating, and using a "detailed" technology plan if that is
your need.

Disaster Preparedness Plan for Small Public Libraries
http://winslo.state.oh.us/services/LPD/dis_biblio.html
Bibliography of helpful resources on disaster planning
from the State Library of Ohio.

Goddard, Lisa. "Hardware Renewal Planning." *Feliciter* 50, no.
2 (2004): 46–47.
Article discussing the topic of hardware renewal
planning.

Hale, Martha, Patti Butcher, and Cindi Hickey. Northeast
Kansas Library System. "New Pathways to Planning." 2003.
http://skyways.lib.ks.us/pathway/
This resource grew out of a series of workshops
sponsored by the Northeast Kansas Library System in 1998.
It was intended for small and medium Kansas libraries
to meet a system requirement for a written library plan,
including a vision statement, goals, and objectives, but it is
a good basic planning resource for any small or medium-
sized public library.

Halstead, Deborah, Richard Jasper, and Felicia Little. *Disaster Planning: A How-to-Do-It Manual with Planning Templates on CD-ROM*. New York: Neal-Schuman, 2005.

Information on how to develop a clear, logical, and revisable plan before an emergency strikes. The authors take you step-by-step through the basics and then beyond them. The companion CD-ROM is full of tools you can use, including sample disaster plans, a downloadable and customizable template for creating your own disaster plan, links to disaster planning websites, a comprehensive directory of electronic resources and planning aids, and a disaster planning database with links to national agencies.

Libweb

http://lists.webjunction.org/libweb/

A list of libraries that have a presence on the Web. It currently includes over 7,300 web pages from libraries in more than 125 countries and is updated daily. Great for finding other libraries similar to your own.

Matthews, Joseph R. *Technology Planning: Preparing and Updating a Library Technology Plan*. Portsmouth, NH: Libraries Unlimited, 2004.

Chapters cover the purpose and need for a technology plan, the description of the library in the plan, current challenges facing the library, emerging technologies, current technology, assessment, and evaluation.

Mayo, Diane, and Sandra Nelson. *Wired for the Future: Developing Your Library Technology Plan*. Chicago: American Library Association, 1999.

Aims to assist public librarians in developing a cogent technology plan.

National Center for Technology Planning

http://www.nctp.com

A clearinghouse for the exchange of information related to technology planning. This information includes school technology plans available for downloading online; technology planning aids (checklists, brochures, sample planning forms, public relations announcement forms); and electronic monographs on timely, selected topics.

Solinet—Contents of a Disaster Plan

http://www.solinet.net/preservation/leaflets/leaflets-fs.cfm?leafletpgname=leaflets_templ.cfm?doc_id=116

Provides the content basics behind disaster planning. There is also a downloadable "Disaster Prevention and Protection Checklist" available at http://www.solinet.net/emplibfile/prevlist.pdf.

Stephens, Michael. "Technoplans vs. Technolust." *Library Journal* 129, no. 18 (November 1, 2004): 36–37.

Article on technology planning that reminds us that technology is not an end in itself but a tool to help us meet our libraries' service goals. Includes some very good pointers for creating and implementing technology plans.

Chapter 5: Staff IT

Anderson, Joseph. "Call and Response: Rural Libraries Take on Their Challenges." March 5, 2004.

http://webjunction.org/do/DisplayContent?id=1231

Describes how rural libraries are addressing their funding, staffing, and tech support challenges.

Blanchard, Ken, and Sheldon Bowles. *High Five! The Magic of Working Together*. New York: William Morrow, 2001.

A management book that is easy and fun to read. Discusses why teams are important and what individuals and organizations of every sort can do to build successful ones.

Connecticut State Library—Automation/Technology Librarian Job Descriptions

http://ct.webjunction.org/do/DisplayContent?id=7397

The Connecticut State Library, in conjunction with WebJunction, has posted several of its job descriptions, including ones for coordinator of library automation, library computer technician, gateway center assistant and manager, head of technology services, and head of systems librarian.

Gaston, Michael R. "Unlocking Potential Staff Development at Deschutes Public Library District." *OLA Quarterly* 5, no. 4 (Winter 2000). http://www.olaweb.org/quarterly/quar5-4/gaston.shtml.

Talks about how the Deschutes Public Library perceived that the key to library evolution, in this period of rapid change, is staff development.

LibraryConsultants.org

http://libraryconsultants.org

An online directory for libraries and library consultants. You can even list RFPs here.

Oakland Public Library—Technology Competencies for Library Staff

http://www.oaklandlibrary.org/techcomp.htm#TECHNOLOGY

Provides a nice overview of what skills this library requires its staff to have, as well as some ideas to get you started with staff assessment at your own library.

Profiler Online Collaborative Tool
> http://profiler.hprtec.org
> Staff collaborative and self-assessment tools for educators that allows for the evaluation of knowledge, attitude, and skill based on simple surveys implemented via the Web.

Rochester Regional Library Council—Technology Competencies for Library Staff
> http://rrlc.entrexp.com/orgmain .asp?orgID=23&storyID=202
> A listing of various categories and questions to get you thinking about staff competencies. Great for incorporating into a staff self-assessment questionnaire.

Chapter 6: Pay for IT

Anderson, Rick. *Buying and Contracting for Resources and Services: A How-to-Do-It Manual*. New York: Neal-Schuman, 2004.
> A practical guide for librarians and frontline staff on dealing effectively with everyday problems and challenges that arise when working with vendors and publishers.

E-Rate Central
> http://www.e-ratecentral.com
> Specializes in providing consulting, compliance, and forms-processing services to E-rate applicants and service providers. Provides news, bulletins, and special features.

GrantStation
> http://www.grantstation.com
> An interactive website that allows grant seekers to identify potential funding sources for their programs or projects and mentors you through the grant-seeking process.

Howden, Norman. *Buying and Maintaining Personal Computers: A How-to-Do-It Manual for Librarians*. New York: Neal-Schuman, 2000.
> Written in language designed for librarians with all levels of expertise, this resource covers purchasing and maintaining computers in both PC and Mac formats for public access and staff use. Hardware and software issues, security, common repair tools, licenses, warranties, inventories, wiring, backup systems, preventive maintenance, costing, staffing, and vendors are discussed.

Institute of Museum and Library Services
> http://www.imls.gov/grants/library/lib_gsla.asp
> Grants for libraries for technology and technology-based information.

OpenRFP
> http://www.openrfi.com/cfm/si_pd.cfm?PID=6
> An open marketplace designed to increase the efficiency of the market for library software. OpenRFP is vendor neutral.

Satin, Seymour. "Negotiating: From First Contact to Final Contract." *Searcher* 9, no. 6 (June 2001): 50–54.
> An article discussing the importance of negotiation skills for information professionals. Includes simple steps and golden rules to help achieve the skills necessary in this area.

TechAtlas Tools
> http://techatlas.org/tools/features.asp#eventtracker
> Many nonprofit tools are offered by the TechAtlas Planning Center. Includes budget templates, a Total Cost of Ownership Tracker, and more.

Technology Grant News
> http://www.technologygrantnews.com
> Provides information on technology grants, free technology resources, technology partnerships, strategic alliances, and technology advancement.

TechSoup.org
> http://www.techsoup.org
> Powered by CompuMentor, TechSoup.org offers nonprofits a one-stop resource for technology needs by providing free information, resources, and support. It also connects nonprofits with donated and discounted technology products.

Universal Service Administrative Company
> http://www.sl.universalservice.org/apply/step2.asp
> This organization administers the Universal Service Fund, which provides communities across the country with affordable telecommunication services. Here you will find information on E-rates and technology planning.

Chapter 7: Implement IT

Anderson, Joseph. "The Puss-in-Boots Formula for Success." March 5, 2004.
> http://webjunction.org/do/DisplayContent?id=1233
> Discusses how a children's classic provided the inspiration for moving the Hennessey (OK) Public Library directly from the 1950s into the new millennium.

Computer Hope
> http://www.computerhope.com
> A collection of free services and computer-related information.

D'Aguiar, Kenji. "Securing USB Thumb Drives Using Software Restriction Policies." January 12, 2005.

> http://webjunction.org/do/DisplayContent?id=8896
> Find out how to use software policies to restrict the use of USB thumb drives on public access computers.

"Demonstrating Impact: Strategizing." January 10, 2004.

> http://webjunction.org/do/DisplayContent?id=1202
> Up-front planning will help you put together a potent message about what your library offers the community.

Event Tracker Helpdesk

> http://techatlas.org/tools/features.asp#eventtracker
> One of the many nonprofit tools found in the TechAtlas Planning Center. Event Tracker is a basic help desk, allowing nontechnical staff to alert "techie" staff to what needs to be done while allowing technical personnel to track progress and report on what has been completed.

GameFest

> http://www.bloomingtonlibrary.org/gamefest/
> The Bloomington (IL) Public Library's GameFest site. Includes information on electronic games in libraries (handouts, presentations, pictures, videos, podcasts, and more).

Jurewicz, Lynn, and Todd Cutler. *High Tech, High Touch: Library Customer Service through Technology*. Chicago: American Library Association, 2003.

> Illustrates technical solutions that really work, inspired by effective customer service strategies used by businesses. These are unique technology solutions—based on digital libraries, portals, e-mail notifications, and database interfaces to the Web—to solve everyday public library problems.

Landsbaum, Mark. *Low-Cost Marketing: Savvy Strategies for Maximizing Your Marketing Dollars*. Avon, MA: Adams Media, F&W Publications, 2004.

> Shows how to create "buzz" through good customer service, strong promotional materials, and smart use of the Internet.

Lavasoft

> http://www.lavasoftusa.com
> Company providing tools for protection against data-mining, aggressive advertising, Trojan horses, dialers, malware, browser hijackers, and tracking components.

MajorGeeks.com

> http://www.majorgeeks.com
> Informative site with a multitude of files for your computer that tweak, repair, back up, enhance, protect, and more.

McAfee

> http://www.mcafee.com/us/
> Company that provides tools for computer security and pest control technology. They have a line that specializes in small and medium "business" products and services.

Microsoft Help and Support

> http://support.microsoft.com
> Resource for support and troubleshooting of Microsoft products.

Note: Go to your vendor's website to find similar help, support, and troubleshooting guides such as this one.

Northeast Texas Library System—Continuing Education

> http://www.netls.org/ContinuingEducation/cedefault.htm
> A good example of a continuing education program that believes "the results of effective continuing education are informed library employees that provide better services to their patrons."

Public Library Advocacy: Goals and Tactics

> http://www.oclc.org/advocacy/public.htm
> Advocacy resource brought to you by OCLC.

Screenvision Cinema Advertising

> http://www.screenvision.com
> Provides cinema marketing solutions on a national and local basis through on-screen sight, sound and motion, cinema spots (still image advertising), cinema slides (in-theater promotional opportunities), and more. A variety of packages are available.

Song, Yuwu. *Building Better Web Sites: A How-to-Do-It Manual for Librarians*. New York: Neal-Schuman, 2003.

> This book provides in-depth information on developing your library's website. It presents a practical introduction to web design in a library setting, beginning with a nontechnical overview of the various functions that library websites can serve and then presenting a process for planning, designing, and developing them.

SpyBot

> http://www.spybot.info
> Resource that provides tools for the detection and removal of spyware.

Symantec

> http://www.symantec.com
> Resource for virus, pest, and security information and much more.

University of Texas System

> http://www.utsystem.edu/ogc/IntellectualProperty/cprtindx.htm#top
>
> Contains a range of resources related to copyright in the library. Includes an interactive "Software and Database License Agreement Checklist."

Wallace, Linda K. *Libraries, Mission, and Marketing*. Chicago: American Library Association, 2004.

> When designed to enliven and inspire staff and customers, the best mission statements energize organizations from restaurants to airlines. This book shows how to utilize mission statements as tools in planning and marketing and provides winning models to help you better communicate why your library is important and how it makes a difference in the community. A book for every library director and administrator.

Web Help for Public Libraries

> http://www.kdla.ky.gov/libsupport/libwebhelp.htm
>
> From the Kentucky Department for Libraries and Archives, this site includes many useful resources, including information on effectively creating a website and incorporating it into your marketing plan.

Website Supporter

> http://www.cgiadmin.com/scripts/ws/
>
> A CGI application designed to increase customer support by generating a unique ticket number for each support request and allowing customers to track the support progress.

Note: Customer service–oriented vendors will provide marketing kits or tools to assist their customers, so see your individual vendors for information on how to market their products to your customers. See, for example, Thomson Gale's "How to Market Your Library" at http://www.gale.com/free_resources/marketing/support/, or e•vanced solutions' "Marketing Tools" at http://www.e-vancedsolutions.com/manuals.html.

Chapter 8: Teach IT

Computer Basics Online Tutorials

> http://www.queenslibrary.org/techhelp/comptutorial.asp
>
> Created and maintained by the Queens (NY) Library's Cyber Center Staff, this resource links to a variety of websites dealing with basic computer tutorials, including interactive training and practice, keyboarding and typing, and computer buying guides, among others.

Computer Tutorials Online

> http://www.npl.org/Pages/InternetResources/SubjectGuides/comptut.html
>
> Resource page developed by the Newark (NJ) Public Library includes links to mousing, Internet, e-mail, MS Word, Excel, Access, and PowerPoint tutorials.

Costley, Enid. "Creating Lesson Plans for Teaching the Public." March 1, 2004.

> http://webjunction.org/do/DisplayContent?id=1243
>
> Follow the tale of how the Hibbing (MN) Public Library created lesson plans to teach patrons, and access the lessons themselves to teach patrons at your library.

Gordon, Rachel Singer. *Teaching the Internet in Libraries*. Chicago: American Library Association, 2001.

> Practical guide offering a step-by-step plan for creating a formal training program geared toward the needs of your library and its users. Classes range from focused, half-hour tutorials to full-day workshops for library users young and old. Packed with ready-to-use instruction, this helpful book is flexible enough to adapt to libraries of all types and sizes.

Hollands, William. *Teaching the Internet to Library Staff and Users*. New York: Neal-Schuman, 1999.

> A guide to help librarians teach their staffs to be Internet trainers. It includes seven scripted workshops tailored for library users.

NetTrain

> http://listserv.acsu.buffalo.edu/archives/nettrain.html
>
> Electronic discussion list for library technology and training news.

New Horizons Computer Learning Centers

> http://www.newhorizons.com/content/
>
> One of many IT training companies providing solutions for small, medium, and large organizations. A variety of training sessions are offered at locations across the United States. Free web seminars are also available, as well as a sign-up for free tips, tricks, and time-saving techniques designed to increase your productivity and expertise with the software applications you use each day—delivered weekly to your e-mail in-box.

Northville District Library—Public Tutorial

> http://www.northville.lib.mi.us/tech/tutor/welcome.htm
>
> Sample computer tutorials in English and Spanish.

Office of Leadership and Management Services—Training Support Skill Site
http://www.arl.org/training/
Training resources geared at academics but also helpful to public libraries in thinking about and developing effective training events and programs.

Stephens, Michael. "Here Come the Trainers!" *Public Libraries* 43, no. 4 (July/August 2004): 214.
Article dealing with librarians as trainers. Includes information on training staff as well as the public. Supplemental resources and reference also provided.

———. *The Library Internet Trainer's Toolkit*. New York: Neal-Schuman, 2001.
Provides everything you need to successfully teach others how to navigate the world of online information.

———. "Mastering a Public Training Program." In proceedings of *Computers in Libraries 2002* (March 15, 2002).
Information on establishing a public training program. Includes how-to tips, marketing ideas, and resources.

WebJunction—Learning Center
http://webjunction.org/do/Navigation?category=372
A source for library staff training: online courses, downloadable lessons, training tips, and other tools to enhance your technical and policy knowledge and skills. You can also use Learning Center resources to develop and conduct technology courses for library patrons.

Westlake Porter Public Library—Connect Fast @ Your Library!
http://www.westlakelibrary.org/connectfast/index.html
Great informational technology page created by the Westlake Porter (OH) Public Library for the public.

Chapter 9: Regulate IT

American Library Association—Policies and Guidelines
http://www.ala.org/ala/oif/statementspols/otherpolicies/Default2544.htm
Includes information pertaining to the development of a public library Internet use policy, user behavior and library usage, and more.

Arapahoe Library District
http://www.arapahoelibraries.org/FamilyOfSites/InternetAccess.cfm *and* http://www.arapahoelibraries.org/Disclaimer.cfm#au
Examples of an Internet access page and an electronic/resources/Internet policy.

Best Practices in Public Libraries
http://www.ala.org/ala/pla/resources/bestpractices.htm
Compiled by the Public Library Association's Electronic Communications Advisory Committee, this page includes a collection of best-practice policy resources.

Connecticut State Library—Policies and Practices
http://ct.webjunction.org/do/DisplayContent;jsessionid=6E3CDDAD7EF34B50797FA11F5468A8FE?id=7050
Includes a wide range of sample policies from Connecticut public libraries as well as from Indiana, Ohio, Massachusetts, and Wisconsin. Also includes links to sample collections and policy development resources.

DeGroff, Amy Begg. "Howard County Library Wi-Fi Policy." July 25, 2005.
http://webjunction.org/do/DisplayContent?id=11059
A friendly and informative handout to help staff support wireless patron computing, from a suburban Maryland library.

gPhotoShow
http://www.gphotoshow.com
Software for creating slide shows and screen savers. Good for creating policy screen savers and more for your public computers.

Indiana State Library—Computer Policies
http://www.statelib.lib.in.us/www/isl/ldo/pol/computer.html
A selected list of Indiana public libraries and policies that can be accessed from the library's home page. It is not a complete list, as libraries add new information daily to their home pages.

Mid-Hudson Library System—Sample Public Library Policies and Development Tips
http://midhudson.org/department/member_information/library_policies.htm
An informational page for trustees and administrators dealing with policy development.

MP3 Player Guidelines
http://www.kpl.gov/collections/av/ab_mp3Players.aspx
The Kalamazoo (MI) Public Library's guidelines for its MP3 player collection.

Nelson, Sandra, and June Garcia. *Creating Policies for Results*. Chicago: American Library Association, 2003.
Covers governance and organizational structure, policy management, and services relating to customers, circulation, information, and groups. Provides guidelines to assess existing policies, develop new ones, and communicate all changes to improve consistency.

Richey, Cynthia K. "Molding Effective Internet Policies." *Computers in Libraries* 22, no. 6 (June 2002): 16. Available online at http://www.infotoday.com/cilmag/jun02/richey.htm.

> After moving into a renovated facility that had fifty new computers, all with Internet access, this library's staff members realized they would need to reshape their existing general Internet policy. They pulled together examples of other libraries' guidelines, and from these, along with the existing policy, the staff crafted a well-defined, flexible policy and workshops for staff and the public.

Sauers, Michael. "Don't Doesn't Work." August 20, 2004.

> http://webjunction.org/do/DisplayContent?id=7202
> Should Internet access policy really be any different than policies for access to other types of library materials?

———. "A Library Policy for Public Wireless Internet Access." July 1, 2005.

> http://webjunction.org/do/DisplayContent?id=11033
> Looks at how one library has handled policy for public wireless Internet access.

State Library of Louisiana

> http://test.state.lib.la.us/la_dyn_templ.cfm?doc_id=42
> Several Louisiana public libraries have made their Internet and electronic resources policies available on the state's website.

State Library of Ohio—Sample Library Policy Statements

> http://winslo.state.oh.us/publib/policies.html
> Sample policies currently being used by Ohio public libraries. Although not a complete listing, these model policies can serve as patterns or examples in developing your own library policies.

Tippecanoe County (IN) Public Library—Staff Computer Use Guidelines

> http://www.tcpl.lib.in.us/admin/scu.htm
> Example of the Tippecanoe County Public Library's staff computer use guidelines.

Walter, Virginia A. "Becoming Digital: Policy Implications for Library Youth Services (Children and the Digital Library)." *Library Trends* 45, no. 4 (1997): 585–602.

> Interesting article that discusses the policy issues surrounding children and digital libraries. The decision to digitize libraries for youth should be based on the ability to provide access to information more easily and the ability to provide better service. Some people object to electronic libraries because of children's potential exposure to pornography or marketing campaigns.

WebJunction—Policies and Practices

> http://webjunction.org/do/Navigation?category=327
> Provides information on a wide variety of policy topics, including how-to articles, best practices, and samples for all aspects of library policy.

Wi-Fi Locator Sites

> http://www.wi-fi.org
> http://www.wififreespot.com
> http://jiwire.com
> http://anchorfree.com

Resource Libraries

C

Disclaimer: The information presented here was submitted by each resource library. The inclusion of the following resource libraries does not indicate the authors' endorsement or recommendation of them. This is for informational use only. The authors disclaim any liability for any content errors or omissions. The intent is to simply make readers aware of potentially helpful technology-oriented libraries.

RESOURCE LIBRARY	CONTACT INFORMATION	POP. SERVED	VOLS. IN COLLECTION	LIBRARY BUDGET	TECH. BUDGET	NO. OF BRANCHES	NO. OF PUBLIC PCS	NO. OF STAFF PCS	OS	NO. OF STAFF WITH PRIMARY TECH DUTIES	NO. OF STAFF WITH SECONDARY TECH DUTIES
Bloomington Public Library	205 E. Olive, P.O. Box 3308 Bloomington, IL 61702 Contact: Matt Gullett, Manager, IT Services http://www.bloomingtonlibrary.org/	73,000	230,000	$4,250,000	$65,000		55	65	MS, Linux, Panther		
Carrollton Public Library	4220 North Josey Lane Carrollton, TX 75010 Contact: Kam Hitchcock-Mort, Technical Services Manager http://www.cityofcarrollton.com/library/	117,250	245,585	$4,352,295	$250,000	2	90	60	MS	1 FT Systems Librarian, 2 Library Assistants (1/2 their time on systems work)	5 FT
Cedar Park Public Library	550 Discovery Boulevard Cedar Park, TX 78613 Contact: Pauline Lam, Library Director http://www.ci.cedar-park.tx.us/index.asp?NID=28	40,000	80,000	$906,700	$20,000 (city) / $15,000 (Dell grant)		36	20	MS	1 FT	4 FT
Cleveland Heights–University Heights Public Library	2345 Lee Road Cleveland Heights, OH 44118 Contact: Catherine Hakala-Ausperk, Deputy Director http://www.heightslibrary.org/	64,896	350,072	$7,458,671	$75,000	4	112	82	MS, Linux, Redhat	3	
Delton District Library	P.O. Box 155 Delton, MI 49046 Contact: Edward Elsner, Director http://www.deltonlib.org/	13,000	34,000	$160,000	$8,000		9	5	MS		1
Euclid Public Library	631 East 222nd Street Euclid, OH 44123-2091 Contact: Matthew Augustine, Technology Manager http://www.euclidlibrary.org/Public/home.asp	52,717	243,175	$6,000,000	$270,000		40	67	MS, Mac OSX, BeOS (Zeta), PickOS	2 FT	

Library	Address & Contact										
Fayetteville Public Library	401 W. Mountain Street Fayetteville, AR 72701 Contact: Louise Schaper, Director http://www.faylib.org/	58,047	90,000	$2,600,000	$85,000		110 approx.	70 approx.	MS, Linux	2 FT	2 FT
Guilderland Public Library	2228 Western Avenue Guilderland, NY 12084 Contact: Barbara Nichols Randall, Director http://www.guilderlandpublic.info/index.html	33,475	57,323	$2,318,000	$36,225		26	38	MS	1 FT and 1 PT	All librarians do some trouble-shooting on the fly
Kent District Library	814 West River Center NE Comstock Park, MI 49321 Contact: Cheryl Garrison, Assistant Director http://www.kdl.org/	362,312	673,850	$13,403,684	$642,380	18	240 plus 1 Mac		MS and Linux	5 FT	
McMillan Memorial Library	490 East Grand Avenue Wisconsin Rapids, WI 54494 Contact: Andy Barnett, Assistant Director http://www.mcmillanlibrary.org	37,000	26,323	$1,256,000	$100,000		33	17	MS	3	
Mt. Prospect Public Library	10 S. Emerson Street Mount Prospect, IL 60056 Contact: Marilyn Genther, Executive Director http://www.mppl.org/about-jobs.html	56,000	340,266	$5,500,000	N/A		63 public, 26 OPAC only	111	MS and Linux	7	10
Nappanee Public Library	157 N. Main Street Nappanee, IN 46550 Contact: Linda Yoder, Director http://www.nappanee.lib.in.us	8,973	57,078	$1,198,000	$150,000		27	12	MS, SQL	2 PT	1 FT, 1 PT
Newburyport Public Library	94 State Street Newburyport, MA 01950 Contact: Nancy K. Alcorn, Assistant Director http://www.newburyportpl.org/	17,504	113,230	$1,075,000	$41,000		33	17	MS	1 FT	2 FT

185

RESOURCE LIBRARY	CONTACT INFORMATION	POP. SERVED	VOLS. IN COLLECTION	LIBRARY BUDGET	TECH. BUDGET	NO. OF BRANCHES	NO. OF PUBLIC PCS	NO. OF STAFF PCS	OS	NO. OF STAFF WITH PRIMARY TECH DUTIES	NO. OF STAFF WITH SECONDARY TECH DUTIES
Oak Park Public Library	834 Lake Street Oak Park, IL 60301 Contact: Ed Byers, Executive Director http://www.oppl.org/	52,524	263,719	$4,933,125	$102,000	2	111	108	MS	3 FT	3 FT
Ogden Farmers' Library	269 Ogden Center Road Spencerport, NY 14559 Contact: Patricia Uttaro, Director http://www.ogdenny.com/TownGovernment/Departments/Library/	18,492	68,000	$389,000	$20,000	Adding branch in 2005-06	16	8	MS	Outsourced	Everyone pitches in
Palm Harbor Library	2330 Nebraska Avenue Palm Harbor, FL 34683 Contact: Gene Coppola, Director http://www.palmharborlibrary.org/	60,000	155,000	$1,000,000	$50,000		49	29	MS	2	
Polk County Public Library	51 Walker Street Columbus, NC 28722 Contact: Mark Pumphrey, Director http://www.publib.polknc.org/	18,324	61,484	$399,000	$15,000	1	23	9			
Portage County District Library	10482 South Street Garrettsville, OH 44231 Contact: Pam Hickson-Stevenson, Director http://www.portagecounty.lib.oh.us/home2.htm	100,000	240,000	$2,600,000	Not given	6					
St. Joseph County Public Library	304 S. Main Street South Bend, IN 46601 Contact: Debra Futa, Assistant Director http://sjcpl.lib.in.us/	172,627	521,968			8	146	210	Mac 10.3, Novell, Linux, Unix XP, MS	5 FT	6 FT

Salem–South Lyon District Library 9800 Pontiac Trail South Lyon, MI 48178 Contact: Derek Engi, Network Administrator http://salemsouthlyonlibrary.info	16,000	60,000	$765,000	$12,500		31	15	MS	1 network administrator	
Westlake Porter Public Library 27333 Center Ridge Road Cleveland, OH 44145 Contact: Anita Woods, Asst. Director for Support Services http://www.wes-lakelibrary.org/	37,719	237,333	$4,000,000			77	58	MS	2	2
Whitman County Rural Library District 102 S. Main Street Colfax, WA 99111 Contact: Kristie Kirkpatrick, Director http://www.whitco.lib.wa.us/	15,795	72,000	$575,000	$56,450	13	34	30	MS	2 PT	All staff have a secondary tech responsibility
Wood County District Public Library 251 N. Main Street Bowling Green, OH 43402 Contact: Elaine Paulette, Director http://wcdpl.lib.oh.us/	65,000	78,000	$1,500,000	$35,000	1	60	27	MS	1 FT and 1 PT	Ref. staff teach tech classes; tech lab monitors (pages) cover evening and weekend shifts
Yorba Linda Public Library 18181 Imperial Highway Yorba Linda, CA 92886 Contact: Danis Kreimeier, Director http://www.ylpl.lib.ca.us/	63,931	145,787	$2,905,800	Not given		36	28	MS and Linux	1 FT	

The following libraries are mentioned in the text but did not send in official resource library submission forms.

LIBRARY	CONTACT INFORMATION	URL
Arapahoe Library District	Administrative Offices, 12855 E. Adam Aircraft Circle, Englewood, CO 80112	http://www.arapahoelibraries.org/default.cfm?aldredirect
Baldwin Public Library	300 W. Merrill, Birmingham, MI 48009	http://www.baldwinlib.org/
Brownsburg Public Library	450 South Jefferson Street, Brownsburg, IN 46112	http://www.brownsburg.lib.in.us/
Delaware County District Library	84 E. Winter Street, Delaware, OH 43015	http://www.delaware.lib.oh.us/
Deschutes Public Library District	Administrative Offices, 507 N.W. Wall Street, Bend, OR 97701	http://www.dpls.lib.or.us/Index.asp
Hennessey Public Library	525 S. Main Street, Hennessey, OK 73742	http://hennessey.lib.ok.us/
Hibbing Public Library	401 East 21st Street, Hibbing, MN 55746	http://www.hibbing.mn.us/
Howard County Public Library	Administrative Offices, 6600 Cradlerock Way, Columbia, MD 21045	http://www.howa.lib.md.us/
Kalamazoo Public Library	Central Library, 315 South Rose Street, Kalamazoo, MI 49007	http://www.kpl.gov/
Kansas City Public Library	Central Library, 14 West 10th Street, Kansas City, MO 64105	http://www.kclibrary.org/
Lee County Library System	Administrative Offices, 2345 Union Street, Fort Myers, FL 33901	http://www.lee-county.com/library/
Liverpool Public Library	310 Tulip Street, Liverpool, NY 13088	http://www.lpl.org/
Manatee County Public Library–Island Branch	5701 Marina Drive, Holmes Beach, FL 34217	http://www.co.manatee.fl.us/library/master.html
Moline Public Library	504 17th Street, Moline, IL 61265	http://www.molinelibrary.com/
Morrisson-Reeves Library	80 North 6th Street, Richmond, IN 47374	http://www.mrlinfo.org or http://mrl.lib.in.us/
Peoria Public Library	8463 W. Monroe Street, Peoria, AZ 85345	http://www.peoriaaz.com/library/library_main.asp
Pierce Free Public Library	208 S. Main Street, Pierce, ID 83546	http://www.lili.org/clearwater/Piercepl.html
Rochester Regional Library Council	390 Packett's Landing, Fairport, NY 14450	http://www.rrlc.org/
St. Louis County Library	Headquarters Branch, 1640 S. Lindbergh Boulevard, St. Louis, MO 63131	http://www.slcl.lib.mo.us/
South Central Regional Library Council	215 North Cayuga Street, Ithaca, NY 14850	http://www.lakenet.org/
Tippecanoe County Public Library	627 South Street, Lafayette, IN 47901	http://www.tcpl.lib.in.us/

Head of Technology and Patron Services (Full-time Librarian)

Immediate Supervisor

Library Director

Duties and Responsibilities

Administration/Management

1. Acts as resource person for daily operations and for Library Director in his/her absence.
2. Represents library at system and community meetings and serves on library system committees.
3. Assists the Library Director in personnel, budget, building, and administrative matters.
4. Recommends technology-related and patron-related policies and procedures to Library Director and advises on long-term needs in relation to these areas.
5. Provides reference and readers/audiovisual/technology advisory service to the public.
6. Oversees technical services department and coordinates materials budgets for all library departments.
7. Gathers statistics for the New York State Annual Report, Town insurance inventory, and other reports as needed.
8. Attends monthly meetings of the library's Board of Trustees and prepares narrative reports as required.
9. Participates in long-range planning process for the library, including recommending changes or improvements and developing new types of services and operations.

10. Provides assistance to Library Director in oversight of physical plant.
11. Develops grants for library programs and services as appropriate and available.
12. Stays up-to-date on professional developments through participation in professional organizations, system meetings, workshops, and continuing education opportunities.

Personnel

1. Interviews, selects, trains, supervises, and schedules staff in network and technical services departments.
2. Maintains payroll and attendance records for network and technical services departments.
3. Conducts staff meetings for network and technical services departments.
4. Supervises staff training of online catalog, databases, online reference service, and web page.
5. Holds performance reviews for network and technical services staff as well as participates in reviews for other staff as determined by the Library Director.

Computer/Network Administration

1. Acts as administrator for LAN/WAN.
2. Serves as webmaster, coordinating the design and maintenance of the library's web page.
3. Evaluates, purchases, installs, and maintains library hardware and software and all related items.
4. Oversees automation of library administrative functions.
5. Develops technology assessments and plans based on customer, library, and staff needs.
6. Retains software and databases licenses as well as service contracts for all network-related equipment.

Collection Development and Training

1. Selects and maintains audiovisual collections including videos, DVDs, audiobooks, circulating software and hardware, and other technologies as relevant.
2. Serves as Training Coordinator for public computer classes.
3. Develops technology competencies for staff, creates staff training and troubleshooting manuals, and holds staff training sessions as needed.

Qualifications and Requirements

- Librarian with an MLS from a graduate library school accredited by ALA and 5 years progressively more responsible professional library experience required.
- A strong background in computers/technology and non-print materials formats.
- Patience, tact, and excellent communication skills.
- Enjoys learning as well as teaching.

- Ability to train and supervise library staff.
- Strong organizational talents.
- Demonstrates creativity, flexibility, and a positive attitude.
- Poise in a busy setting serving patrons and staff with high expectations.
- Excellent reference skills and ability to relate to patrons of all ages.
- Ability to exhibit good judgment and establish effective working relationships with staff, colleagues within the library system, local government personnel.
- Ability to plan and coordinate the work of others.
- Ability to exercise leadership and motivate others.
- Ability to establish effective working relationships with community organizations.
- Warm, outgoing personality.

Manager, Information Technology

Immediate Supervisor

Executive Director

Job Summary

Provides a reliable, accurate, responsive, efficient, safe and secure information systems platform for library service delivery. Manages data and voice network operations including staff and public computing, application software and telecommunications, as well as specific facility, meeting room and materials management systems. Responds to staff calls for help, troubleshoots and solves hardware and software problems, monitors overall system performance, implements improvements and works with the management team to develop long-range technology plans. With management team develops technology plans. Supervises occasional volunteers and temporary employees and/or interns.

Duties and Responsibilities

1. Manage a 100+ device data network plus 45+ voice network. Develop, document and implement network administration policies and processes. Maintain and troubleshoot hardware, software, and network issues. Ensure system integrity, reliability, responsiveness, security and compliance with library policies, e.g., Internet use. Maintain a regular backup schedule and off-site backup storage. % of time: 40%

2. Manage help desk functions by cataloging and responding to requests. Ensures that systems serving library customers are first priority for trouble calls. Assists staff with system and application software training and development needs. Working with library staff on web development issues. % of time: 30%

3. Develop and implement technology plans. Deploy sound project management practices including goal/problem identification and decision analyses. Using City of Fayetteville purchasing guidelines, prepares RFPs, bids or requests written quotes. Budget responsibility ranges from $30,000–$100,000. % of time: 20%

4. Manage other automated systems including building security, HVAC, conveyor etc. as needed. Supervise interns, volunteers, temporary employees. % of time: 10%

Qualifications and Requirements

1. Education
   a. B.S. in computer science or equivalent.
   b. M.C.S.E. or M.C.S.A. desired.
   c. Cisco CCNA desired.
2. Must have:
   a. Ability to administer MS (2000, 2003) solutions, an active directory domain, group policies, roaming profiles, remote desktop terminal services, firewalls, Cisco VOIP, backups, content filtering, MS Exchange, meeting room control systems, library automation systems.
   b. Positive, upbeat attitude and good interpersonal skills.
   c. Ability to work and communicate effectively with library management and staff.
   d. Proven project management, troubleshooting and problem resolution skills.
   e. Ability to simplify complex technological topics for novices.
   f. Ability to develop and maintain effective knowledge-based relationships with vendors.
   g. Ability to work independently.
3. Must be able to learn how to administer additional specific applications including building systems, TechLogic conveyor and other smart library solutions such as Internet queuing, print payment, RFID-based self-check.
4. Web development skills and ASP desired.

Equipment Operation

Servers, PCs, printers, library automation system, scanners, RFID scanners, self-check machines, faxes, conveyor, self-check equipment, building systems, application software specific hardware.

Work Week

40 hour work week, pager accessible with additional hours as needed.

Used with permission from the Fayetteville Public Library, AR

Computer Support Specialist, Information Technology

Immediate Supervisor

IT Manager

Job Summary

Provides reliable and responsive support to FPL staff and patron workstations. Responds to calls for help, troubleshoots and solves hardware and software problems. Provides support for Crestron audiovisual system for FPL meeting room. Setup and takedown of AV equipment such as laptops, digital camera, and digital projector. Consults IT Manager on best practices and implementation methodology.

Duties and Responsibilities

1. Provide support to staff and public workstations. Primary responsibility of this position is to support staff and public workstations by investigating and resolving computer hardware and software problems of end users. Much of this work is done remotely with occasional need for physical visits to another area of the facility. % of time: 80
2. Secure and lockdown workstations through use of security and lockdown tools. % of time: 5
3. Identify and correct printing problems through use of web interfaces. % of time: 5
4. Document workstation changes and configuration. Thorough understanding of documentation principles and updates. % of time: 2
5. Software installations. % of time: 5
6. Serve as backup for other IT staff. % of time: 1
7. Training staff on new software and technologies. % of time: 1
8. Other duties as assigned, including conveyor troubleshooting. % of time: 1

Qualifications and Requirements

1. Education
   a. B.S. in Computer Science, Computer Engineering, Information Technology or equivalent.

b. Microsoft Certified Professional (MCP) or CompTIA A+ certification desired.
2. Must have:
   a. Ability to effectively and easily communicate technical topics to novices.
   b. Ability to project a positive, upbeat attitude and excellent interpersonal skills even under stress.
   c. Ability to work and communicate effectively with library management and staff.
   d. Ability to work in a team environment.
   e. Ability to learn new and emerging technologies.
   f. Understanding and utilize IT best practices.
   g. Ability to troubleshoot Windows 2000 and Windows XP workstations.
   h. Ability to troubleshoot Dell print devices.
   i. Ability to develop and maintain effective knowledge-based relationships with vendors.
   j. Thorough understanding of PC hardware, components and parts.
   k. Ability to document any and all workstation changes and updates.
   l. Understanding of troubleshooting ticket systems.
   m. Solid understanding of NTFS and Share permissions.
   n. Ability to configure TCP/IP.
   o. Knowledge of workstation imaging software.
   p. Knowledge of workstation security software.
   q. Understanding of Windows Registry and important keys.
3. Experience with enterprise management software strongly desired.
4. Web development skills strongly desired.
5. Strong command line experience desired.

Equipment Operation

PCs, printers, library automation system, scanners, RFID scanners, self-check machines, faxes, self-check equipment, application software, and some PC hardware. Must be able to lift 50 pounds.

Work Week

40 hour work week, pager accessible with additional hours as needed.

Used with permission from the Fayetteville Public Library, AR

Electronic Resources Coordinator (Librarian)

Position Summary

Coordinates all activities having to do with the library's automated system and access to all electronic resources. Works closely with supervisors and Training Team to manage library software training for library employees. Represents Carrollton Public Library with selected system software vendor for applications and software upgrades and at user group meetings. Manages the Library Information Systems Group that coordinates automation activities in each of the library's service areas: Technical Services, Access Services, Adult and Youth Information Services. Works closely with assigned ACS, Inc. staff to solve technical problems and recommend solutions to library management. Manages "Computer Support Crew" a library-wide group who receive computer training in order to facilitate staff and patron use of our system. Serves as advisor to the Library Web Page Committee. Provides professional reference services at the Adult Reference Desk as needed. This position reports to the Technical Services Manager.

Essential Job Functions

Coordinator

- Works closely with Innovative Interfaces to configure, test and adjust library software to meet policy and procedural requirements of library.
- Works closely with Systems Assistant to maintain library database: reports, global updating, etc.
- Manages all electronic resources processes (CD ROM, web access, electronic journal access, library OPAC, and e-books) that provide 53 hours of service each week in the library and 24/7 via the Internet.
- Acts as communication conduit for ACS, Inc. City Network Help Desk, recording and following through on all problems reported to her team.
- Serves as contract compliance coordinator between software vendor, City IT Services provider, and library.
- Manages staff users in library automation system, sets up user parameters within the software, maintains documentation on all library decided parameters, institutes security policies and procedures.
- Works with library electronic resources vendors to make selected databases available to Carrollton users and maintains records of use.
- Represents library with software vendor, the Library Web Page Committee and other libraries in the area in cooperative ventures.
- Manages all general training on the library information system and serves as backup for all departmental training functions.
- Manages Electronic Classrooms at all locations.

- Implements semi-annual software upgrades from ILS vendor, tests software and trains staff on changes in software procedures.
- Provides statistical reports on a monthly basis to Technical Services Manager, responds to requests for reports from library and city staff and submits an annual report on system and Computer Support Crew activities.

Trainer/Supervisor

- Trains and oversees the Library Computer Support Crew, a group of 10–15 staff members from all over the library who have volunteered to learn more about our computers and the library/city network in order to facilitate the work for both patrons and staff.
- Contributes to the evaluation of Preservation Clerk, Senior Bibliographic Services Assistant, and other members of the Library Computer Support Crew annually.

Equipment

- Operates microcomputers and printers within citywide WAN-LAN network environment with Microsoft Office 97/2000/XP.
- Systems Administrator responsible for library automation system software, 3M Self-Check machines, bar code readers, receipt printers, subnet servers, and third-party software.
- Works with FTP and Telnet software, web software (Dream Weaver).
- Works within web environment to facilitate connection with vendors and electronic databases.
- Microfiche/film reader printers, copy machines, VCR.
- Use MS Word, MS Outlook, Internet/World Wide Web daily.

Minimum Qualifications

- Five years of progressively more responsible professional library experience required.
- Relates and applies expert knowledge of contemporary library theory, practices, methods, trends.
- Communicates effectively to patrons and co-workers both orally and written.
- Knowledge of computer hardware and peripherals preferred.
- Prepares written and oral reports including conclusions and recommendations.
- Experience with Windows 95-2000, MS Office software in course of daily work activity.
- Ability to work in a team-based office structure required.
- Must possess a valid Texas Class C driver's license.
- Must pass pre-employment drug test, motor vehicle record's check, and criminal history check.

Knowledge/Training/Experience/Skills Preferred

- Accurate keyboarding skills are required.
- Microsoft Office 97: Word, Excel, Access required.
- Knowledge of computer hardware and peripherals required.

Job Requirements

- Some evening and weekend work will be required: Incumbent or designated substitute responds to problems with the system for the entire time the library is open.
- Incumbent is required to travel to participate in training at all levels of library automation.
- Incumbent will carry a cell phone for emergencies within the Metroplex area.

Used with permission from the Carrollton Public Library, TX

Network Systems Administrator

Immediate Supervisor

Technology Manager

Job Responsibilities

Under direction, the Network Systems Administrator provides technical support to the Technology Manager to implement and coordinate the library's electronic environment.

Qualifications

A Bachelor's degree in Computer Science or related degree, or a combination of education, training, and significant work experience. A working knowledge of database development and administration, Microsoft server administration and maintenance. Experienced development in Windows and web-based applications. Library experience preferred.

Knowledge of

- Backup technology
- CLEVNET system*
- Computer network operations and maintenance
- Customer service methods*
- Developing and administering databases
- Experience in creating and maintaining websites
- Experience in creating Windows and web applications

- Hardware/software purchasing, installation, configuration, and maintenance
- Internet
- LAN/WANs
- Library policies and procedures*
- Microcomputer hardware and software
- Microsoft Office and Internet applications
- Portable computing*
- Computer programming languages
- Telecommunications
- Windows and MacOS networking
- Wireless technologies*

*May be acquired after hire

Skills and Abilities to

- Communicate effectively
- Develop and maintain effective working relationships with departments
- Interpret needs and design/create appropriate working software solutions according to library needs
- Maintain confidentiality
- Assists with maintaining and operating network system
- Plan, schedule, and organize work
- Prepare accurate and complete reports
- Present a professional image to the public
- Read and understand technical manuals and online documentation
- Spend extended time at a keyboard/monitor
- Tactfully interact with and respond to staff and patron technical problems
- Understand computer specifications
- Work a flexible schedule
- Work in a team-based, cooperative environment

% of Time   Illustrative Duties

(The duties listed below are intended to depict tasks performed by this classification. An asterisk denotes an essential function of the job.)

45%   Maintenance

- Acts in the absence of the Technology Manager.*
- Assists library staff with technical difficulties arising from hardware and/or software.*
- Assists with maintaining the daily operation of the library computer systems including but not limited to: Resolves and troubleshoots problems with computer hardware, software, networks, and LAN/WAN connectivity.*
- Assists with the purchase and installation of compatible hardware and software applications.*

- Performs computer system diagnostics, maintenance, and backup routines.*
- Assists with implementation and maintains network and workstation stability, security, and performance.*

45%   Development

- Develops and implements working software applications according to library needs.*
- Participates in the design, development, implementation, and maintenance of the library's website.*
- Participates in the development of procedures and network resource acquisition.*

10%   Miscellaneous

- Attends meetings and serves on committees, as requested.
- Maintains and increases knowledge and skills through attendance at meetings, conferences, training seminars, and in-service training sessions.
- Performs additional duties and assignments, as requested.

Used with permission from the Euclid Public Library, OH

Technology Support Clerk/ Technician

Immediate Supervisor

Network Manager

Note: This could be PT or FT. Major Duties will need to be adjusted accordingly.

Job Summary

The Technology Support Clerk/Technician is responsible for installation, preventative maintenance, and minor repair of all computers and their peripherals, and miscellaneous office equipment. In addition, the position performs on-call computer help desk duties for Library staff and patrons involving computer hardware, applications, and office equipment. It requires the ability to access, input, and retrieve data from the computer; ability to perform light to medium work; ability to use phone effectively.

Major Duties

1. Under the supervision of the Network Manager, handles day to day installation, maintenance, minor repair,

and troubleshooting of the library's network hardware and software, peripherals, office equipment, and other technology-related areas.

2. Performs help desk duties for staff and patrons.
3. Generates system reports from the Integrated Library System and others as needed.
4. Maintains written maintenance logs for the computer work as completed.
5. Under the supervision of and with instructions from the Network Manager, prepares specifications for the purchase of computer software, hardware, supplies, and other equipment.
6. Assists in monitoring server logs and events.
7. Prepares, delivers, and picks up equipment that is sent out of the building for repair.
8. Provides assistance in use of equipment and software to both patrons and staff.
9. Remains aware of new technologies which have application to library operation.
10. Attends appropriate meetings, workshops, and seminars.
11. Serves on committees as assigned.
12. Other duties as assigned.

Desired Skills

■ Background and interest in working with computers, both hardware and software.
■ Knowledge of computer networking concepts and applications (preferably Microsoft Operating Systems).
■ Willingness to explore and research solutions to computer problems as they arise.
■ Ability to interpret and communicate computer problems.
■ Ability to organize workload and multi-task effectively.
■ Good communication skills, both verbal and written.
■ Ability to work neatly, pay attention to detail, and follow directions.
■ Ability to climb, stoop, kneel, crouch, and crawl and lift and handle a minimum of 50 lbs.
■ Ability to follow directions.
■ Ability to interact with patrons and staff openly, courteously, skillfully, and accurately.
■ Ability to train/assist others in use of equipment, software, and related items.
■ Ability to work as a member of a team.

Education and Training

■ High school diploma required.
■ A minimum of two years experience in computer or technology-related services.
■ College/technical training in computer science is desirable, but not required.

Hours

20 hours per week. Must be able to work mornings with the option of five 4-hour days or three 6- to 7-hour days.

Library Assistant–Computer Technician (Part-time)

Definition

Performs basic setup, support, maintenance and trouble-shooting of stand-alone and networked PC's software, terminals and peripherals. Responsible for technical work requiring application of principles of computer technology. Work is performed under general supervision of the System Administrator.

Minimum Qualifications

■ Associate's degree in computer science or related field and up to two years of related experience.
■ Good knowledge of microcomputer hardware, operating systems and applications.
■ Good knowledge of network technology, especially Windows NT.
■ Must be well organized and able to work well with non-technical staff and patrons.
■ Ability to install, configure and troubleshoot PC and network-related hardware.
■ Ability to work in a team environment.

Used with permission from the Palm Harbor Public Library, FL

APPENDIX

Publication Samples

E1 Sample Press Release

E2 Brownsburg Public Library's Wireless Access Brochure

E3 Morrisson-Reeves Library's Disc Repair Brochure

E4 Westlake Porter Public Library's Newsletter

E5 Staff Memo: Howard County Library WiFi Policy

Press Release

FOR IMMEDIATE RELEASE

[Your Library's Name] adds online access to program calendar and meeting room schedule

[City, State] [Date]:   Patrons of the **[insert library name]** can now search and register for programs and book a meeting room online, 24 hours a day, 7 days a week. This convenient, up-to-date information is accessible to anyone with access to the library's website **[insert library's URL]**.

View an up-to-the-second program and activity schedule. Simply go to **[insert library's URL]** and click on **[insert appropriate directions]**. The best part, no more waiting in line!

Tired of spending time on the phone going through room availability to book your group's next monthly meeting? View the **[insert library name]**'s room schedule at **[insert library's URL]** and request a room right then and there. It's quick and it's easy

[Insert quote from staff member if appropriate. Refer to the "News and Events" section of the e•vanced solutions' web page for examples.]

The **[insert library name]** is committed to providing a variety of service options to its patrons, from direct staff assistance to online self-service. Feel free to stop by the library at **[insert address]** for a quick demo or for more information on these or any other library services, contact **[contact name, title]**, **[library name]** at **[contact's phone number]**.

These solutions were provided by *e•vanced solutions*, inc. a leading provider of web-based software solutions for library event management, meeting room reservation management, study room booking, genealogy, and reading program management. Visit them at www.e-vancedsolutions.com.

Press release courtesy of e•vanced solutions, inc.

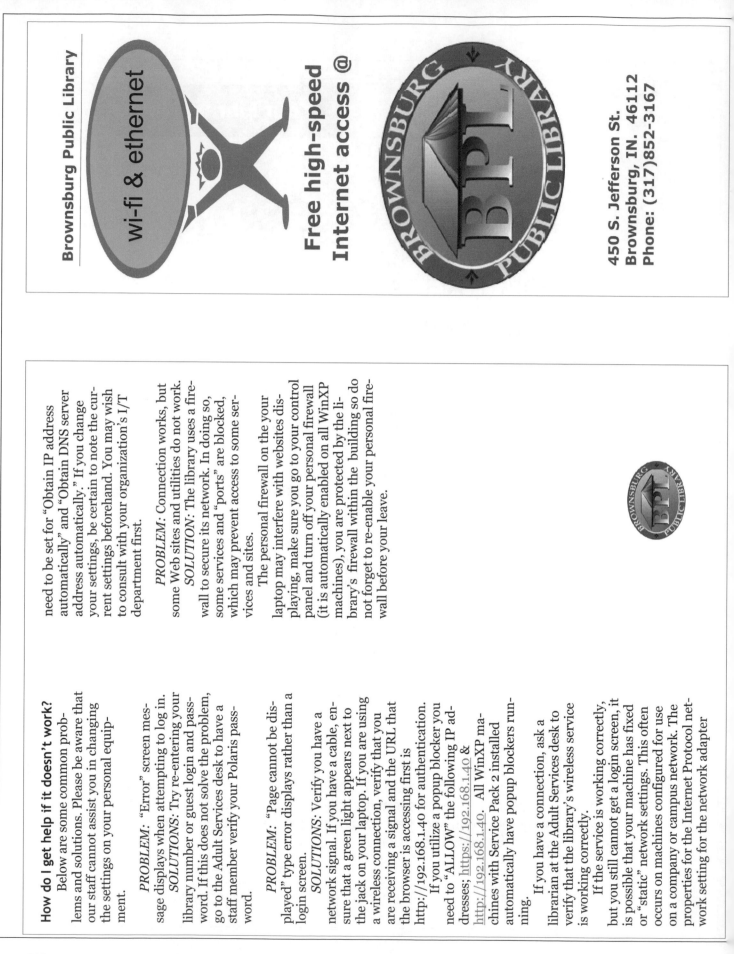

How do I get help if it doesn't work?

Below are some common problems and solutions. Please be aware that our staff cannot assist you in changing the settings on your personal equipment.

PROBLEM: "Error" screen message displays when attempting to log in.
SOLUTIONS: Try re-entering your library number or guest login and password. If this does not solve the problem, go to the Adult Services desk to have a staff member verify your Polaris password.

PROBLEM: "Page cannot be displayed" type error displays rather than a login screen.

SOLUTIONS: Verify you have a network signal. If you have a cable, ensure that a green light appears next to the jack on your laptop. If you are using a wireless connection, verify that you are receiving a signal and the URL that the browser is accessing first is http://192.168.1.40 for authentication.

If you utilize a popup blocker you need to "ALLOW" the following IP addresses; https://192.168.1.40 & http://192.168.1.40. All WinXP machines with Service Pack 2 installed automatically have popup blockers running.

If you have a connection, ask a librarian at the Adult Services desk to verify that the library's wireless service is working correctly.

If the service is working correctly, but you still cannot get a login screen, it is possible that your machine has fixed or "static" network settings. This often occurs on machines configured for use on a company or campus network. The properties for the Internet Protocol network setting for the network adapter need to be set for "Obtain IP address automatically" and "Obtain DNS server address automatically." If you change your settings, be certain to note the current settings beforehand. You may wish to consult with your organization's I/T department first.

PROBLEM: Connection works, but some Web sites and utilities do not work.
SOLUTION: The library uses a firewall to secure its network. In doing so, some services and "ports" are blocked, which may prevent access to some services and sites.

The personal firewall on the your laptop may interfere with websites displaying, make sure you go to your control panel and turn off your personal firewall (it is automatically enabled on all WinXP machines), you are protected by the library's firewall within the building so do not forget to re-enable your personal firewall before your leave.

Frequently Asked Questions

What do I need to connect my laptop to the Internet in the library?

1. A laptop with an Ethernet network card or wireless card.

2. A network connection configured for DHCP (more information available under help in your start menu).

3. A valid BPL library or a guest logon and password. Ask at the Adult Services Desk across from the front entrance if you need a card. A Polaris PIN number or password, assigned at the time you received your card.

4. A Polaris PIN number or password, assigned at the time you received your card.

Is there an access fee?

This service is free to all residents and guests. If you do not have a library card, then please go the Adult Services desk for a guest logon and password.

Where can I connect?

The Study Rooms in the library have at least one network jack for connecting a cabled network card. Often these are located on the wall near a power outlet.

There is a wireless access point in the center of the building for wireless access. Signal strength is dependent upon a variety of factors, and you may need to try a couple of locations to get the strongest signal.

Can I print?

Printing is not available via personal laptops You may wish to transfer documents to a Web-based personal e-mail account and then log into one of the library's Internet stations to print out your documents.

How do I connect?

1. If you are using a **cable connection**, connect your laptop to any data jack in a study room, you may need to visit the computer lab desk to make sure the specific jack you are connecting to is live on the network. If you are using a **wireless connection**, find a location with a strong signal.

2. Turn your laptop on.

3. Once your desktop is up, start your Web browser. If you see a "Security Alert" message, click the "yes" button to continue.

Wireless Access

4. You should see the following login screen for wireless access:

5. Enter your 12-digit library card number (starts with 12010) or guest logon in the Library card barcode number field.

6. Enter your Polaris password in the Password/PIN field. Note that this password was created by you when you received your library card.

7. Click on the "Enter" button. You should see the following

8. Leave the success screen open (you may minimize it) until you are finished with your session. Click the "Logout" button to close the connection.

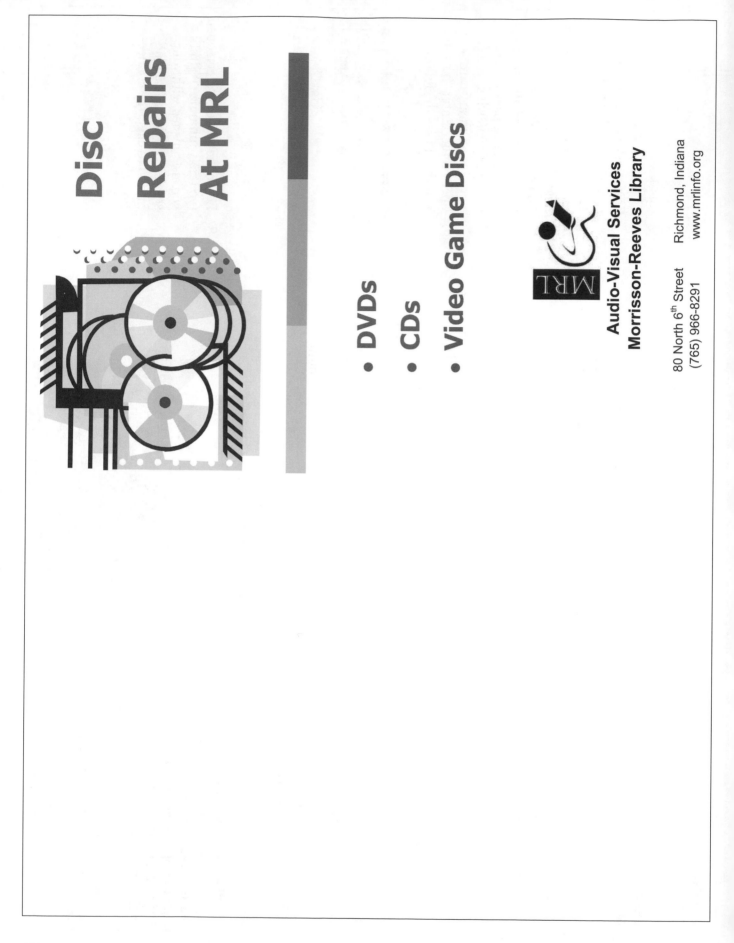

Disc Repairs Available Through Morrisson-Reeves Library's Audio-Visual Services

Disc Repair Procedures

- For a $5 donation to the Audio/Visual Services materials fund, a patron is entitled to have either 1 DVD, 1 Video Game Disc, or 2 CDs repaired by the A/V Services RTI Eco-Senior Disc Repair Machine. The donation only entitles the disc(s) to one run through the machine. If another cleaning/repair is desired, another $5 donation will be required.

- The disc(s) will be run through the RTI Eco-Senior Disc Repair Machine on the Medium mode, unless otherwise requested by the patron. The other modes that are available are Very Light (removes stains), Light (for a disc with light scratches), and Deep (for a disc that has been deeply gouged)

- The RTI Eco-Senior Disc Repair Machine is only run once a week. By nature this cannot be a pay and wait service. Discs should be dropped off at the time of donation and will be available for pickup after the following Wednesday. If you are unsure when your disc will be available for pickup, please inquire at the A/V Services Desk.

Guidelines for Disc Repair

- The Audio/Visual Services staff does not guarantee the playability of a disc after it is run through the RTI Eco-Senior Disc Repair Machine. While the machine is designed to eliminate scratches on discs, it does not repair cracks or pre-existing faults in them that may have been a result of a manufacturing error.

- The Audio/Visual Services staff also does not guarantee the ability to fix a disc if it has already been through another disc fixing machine. Many of the commercially sold disc repair machines buff discs and do more harm than good. The RTI Eco-Senior Disc Repair Machine may not be able to reverse the damage already done by one of these machines.

- The Audio/Visual Services staff does not recommend a disc be run through the RTI Eco-Senior Disc Repair Machine more than 10 times on the Medium mode. The machine removes layers of the disc in an effort to eliminate scratches. If a disc is repaired this way too many times, the disc becomes too thin to be read by laser. For this reason, we cannot guarantee the playability of a disc if it has gone through this type of process more than a few times.

Notes

We're #2 in the Nation!

Westlake Porter Public Library • 27333 Center Ridge Road • Oct. - Dec. 2004

Know-It-Now 24x7 = 24 Hour Reference for Westlake

Know-It-Now 24x7 Statewide Virtual Reference debuted in September, giving Westlake residents access to 24-hour online reference services.

The online service, *www.KnowItNow.org*, is part of a statewide initiative that assists residents of the State of Ohio with access to information on an as-needed basis, regardless of the time of day. WPPL staff members are among the library professionals across the state who will be sharing the responsibilities for providing this service. *KnowItNow.org* is one of only a few virtual reference services made available through a statewide public library system in the United States.

All that Westlake residents need to do to use the service is log on to the library's website (*www.westlakelibrary.org*) and click on the *KnowItNow* icon. From that point, the Web site guides a user to access various locations within

Continued on page 4

Woods Named Assistant Director for Support Services

Anita Woods, the library's Community Education Librarian for nine years, is the library's new Assistant Director for Support Services.

Woods started at WPPL in July, 1995 as a reference associate, and became the Community Education Librarian in November, 1995. Before coming to Porter Library, she was the University Librarian at Johnson and Wales University in Charleston, South Carolina. She received her Masters degree in Library and Information Science from the University of South Carolina.

As Assistant Director for Support Services, Woods oversees the technical aspects of library operations — such as the library's computerized catalog

Continued on page 4

Our mission:
"...to educate, empower, enlighten, and excite..."

Hours:
Monday - Thursday:
9:00 a.m. - 9:00 p.m.
Friday and Saturday:
9:00 a.m. - 5 p.m.
Sundays (September - May):
1 - 5:00 p.m.

Westlake Porter Public Library
27333 Center Ridge Road
(440) 871-2600
www.westlakelibrary.org

Director's *Notes:*

The Whole (Reading) Enchilada

The National Endowment for the Humanities recently released a study that has rocked the reading world! "Reading at Risk" shows a two decade decline in 'literary reading,' with the most vulnerable group being 18 – 34 year olds. In other studies, projections show that the average American will spend 213 hours on the Internet in 2006, while only spending 106 hours reading trade books (PW, Aug. '04).

The Plain Dealer has responded with a year-long series called "The Read on Cleveland." A variety of writers in publishing trade magazines have also joined in expressing their horror that reading may become a lost skill.

While the NEA study and other statistics paint us into a reading crisis corner, however, there is hope. The number of books published last year, for instance, was 19% more than the year before. Book sales *have* increased a bit. Borrowing of print materials has increased here at Westlake Porter Library by 38% over the last decade, and it has increased at many other libraries as well. Interest in book discussion groups has never been stronger. In the last decade, we witnessed the success of Oprah's Book Club, and the launching of "Book-Span" TV. There has also been a resurgence of interest in poetry and in creative writing since 9-11.

So, where's the disconnect? Should we be panicked about the demise of reading and literature, or is everything really okay? To answer that question, perhaps we need to look at 'the whole reading enchilada.'

The NEA study, first of all, measured only 'literary' reading. It excluded nonfiction. Yet magnificent nonfiction books (some quite literary) are published and read — not just for facts, but for pleasure — each year. A huge part of our borrowership at WPPL is of nonfiction books.

Another huge proportion of reading these days occurs in *other* than the

book format — newspapers, magazines, electronic downloads, and on-screen reading. These alternatives offer new forms of literature exposure and reading 'competition' in what is now a format-diverse, information-rich, and media-driven society.

Audiovisual formats are frequently disdained and dismissed by serious 'readers.' However, these new formats allow people to multi-task - i.e., to be exposed to literature *and* do something else at the same time. One of our most popular formats, for example, is the book on CD, used heavily by commuters and travelers. New listening and viewing formats provide the opportunity for connecting with literature or novels — in a different way, certainly. But one can still absorb and appreciate the beauty of the words, characterization, and thoughts within them. That experience may encourage individuals to read the book or to pur-

sue something else by that author. Multiple formats *can* 'feed' each other.

Is reading at risk? Yes. The traditional vision of a reader with novel in hand will undoubtedly diminish as our boomer generation ages and as the multimedia generations mature. And is that something to mourn? Absolutely! But perhaps we should acknowledge that our echo-boomer cohorts are already well-entrenched into a multimedia society and that their way of life is and will continue to be radically different from ours – whether we want it to or not, whether we mourn it or not. Reading looks much different today than the way it looked twenty years ago, and it will certainly look immensely different twenty years hence.

One bookseller recently stated, "... we should work harder to inspire and nurture the readers we still have instead of helplessly mourning the ones we've lost." While I agree with that, I will go one step further.

Perhaps it is also time for us to expand our definition of 'reading.' *Perhaps* we should not be so quick to superimpose a stilted and narrowly defined perception of reading onto a new generation of multimedia 'readers,' lest we scare them away entirely. Much as Gutenberg's invention of the printing press gave way to a whole new world of readers, perhaps we are simply witnessing a "passage" – into a new era of reading and media coexistence. Perhaps we should embrace readers, of whatever age and format and reading inclination ...and just let reading happen.

Paula Miller,
Library Director

2

Renewals and DVD Loan Period Increased; Non-Fiction DVDs Now on Non-Fiction Shelves

In order to provide more user-friendly service to customers, the library has changed its renewal and DVD loan period policies. Effective immediately, customers are allowed three renewals instead of just one, *unless* the item is on hold for someone else. In addition, the loan period for DVDs (with the exception of new feature film DVDs) has been increased to three weeks.

The change in the renewal policy is being implemented to provide better service. In many cases, an item being returned is one of several copies the library owns, making it available to others who need that title. Sometimes individuals need certain items longer in order to complete homework, a research paper, or a business project. You'll save on trips to the library by being able to renew three times from home by phone or through the library's online catalog.

Extending the loan period for some DVDs also serves you better. When you check out a non-fiction DVD (such as an exercise DVD) or an older feature film, you no longer have to worry about running back to the library within a week to return it. Keeping track of due dates is simplified, because you'll only have one for *all* of your items (with the exception of the one-week loan items, such as the *EXPRESS* collections and the new feature film DVDs).

The library has also made a change in shelving non-fiction DVDs (such as exercise DVDs). They are now on the non-fiction shelves, along with the non-fiction books and VHS videotapes on the same subject. This will make it easier for you to find material on a specific subject in *any* format just by browsing the non-fiction shelves — instead of having to check the catalog and go to several *different* locations in the building.

Why Does/Did the Library...?

The library's policies and procedures are the result of much research, information gathering, and deliberation. They are instituted to give you good, efficient, sensible service; to protect your investment in the library; and to make the library a more pleasant environment for all. This feature clarifies various policies and procedures.

How Long Are You Going to Continue Providing VHS Videotapes and Books-on-Tape?

For the time being, the library will continue purchasing VHS videotapes and books-on-tape. However, as these formats are phased out by manufacturers, and as more people purchase DVD players and autos with CD players, the library will reduce its purchases of these formats.

While all <u>new</u> autos are being manufactured with CD players, there are many older and used autos without CD players still in use. For the convenience of those with vehicles still having tape players, phasing out of books-on-tape is not scheduled until 2007.

And, of course, not everyone owns DVD players yet, so we'll continue to purchase a limited number of VHS videotapes in 2005. However, since the number of DVDs being requested and checked out is growing at a rapid pace, and since many new movies aren't even being offered on VHS, the library will purchase more films in DVD format. According to vendors, in fact, the VHS format will most likely be gone from the market by mid-2005.

If you have any questions about library policies or procedures, you are always welcome to call us at (440) 871-2600.

Portables Holiday Preview

October 31, 1 - 4:30 p.m.

Stop in for an early look at our new holiday decorations, gifts, cards, and more.

(All "Portables" Gift Shop sales benefit the library.)

3

Special Programs on Fall Schedule

Join us this fall for these special programs:

Tuesday, November 16 (7 p.m.) *Booktalk with author Daniel Chaon.* The Oberlin resident will read from and take questions about his acclaimed novel *You Remind Me of Me.* Copies will be available for purchase and signing.

Friday, November 26 (2 p.m.) *Ken Brown of Turbine Games.* Teenz: meet the Elyria native, who's currently working on the *Lord of the Rings* online computer game, and hear about his career. Call 440/250-5471 to sign up.

November 21 (2 - 4 p.m.) and Wednesday, December 15 (6 - 8 p.m.) — *Joyful Noise at the Library music programs.*

Arts Council Announces Show at Library

The Westlake-Westshore Arts Council is pleased to present the artwork of Lillian Bialosky in its first one-person show of the 2004-'05 season. The show runs from through October 31st at Westlake Porter Public Library.

Lillian was a member of the Westlake Art Society from 1963 to 1993, and was taught by art teachers from American Greetings and the Cleveland Institute of Art, among others. She works primarily in watercolor and acrylics. Bialosky's work has been displayed in many shows, including Beck Center, Higbee's Downtown, Emerald Necklace juried shows, and Hixon's.

Lillian gives credit to WPPL for her continued interest in art education, for art classes held here over the years, in addition to the excellent art resource section.

This is the first exhibit to be displayed at the library since its return to the renovated facility. Donations enabled the library to purchase and install a complete hanging system, allowing artwork displays in the meeting room wing.

Artists who are interested in being considered for a display should pick up a policy sheet and application packet at the library.

Anita Woods (Continued from page 1)

system, building services, circulation functions, and meeting rooms.

"Anita's experience here at WPPL with internal operations and her technology expertise enable her to handle the challenge of overseeing these complex systems," said Library Director Paula Miller.

Reading Garden Fundraiser Set for Spring

The Westlake Garden Club and Westlake Porter Public Library are planning a spring fundraiser for the Reading Garden. Look for details in the next *Notes.*

Know-It-Now (Continued from page 1)

the site. Users can ask questions on a variety of topics, chat in real time with a librarian, get help with their homework, and find answers to their questions.

Resources on business and finance, health and medicine, science and technology, and genealogy are accessible from the site. Librarians will staff the service for real time answers to questions from users. Homework assistance is available from 2:00 p.m. to 10:00 p.m. seven days a week, utilizing teacher subject specialists. Access to the Web site is obtainable from a home computer, a personal laptop, a computer at work, or inside your local library.

Know-It-Now 24x7 statewide virtual reference service was created through a grant from the federal Institute of Museum and Library Services (IMLS) awarded by the State Library of Ohio.

Opening in November!

PICC-A-DELI Café
At Porter Library

This coupon good for a free cookie with the purchase of a beverage

27333 Center Ridge Road, Westlake, Ohio 44145

Hours
Monday - Thursday: 9 a.m. - 1 p.m. & 4-8 p.m
Friday and Saturday: 9 a.m. - 4:30 p.m
Sunday: 1 -4:30 p.m.

4

Meet The Library's New Youth Services Coordinator!

Bay Village native Carolyn Fain is the library's new Youth Services Coordinator. She replaces Mary Worthington, who was promoted to Assistant Director of Public Services in May.

Carolyn received a Master's in Library Science from St. John's University in Queens, New York. Before coming "home" to WPPL, she served at the Queens Borough Library for four years, first as a librarian trainee in the Central Library's Film Division, then as a children's librarian at several branches. More recently she worked at the Fountaindale Public Library District in Bolingbrook, Illinois, for over seven years, first as a children's librarian and eventually as the Assistant Coordinator of Children's Services.

Carolyn is thrilled to be back in the Cleveland area, and to take on the challenges of running the Youth Services Department for a busy and forward-thinking library like WPPL. Upon starting in July, she immediately plunged into planning the grand opening of the Homework Help Center — see the article on the opposite page.

The library is happy to have Carolyn. "her experience, enthusiasm, and commitment to children make her a wonderful addition to our staff," said Library Director Paula Miller.

Youth Services Makes Learning Fun

The library's creative Youth Services Staff is a large part of the "excite" in WPPL's mission statement — "to educate, empower, enlighten, and excite...."

This talented group is behind the weekly storytimes, Pickle Tree Club, Super Science Saturday and MITIcraft Saturday, as well as the Summer Reading program, cool programs and activities for "Teenz", the new Homework Help Center, and the Imagination Stations.

Every week, in addition to ordering new books and materials for kids and teens, and providing reference services and assistance to children and their parents, this group is busy planning these programs.

The Youth Services Staff: Back row (left to right) - Nancy Kendall, Mary Beth Major, Denise Steve, Karen Marino, and Joyce Igel. Seated (left to right) - Maureen Ring, Nancy Sabo, Cathy McCAnn, and Carolyn Fain. Not pictured: Jane Barker, Christine Bettinger, Therese Schwind, Laura Ploenzke and Kate Tuthill.

On top of all of that, they're also called upon to help with other library activities and initiatives, from the Homework Help Center to a new Chautauqua program for young readers ages 10 - 14.

Other creative ideas enhancing the department are the Imagination Stations, and the recent re-design of the preschool room.

Youth Services staff also worked closely with Mr. and Mrs. Dae-Jin Ryook to design "Christina's Corner," a memorial to their daughter, Christina, who was among those who perished in the World Trade Center during the September 11, 2001 terrorist attacks.

Be happy? Excite? No problem. The staff always has time for a smile or word with their young customers and their parents or caregivers.

Partnership with Celebrate Westlake
Refreshes *and* Educates
Homework Help Center - "H2C" -Now Open!

For 14 years, Westlake has gathered at St. John West Shore Hospital the Saturday before Labor Day to raise funds for charity, celebrate the community, and learn about and embrace health and fitness. For nine of those years WPPL staff and family members have been on hand to refresh the runners, skaters and walkers at all of the water stops for the races. This year was no exception, as 39 library staff members, volunteers, and their families staffed the water stations, providing much-needed refreshment to the dozens of race participants.

For the last several years the library has been the recipient of a portion of the funds raised by

Celebrate Westlake. Along with other donations, Celebrate Westlake funds received in 2003 and 2004 have been used to develop the Homework Help Center (H$_2$C), which opened on October 5.

H$_2$C is a place students in grades K-12 can go to access Westlake City Schools' math, science, and social studies text-

books. Once inside they can get help from student learning coaches, and use laptops connected to the library's wireless network where research databases, the Internet, the library catalog, and HomeworkNow.com, an online tutoring service, will be available.

"We are extremely grateful to Celebrate Westlake and our other donors for helping us to create this resource," said Paula Miller, Library Director. "We are pleased to support schools, students, and their parents through this service."

The H$_2$C will be open from 6:30 - 8:00 p.m. on Tuesdays and Thursdays, and 1 - 3 p.m. on Sundays, when the Westlake City Schools are in session.

Chautauqua Young Readers Program
Coming to Westlake

The Cleveland Metropolitan Library System (CAMLS) and its member public and school libraries — including Westlake Porter Public Library — are bringing Chautauqua to northeast Ohio. This pilot program, part of the Chautauqua Literary and Scientific Circle's outreach efforts, is aimed at young readers ages 10-14, and

will include programs tied into the books selected for reading. The aim of the program is to encourage the enjoyment of good reading. The program will take place over a seven month period starting this fall.

Among the titles selected for focus events here at Westlake Porter Public Library are *The Tale of Despereaux* by Kate DiCamillo, *The Kite Rider* by Geraldine McCaughrean, and *Eragon* by Christopher Paolini — selections

which will delight older as well as younger readers.

Westlake Porter Public Library's staff have planned several special programs revolving around these books, such as a "stone soup" making program, a visit from the illustrator of *Eragon* in March, and a kite program in April.

Watch for details about programs in the library and on our website (*www.westlakelibrary.org*).

6

User Spotlight:
Karen Jones

Karen Jones (center left) and family.

Bio: I was born and raised in Savannah, Georgia, and attended Santa Fe Community College in Gainesville, Florida from 1983-1996. My husband, Garrett, and I were married in 1996. His Coast Guard career took us to Boston for three years before we moved to Cleveland. When Garrett completed his Coast Guard career two years after moving here, we decided to stay.

Family: Garrett and I have two children, Alexandra and Jacob. Let's not forget Max, our mixed-breed dog, who just turned 1 in July.

All-time Favorite Book: Stuart Woods' collection of books

What I Don't Like: Anything historical or political

Reading Influences: My mother and father, who always had a book in their hands when I was growing up.

Why I Use the Library and its Services: The incredible media collection and the friendly staff have me returning several times weekly. I find something new with every visit.

Hobbies and Other Activities: Camping, beach activities, walking, and biking. I'm also a room mother for Jacob's class, and am on a committee for the Holly Lane Elementary PTA.

On Karen's Reading List:

- Anything by Stuart Woods
- Mystery
- Romance
- Some self-help

View the Lunar Eclipse @ Your Library!

Celebrate the total lunar eclipse with a special program and webcast on Wednesday, October 27. "Kids" elementary school age and up will learn what causes lunar eclipses and what to watch for during the program, which runs from 7:30 - 8:15 p.m. Then, for great viewing (weather permitting), visit the the library's website — *www.westlakelibrary.org* — for an eclipse webcast from 9 p.m. on October 27 to 1 a.m. October 28.

Helping Our Community...

Did you know the library is a drop-off site for donations to the Westlake Center for Community Services? Needs for October are: canned fruit, soup, and paper products (such as paper towels). Needs for November and December are: cereal, canned vegetables, canned meat, and personal hygiene products. A big THANK YOU goes to our customers and staff who continue to contribute to this worthy cause. The amount of items collected grows each month — and benefits local families who are in need.

7

WESTLAKE PORTER PUBLIC LIBRARY

27333 Center Ridge Road
Westlake, Ohio 44145-3947

Holidays

The Library will be closed to observe the following holidays:

Thanksgiving (November 25)
Christmas (December 24 - 26)
New Year's Day (January 1)

The library's Board of Trustees normally meets the third Wednesday of the month at 6:30 p.m. Meetings are open to the public. Call in advance to verify date, time and location, as occasionally there are changes.

Thank you, Donors!

We would like to thank the following individuals and organizations for their generous contributions from May 11 through August 18, 2004.

HONOR ROLL (up to $250)

Mr. & Mrs. Fred Antolini
Benik Family
Barbara E. Briggs
Cuyahoga West Genealogical Society
Carol Guilford
Cynthia Hall
Glenda Holmok
Sarah Ellis Jackson
Gary Jones
Anand Mehta
Robert and Jan Ontolchik

Laura J. Peskin
Village 100 Club
WHS Panorama Staff
Westlake Garden Club
Mark Zust

WESTERN RESERVE CLUB ($250+)

Dean's Greenhouse and Flower Shop

CLAGUE CLUB ($1,000 +)

Westlake Early Childhood PTA

DOVER CLUB ($5,000 +)

Westlake Historical Society

The library welcomes gifts of books, other library materials and funds by individuals or organizations, as lasting and useful memorials of friends or family members, and as celebrations of special events such as birthdays, anniversaries, etc.

The library is currently accepting donations for a community reading garden, which will be constructed next spring.

Donations to Westlake Porter Public Library are tax deductible, and may be made by calling the Clerk-Treasurer at (440) 871-2600.

8

Staff Memo: Howard County Library WiFi Policy

Hello and happy summer!

I see and hear that every day, more and more customers are taking advantage of our WiFi services. The result is that many of you are fielding questions about access which you may not be comfortable answering.

Below are a few points to share with you about the WiFi configuration. This information will be posted to the Staff Intranet in the next few days.

(1) **The extent of troubleshooting HCL employees can provide for the WiFi is to confirm that it is available.** This confirmation is accomplished by using a WiFi enabled device to launch a web browser and reach a web site. In order to do this, we will deliver to each branch, a low level laptop with WiFi capabilities. HCL employees can pull out this laptop and confirm the ability to reach the Internet via the WiFi.

(2) IT staff will not provide technical support on customer computers. No exceptions. **Do not page or call IT for WiFi support.** We cannot troubleshoot computers that are not part of our inventory.

(3) Finally, HCL employees are not permitted to configure or troubleshoot a customer computer. No exceptions. **Do not touch a customer computer.**

A few more detailed points . . .

What is WiFi?

According to Wikipedia (don't tell my husband I used Wikipedia because he loathes it) WiFi is a set of product compatibility standards for wireless local area networks (WLAN). When near an "access point" an individual with a WiFi enabled device can connect to the Internet. http://en.wikipedia.org/wiki/WiFi

Sounds freaky and hi tech

According to *How Wireless Works* by Preston Gralla (384.5G, one copy in each branch), wireless is all over the place. Our remote controls, our radios, our beloved cell phones. So, it is here and has been here and given the popularity this summer is HERE AT HCL to stay!

Why does HCL have WiFi?

HCL decided to offer free access to WiFi as a way to provide a public service to the community. We recognize that many of our customers own computers (and many are laptops) and want their information and research all in one place. Also, we moved to WiFi for selfish reasons—anyone bringing in a PC to work is not using one of our PCs—freeing up our PCs for other customers.

How is the WiFi configured?

We configured our WiFi to provide access to the Web and to provide access to information. The WiFi is not as open as our internal network nor is it as open as someone's Internet access at home or at their place of employment. It might also not be as open as another free WiFi provider.

How does someone use the WiFi?

They walk in and their device (laptop or PDA) finds the network and VOILA—they are good to go.

What is the deal with EMAIL via the HCL WiFi?

We've shut down SMTP in order to protect our infra-structure and our customers from a SPAM engine being brought in.

. . . Amy, you now sound like an adult in a Peanuts TV special.

If the email is set up to move messages from a server to a client-based email application (such as Outlook) it will only partially work on the HCL WiFi.

. . . Amy, what the heck does that mean?

Email can be RECEIVED AND READ either via a web browser (like Firefox or Internet Explorer) or via a client (such as Thunderbird, Eudora, Outlook). If a WiFi user is trying to SEND email from a client it will not work. WiFi users MUST send email via a WEB BASED email client.

. . . Goodness, Amy, how will I know?

The way I figure this out is to say, "Are you using Firefox or Internet Explorer to send email?" If they say, "No, I am using Outlook Express," you have your answer.

. . . Amy, more detail, please?

When you read email via OpenWebMail you are on a web browser. If you use Thunderbird at your desk, that is an email client. Is this getting more clear?

. . . Hey, I am almost getting this . . .

If you have ANY software on your computer (other than a web browser) to read email, you are using an email client and you WILL NOT be able to send email via the HCL WiFi. You will be able to read it and receive it. You can also write an email and put it in a DRAFT folder to send later.

If you are ONLY in a browser, your email should work.

What if there is another problem? What if they can't find the WiFi on their computer?

You can always suggest the tried and true step—reboot. I find with my laptop, when I turn it off and then back on, it finds the WiFi network. Otherwise, the customer needs to contact their computer support team.

Amy Begg DeGroff, "Howard County Library WiFi Policy." *WebJunction* (July 25, 2005). http://webjunction.org/do/DisplayContent?id=11059.

INDEX

Kimberly Bolan has worked in the area of network and computer services for small and medium-sized libraries for many years. Most recently, she served as the assistant director in the Webster (NY) Public Library. She currently works as an independent library consultant. Bolan received her M.L.S. degree from the School of Information Studies at Syracuse University. She serves on the Small and Medium-Sized Libraries Committee of PLA.

Robert Cullin is the vice president and co-owner of e•vanced solutions, Inc., a software company that focuses on developing web-based productivity solutions for libraries. The company provides application software for managing library programs and events, registration, meeting and study rooms, and reading programs. Cullin's background is in software and hardware product development, and his passion is public libraries.